Globalization and Transformations of Local Socioeconomic Practices

Routledge Advances in Sociology

Globalization and Transformations of Local Socioeconomic Practices

Edited by
Ulrike Schuerkens

Routledge
Taylor & Francis Group
New York   London

First published 2008
by Routledge
711 Third Ave, New York, NY 10017

Simultaneously published in the UK
by Routledge
2 Park Square, Milton Park, Abingdon, Oxon OX14 4RN

Routledge is an imprint of the Taylor & Francis Group, an informa business

© 2008 Taylor & Francis
First issued in paperback 2013
Typeset in Sabon by IBT Global

Library of Congress Cataloging in Publication Data
Globalization and transformations of local socio-economic practices / edited by Ulrike Schuerkens.
p. cm — (Routledge advances in sociology)
Includes bibliographical references and index.
1. International economic relations—Social aspects. 2. International trade—Social aspects. 3. Globalization—Social aspects. 4. Globalization—Economic aspects. I. Schuerkens, Ulrike.

HF1359.G5843 2007
303.48'2--dc22
2007016170

ISBN13: 978-0-415-96090-8 (hbk)
ISBN13: 978-0-415-54135-0 (pbk)

Contents

Preface

Ulrike Schuerkens

"Globalization and Transformations of Local Socioeconomic Practices" assembles some of the most interesting contributions to the Research Committee 09 "Social Transformations and Sociology of Development" of the International Sociological Association over the last years during my term as President of RC 09 (2002–2006). The largest part of the articles were presented in sessions at the 37th World Congress of the International Institute of Sociology in Stockholm, Sweden, in July 2005 and at the 16th World Congress of the International Sociological Association in Durban, South Africa, in July 2006. Colleagues and PhD students of the editor at the *École des Hautes Études en Sciences Sociales*, Paris, wrote most of the other articles.

This collection of articles offers analytical and comparative insights at the world level, with regard to current socioeconomic practices as well as an assessment of the overall economic globalization phenomenon in the global world. The introductory chapter discusses the notions of *socioeconomic practices* and *competition*—notions which prove to be important in the contemporary global context, where socioeconomic and cultural factors become increasingly intertwined. The concluding chapter reviews from a critical comparative perspective how different regions have dealt with socioeconomic practices and whether global cooperation has played a role in terms of the distinction of different world regions between the *old* bipolar world order and the *new* center, semiperiphery, and periphery status. This publication seeks to assess the overall situation in the world, looking at the world as a socioeconomic system where some countries act as winners, others as losers, and some as both winners and losers of economic globalization. The authors also tentatively offer some predictions for future developments of their research topic.

The overall aim of the book is to provide a comprehensive overview of transformations of socioeconomic practices in the global economy. It is worth noting that although this collection of articles is comprehensive in its coverage of socioeconomic local practices and in its geographical coverage (all major world regions are included), it is also theoretically informed. Hence, additional theoretical or empirical research questions are raised by

single authors for further study but are not discussed in the single chapters, mainly for reasons of space. The volume aims to become a specialized
monograph developing new advances in the field of globalization studies.
We hope that the book will help academic readers, policymakers, and the
larger public to better understand current transformations of local socioeconomic practices and social processes affecting all countries in the world.

The studies in this book refer to economic anthropology and economic
sociology. They contribute to an understanding of social processes that
are most often lived without grasping their real meanings. The book challenges localized cultural anthropology and shows that some current global
processes have caused similarities across the world. What we can find is
a world that has changed some of its local socioeconomic practices on a
global scale. The studies show that the neo-liberal credo had repercussions
all over the world and not only in the core Western countries. Similarities
and differences of this intertwining of local and global elements are shown.
It is argued that a sort of *global modernity* is in the making, even if differences based on local cultural life-worlds continue to exist.

My special thanks for the support of this publication go to Nina Bandelj,
the current cochair of RC 09 "Social Transformations and Sociology of
Development," whose sympathetic support and assistance during the prepa-
ration of the book contributed to a great extent to its successful comple-
tion, and to two anonymous reviewers, who helped with their comments to
clarify the argument.

1 Transformations of Local Socioeconomic Practices in a Global World

A Theoretical Approach and Some Empirical Evidence From Different World Regions

Ulrike Schuerkens

Since the end of the global competition, characteristic of the cold war era, processes of international competition have played a lesser role than domestic ethnic conflicts, which took center stage in areas with weakly developed democratic institutions in the South. Nevertheless, with the increase of *global modernity* during the last decade, the breakdown of most of the communist states, and the spread of the neo-liberal credo, the notion of competition resurfaced as a prominent issue in understanding socioeconomic development in a globalized world. The discussion has centered on the question of whether the economic ideology brought about by *global modernity* would have an impact on countries socially and culturally very different from the Western core countries. As there seems to be no real alternative to the Western economic competition ideal, economists and sociologists have asked whether institutions of competitive markets could be integrated into the social, cultural, and economic systems of Asia, Latin America, and Africa. The answer has largely depended on the social-structural makeup of societies in different world regions. It seems now obvious that some societies are better positioned to become active participants in the global modernity than others. Perhaps such positioning would be best conceptualized by the notion of cultural life-worlds than mere socioeconomic and political constellations (Jacquin-Berdal et al. 1998a; Tetzlaff 2000; Mozaffari 2002; Arjomand and Tiryakian 2004; Nederveen Pieterse 2004). If so, then a reflection on the cultural construction of social life-worlds in global modernity seems to be a precondition for the analysis of discourses and practices on economic globalization in non-Western civilizations. Global players exert pressures for adaptation and efficiency on local and regional cultures. The world market defined by competitive capitalism, the importance of private property, and the virtue of individualism have become the dominant principles introduced by colonial and postcolonial forces in non-Western societies during the last centuries and in more recent years. Civilizations have become defined by their adaptability to global economic processes. The culture as a given system for capital investment and capital use has become the criterion of selection. According to global players, a competition around social systems that permit the highest profits, has become established on cultural values. Societies that are capable to adopt these principles receive higher scores than societies that resist changes required by the capitalist logic.

This briefly outlined approach, which intends to reunite economic interests, cultural preferences, and political institutions in one logical system, permits us to analyze why some societies are more able or willing to negotiate global pressures and to confront world market conditions than others. Within this theoretical framework, we present here empirical case studies of how local socioeconomic practices in different civilizations or cultures intertwine with global economic modernity.

GLOBALIZATION IN HISTORY

The analysis of the origins and consequences of globalization is currently one of the most important debates in the social sciences (Balachandran and Subrahmanyam 2005). The French historian Serge Gruzinski (2004) has argued that globalization had its roots in the Great Discoveries in the East and West in the beginning of the 16th century when Asia, Africa, Europe, and America were linked together. According to Gruzinski, the years from 1480 to 1520 should be considered the first period of globalization. For Williamson and O'Rourke (2002), the *first global century* began only after 1820 and lasted up to 1913. It was linked to the gold standard under the free trade imperialism of the British Empire. During this century, a global commodity market and even an increased labor migration existed. According to Williamson and O'Rourke, the *second global century* began in 1950 and corresponded to the worldwide acceptance of the dollar. The period after 1985, associated with the fall of the Iron Curtain, the opening up of certain markets, and the decline of national economic controls that most of the articles in this book discuss, can thus be seen as belonging to a far longer trend.

Yet Gruzinski's and Williamson's and O'Rourke's views are quite different in relation to cultural or economic questions. For Williamson and O'Rourke, globalization is a form of economic integration verified by an intensification of economic exchanges. After 1492, as said by Williamson and O'Rourke, tariffs, trading monopoly, wars, and not economic exchanges were the driving forces of wider processes. Gruzinski has been more interested in cultural exchanges instead.

There are further scholarly differences on the various waves of globalization: For Richard Baldwin and Philippe Martin (1999) the period from 1870, linked to the expansion of trade from Europe to the rest of the world, represents the *first wave* of globalization. O'Rourke (2002) has even preferred to fix the beginning of globalization at about 1820 because of the higher growth rate of the world trade at that time compared to previous centuries. The interwar years of the 20th century conventionally represent a global disintegration with the dissolution of external links for many countries. The liberalization of financial markets beyond Europe and the decline of national sovereignty in policy areas related to markets and international institutions in the 1980s are often assimilated with the present phase of globalization. There are other views that underline that the Bretton Woods agreement and the reduction of tariffs under the General Agreement on Tariffs and Trade (GATT) set the institutional infrastructure for the reemergence of industrial capitalism, the changes in financial and banking institutions, and the globalizing transformations in culture, communication, politics, and global institutions.

According to these discourses, globalization can be represented as a flow of human history that has prevailed over most of the last 150 years and that is founded on processes that began 500 years ago. The logic of globalization is thus more than the logic of capital imagined by Marx insofar as it has economic, political, and cultural dimensions (Schuerkens 2004; Scholte 2005; Stiglitz 2006). Politicians, scholars, and opponents of globalization have contributed to reify the phenomenon. One might argue that today's globalization is a reinvention of international capitalism that had been politically compromised. But globalization is also promoted by agencies representing the nongovernmental sector, with large implications on individuals and competition regimes. Globalization represents the danger and the opportunity that governments and national elites evoke in order to force opponents to accept reforms. It is a hopeful slogan or a frightened process in developing countries depending on social categories and/or social classes.[1]

ECONOMIC GLOBALIZATION AND ITS STRUCTURAL INFLUENCE ON SOCIETIES

Commercial penetration in different world regions does not unilaterally imply propagation of capitalism. Sub-Saharan Africa receives more aid than the Far East, but it remains of little interest for private foreign capital. Countries in the Near East or in Northern Africa that possess oil do not really industrialize. Yet the multilateral aid of the International Monetary Fund (IMF) and the World Bank is disbursed with the conditionality to develop free market economies in the receiving countries, that is, to propagate capitalism in these regions. Multilateral institutions finance productive or collective projects that promise profitability in the long term. Often, they contribute to the restructuring of sectors, such as agriculture, energy, and communications (Adda 2006: 132). The primary goal of these programs is the systematic introduction of the market mechanism in these economies via external exchanges, the financial system, and other sectors ruled by the state. The creation of these institutional conditions of capitalism lays the ground for further economic processes linked to the global economy (Nicholas 2005).

The question is then how these societies internalize, appropriate, and reshape their particular form of capitalism. It is obvious that cultures react in different ways to these processes. In some societies, capital may enter and propagate a given material culture and consumption styles, but capitalism as a system based on competition may be barely developed. Credits and aid, and not private foreign investment, are thus the dominant forms of the penetration of foreign capital that one can find in regions such as Africa South of the Sahara, the Near East, and Central and South Asia.

In three other regions, capitalist economic structures have been more readily embraced and implemented: Eastern Europe, Latin America, and the Far East. To a large extent, the first two regions could base their development on groups that originated from Europe (refugees, migrants, etc.). The Far East could absorb and internalize global capitalism by focusing on three elements in its national development projects: education, the existence of a local middle class, and economic growth organized by the state. The state served as a leader and assured the functioning of the public bureaucracy (Evans 1995), a condition that has been absent in most African and Latin American countries (Adda 2006: 141).

The empirical facts created in these different world regions put in question the notions of "North/South," "center—periphery," and "First, Second, and Third World." Braudel (1998) emphasized some decades ago that there were stable cultural realities, readapted to structural constraints according to wider civilizations. The development discourse of the last decades let us forget these findings, which were rather unpopular with elites who founded their political measures on an understanding of development as an improvement of socioeconomic conditions in every country. Adda (2006) emphasizes in his book that "the particular characteristics of these regional areas explain the manner of insertion in the global economy and their capacity to profit from the globalization process" (p. 164, my translation) This means that there are winners and losers, and even for those that are situated in between, such as Eastern Europe, which could base economic success on its industrial culture created under the communist regimes, the question continues to exist of whether these societies are capable of assimilating to the Western capitalist logic. The new periphery in the global world seems to be Sub-Saharan Africa, the Arab World, and Central and South Asia. In these regions, we find prevalent poverty, structural unemployment, feeble salaries, and high fecundity rates. Moreover, political structures are weak, and ethnic and religious violence is widespread.

INTERNATIONAL POLITICAL ECONOMY AS A CULTURE OF COMPETITION

Our contemporary world is composed of three regions that claim a Western civilization, namely, North America, Western Europe, and that part of Asia that developed from Japan, such as South Korea (Blancy and Inayatullah 1998). These three regions have spread over the rest of the world common development principles that support *global modernity*. This sort of globalization is defined by the integration of other world territories according to Western perceptions and power logics. But whether this system, even if there seem to be some common dynamics, is characterized by such a political and economical unity, so that regions from all over the world have been trying from their point of origin to integrate in a common system, is largely contested.

Currently, some scholars insist that there is a multiplicity of globalizations (Chang 2007). The case of China is taken as an example of a civilization that imposed itself to the whole region of East Asia. China's capability to found a written language, its values, and a unique social and political system seem to establish the Chinese world as an alternative to the Western world. The political and economical events in China since the first half of the 19th century and the impossibility for China to challenge European and North American modernity have not reduced China to a nation-state that has submitted to Western globalization. As Sanjuan (2004: 123) underlines, Chinese defend three forms of globalization: an imperial model that has conceived China as a political, cultural, and cosmological factor organizing the world from the north of China; a network model founded on the networks of the diasporas; and a coastal model where the big towns from the coast, such as Shanghai and Hong Kong, have become spaces that have integrated China in the world system.

These globalization models have begun to be transformed by Western globalization, but they also, in turn, transform Western globalization, as China has continued to redefine its relations with its neighbors and other countries of Asia and the rest of the world. Let us think, for instance, of the events surrounding the liberalization of textile imports from China into the European Union in 2005. This topic has shown that China has tried to promote its own distinct economy in a world economy characterized by economic competition. The reactions of the United States and the European Union were to reduce Chinese imports in order to protect their textile economy. That has been challenged by China, which wishes to discuss this topic in an organization that defines international economic relations such as the World Trade Organization.

These events show that Chinese political and intellectual elites try to strengthen the economic and political power of China in the world, even if its globalization is not orientated at a universalism trying to create a hierarchy of territories and nations. The current political elite seems to be convinced that the power of China has to be spread globally on the basis of its rapidly growing economy, and not of its culture or politics, as it was the rule under the Empire or under Mao. Since the opening of China in 1978, China seems to have restored the global status of the country. Chinese know that their nation is not the only superpower trying to reorganize the world. Chinese accept the North American model where it seems necessary for them in order to strengthen the place of China in East Asia in opposition to Japan, Southeast Asia, and India. According to Sanjuan (2004), the rivalry between China and the United States is not conceived according to the same notions. Chinese globalization is based on a regional power in Asia and is rather uninterested in far-away conflicts in the Near East or in Africa, even if China has recently expressed concern with the Palestinian cause and has enlarged its economic relations with Africa. China does not try to impose its model on others or to change the West. But Chinese try to adapt pragmatically and realistically to the current state of the world in order to use it for their power project. Globalization, according to Beijing, can only be multipolar. But this Chinese world is global insofar as the Chinese diasporas are spread over the five continents and try to increase Chinese transnational solidarities. Beijing has pursued a politics directed to the Chinese diasporas, asking them to develop China by investments and industrial relocations, and by the promotion of Chinese products and Chinese cultural heritage. Chinese communities in Southeast Asia and in Western Chinatowns now belong to a larger community of a global reach. Furthermore, Chinese towns have to display the success of the reforms in China and an international modernity with urban behaviors and leisure, urban silhouettes and new urban public spaces, foreign banks and commerce, or tourism. The Olympic Games in Beijing in 2008 and the World Fair in Shanghai in 2010 will further accentuate these processes.

All these elements also underline the integration of China in the community of developed states, and affirm its place as a dynamic actor of globalization. This means not only a reformulation of Chinese globalization, but also a reformulation of globalization according to Chinese interests in a global Western order. As such, China should be able to engage other states of the world to reinterpret globalization.

Beside this particular form of globalization that will probably transform our understandings of the world in the coming years, the current Western form of globalization has tried to enlarge its influence after the breakdown of the Iron Curtain in Eastern Europe and in those parts of Central Asia formerly under the influence of the Soviet Union. Cultural products originating from Western countries have methodically confronted these regions. Financial assistance to favor economic development and systemic changes has served to institute political, economic, and social reforms. The discourse of globalization has been introduced by international financial assistance, diplomats, businesspeople, and international experts sent to the different world regions, and by local experts who have supported the implementation of programs by governmental institutes before they were accepted by parliaments and presidents.

In fact, the United States has utilized enormous financial, economical, and human measures in order to accelerate the participation of Central Asia in global processes (Poujol 2004: 146). These have privileged bilateral treaties in important sectors such as defense, economic investment, participation in the oil business, and so on. The United States has promoted democracy, the free market, political stability, and assistance to private industries and to educational programs—all in all a complex program aimed at firmly integrating the new states in the global economic system. Today, thousands of Americans and Europeans are charged to implement a model presented as universal under a global cover. They work as democracy officers, Peace Corps members, or in international nongovernmental organizations (NGOs) that tackle the entire sociopolitical space. USAID is one of the most important instruments to spread the message of globalization. The United States is considered as more or less the only global player. Chinese, Japanese, Indian, and even Russian projects are considered as bilateral efforts that remain national (Poujol 2004: 148).

The rapid spread of these political measures, aimed at integrating these countries into new economic, financial, and strategic networks, has been intentional insofar as it tried to avoid allowing the former Russian power to reconstruct new links to its former Soviet satellites. The new partners of these countries have tried to integrate a total of 50 million inhabitants into Western globalization. The peoples of these regions had to reconsider their place, their history, and their future. They have shown ambivalent feelings and an apparent submission in order to please money lenders. Often, large parts of the population have refused global cultural models that denied national particularities. But the political options of this region are different from antiglobalization movements insofar as its leaders try to strengthen their states while accepting large aspects of globalization.

GLOBALIZATION AT THE PERIPHERY: THE IMPACT ON AFRICA

Globalization refers to intense economic, political, social, and cultural relations across international borders. Barriers in the areas of culture, commerce, and communication are broken down. Free-market economics, liberal democracy, and good governance have become universal values for states. The collapse of the Eastern bloc in the late 1980s and early 1990s led to the emergence of a global economy structured by the interests of mainly Western countries, increasing the integration of most economies in the global economy. Capitalism as an economic system currently dominates the globe. The broadening linkages of national economies into a worldwide market for goods and services characterize globalization. But globalization is also about the international division of labor: developed countries specializing in high-skill manufacturing and services, and developing countries in low-skill intensive manufacturing. This asymmetry has had severe impacts on African countries that primarily produce raw materials for industries in the developed countries that may sell the produced goods in developing countries (Grégoire 2002; Ajayi 2003; Brunel 2005; Rugumamu 2005).

Capitalism and Marginalization

The African continent is currently characterized by marginalization. Already in 1996, Africa's share in world exports had dropped to a meager 1 percent. If South Africa and the oil-producing states are excluded, the percentage is rather by nil. At the end of the last century, growth in African countries slowed down to 1 percent, while official aid was less than $20 per head annually (Akindele et al. 2002). Scholars such as Nigel C. Gibson underline that the world system has been strongly unequal since the beginning of the industrial revolution in the North linked to the exploitation of colored and Black people. According to Gibson, "political power has been employed to gain advantages, exploit inequalities, and crush competition" (2004: 5). Africa, because of its centrality during the triangular trade between this continent, the Americas, and Europe, became marginalized. European colonialism shaped modern Africa, but Africans also contributed to the rising power of Europe.

Africa was linked to other regions, such as China and India, the Middle East, and the Mediterranean, through trade as early as the second century (Beaujard 2005). The Portuguese contributed in the early 16th century to the partial destruction of African mercantilism in modern Mozambique. Some African economies remained in trade with Europe until the period of European colonization in the 19th century. The enormous wealth linked to the slave trade, lasting for nearly 400 years, had strong effects on the African and American continents. Walter Rodney famously wrote that "the development of America meant the underdevelopment of Africa" (Gibson 2004: 6). Other authors, such as Akindele et al. (2002), underline the opinion that globalization is the latest form of capitalist diffusion in Africa. The continent has been opened to capitalism by structural adjustment, privatization, and World Bank and IMF policies. As a result, Africa's consumers and productive forces have dealt with capitalism. It seems thus that the 21st century is characterized by the marginalization of Africa as a continent of increasing inequality.

Globalization and Labor Productivity

For most African countries, the first period of independence did not lead to the realization of the political goals of the anticolonial struggles. Often, national economies functioned more or less successfully by loading the largest share of the burden on the peasantry who produced to low prices. Cheap capital loans led to the high burden of debts while the prices of primary goods diminished. Since the 1980s, African countries were obliged to accept the rules of the international economic system by opening up their national economies to world-market competition. The free movement of capital was in search of markets and cheap labor. Since the 1960s, there has been a constant movement of redundant workers from the African countryside to the overcrowded towns. These men and women may have worked from time to time, but they have often been unemployed or part-time or occasional workers. Export processing zones (EPZs), which see the assembly of products, have been created in twenty-five African countries, but are only important in Tunisia, Egypt, and Mauritius. They have been successful in Mauritius, where they account for 65 percent of exports (Gibson 2004: 10). The rest of the continent is not a source of semiskilled workers from the point of view of international capitalism. But there has been an important brain drain of African intellectual elites to Western countries since the 1960s. Another particular element of the continent's globalization has been that women's unpaid work as subsistence farmers not only has contributed to the national economy, but also has given women a degree of autonomy and independence unknown in other continents. It can thus be argued that Africa's marginalization from the international economy is also a result of gender conflicts.

Since September 11, 2001, there is a renewed interest in Africa's raw materials and specially oil. The United States in particular has looked for a control of these goods. Globalization as a myth is only affordable to an elite minority of Africans, while most other people live situations of unemployment, illness, and starvation. As a result of structural adjustment and the debt regime, the majority of Africa's populations are faced today with a situation that is worse than twenty-five years ago. This means lack of chances for youth, conflicts about resources, and social and political movements against globalization and some Western states.

Globalization and a National Leadership

Africa's populations have been looking for good governance but have often been ruled by political elites who have tended to think more about their privileges than about the improvement of the situation of their populations. In fact, world markets have contributed to the declining power of the nation-state and its elites. Political elites are less and less able to control their national economy. International organizations such as the IMF or the World Bank are more important than national governments. Countries like Nigeria and South Africa have played dominant regional roles, but most other states have been weak. The possibility of instituting socioeconomic change has been rather limited in African states. Even if there is an argument underlining the necessity to have ethical and charismatic leaders, who are responsible for their population's needs, the small political autonomy puts a real challenge to African elites. Yet the current crisis in Africa might be a turning point: All sorts of interior crises appear, such as civil wars, ethnic and political conflicts, and high criminal rates. The youth feel like "the lost generation" and, having nothing to lose, they engage in political upsets, religious fundamentalism, or cultural chauvinism.

Globalization: Its General Impact on African Societies

Globalization influences autochthonous cultures, environment, labor standards, productivity, and other elements of societies. Liberal economic thinking has considered that trade would result in economic welfare for the participating states. The General Agreement on Tariffs and Trade (GATT) played a major role after World War II in reducing tariffs for developed countries, eliminating certain barriers and subsidies, broadening GATT principles to sectors such as services and investment, and applying more rules to agricultural trade. Long-term rules were established and national policies that hindered access to the market were reduced. In 1995, the World Trade Organization began to function and currently 150 countries accept its free trade rules. The worldwide movements of capital and labor have become easier, so that even the last unlinked regions have got their rural migrants who send money back from the region of residence and spend their holidays in the region of origin. But the evidence of whether globalization has been beneficial to most countries is mixed. There are scholars who argue that in the globalization process the destiny of the poorer countries is to become marginalized, except for those countries that can attract subcontracting enterprises. Global companies are concentrated in the global North, and trade is dominated by this same category of countries. The percentage of world trade has been small in the least developed countries, especially in per capita figures. In 1999, the merchandise trade among these countries accounted for 14 percent of the world trade. Some four or five developed countries bought 54% percent of all exports from the least developed countries (Momayezi 2006: 710).

On the other hand, some scholars think that the least developed countries (LDCs) gain from engaging in global interactions. In fact, they gain access to larger markets and consumers gain access to a larger variety of goods and services. Domestic industries may have the possibility of serving global markets, and domestic producers gain access to necessary inputs at lower prices. A further argument is that LDCs may improve their level of technology without the high costs of research and development. They may import capital equipment that raises their productive capacity. These outcomes may engage future growth with higher domestic savings and/or international credits. Another argument is that governments are encouraged to follow international economic policies: Countries that insist on policies that do not favor the market risk no longer to receive international investments.

History suggests that the wealthiest nations of the world have been trade-oriented (Western Europe, the United States, Japan, South Korea, and Singapore). In contrast, the poorest regions of the world, such as some Asian countries and Sub-Saharan Africa, have remained more or less absent from foreign trade. Countries such as India, China, and Poland that have opened their economies could strongly improve their standard of living for parts of their populations. Yet it may be the case that there must be a sort of Marshall Plan for some parts of the developing world in order to benefit from globalization (Goldstein et al. 2006). Only by pursuing the welfare of all can the international community change the negative effects of globalization that the poorer countries currently resent.

ECONOMIC GLOBALIZATION IN LATIN AMERICA

Business and state relations in Latin America have historical roots that are particular for the region. In the current global economy, most firms of Latin American origin are unknown outside their region. Most of the local groups are "multi-company firms under the control of family and friendship cliques" (Conaghan and Malloy 1994: 16). Few economic groups are important, but these "groups are horizontally and/or vertically diversified industrial and financial powers" (Cordey 2005: 79). The particular characteristics of power elites in Latin America are that horizontal networks have linked them: Economic elites are in informal contact via clubs or meetings with political elites so that they may defend common interests.

Economic power concentration has its traditional roots in groups that based their power on land and the enslavement of the population in the 19th century. These families maintained their power until the 1930s. Since the 1920s, new elite groups "began to articulate ideologies and economic programs that assigned a leading role in economic development to the state" (Conaghan and Malloy 1994: 19). The *hacienda* ceased to be an important economic factor but state industries and new private enterprises were appearing. Military governments accessed to power in the following decades. They sought an alliance with economic elites and gave them an influence on the decision-making process. The masses were excluded from political processes. The absence of formal possibilities of interaction between the domestic economic elites and the military governments contributed to a growing unease of the bourgeoisie, who looked for political and economical models better adapted to their visions. From the 1980s, business groups began to support democratization in order to open up political processes to the masses (Conaghan and Malloy 1994: 5). The state began to retreat from state enterprises and reaffirmed the private sector, so that the market power of the business groups grew with their acquisition of state enterprises (Cordey 2005: 82). Yet business elites continued to be closely linked to political power. These domestic elites were regarded as rent-seeking and inefficient, but they had success in adjustment processes by underlining the national reality of the different countries (Conaghan and Malloy 1994: 219). The majority of the population was more or less excluded from these debates. Economics was an "elite affair" (Cordey 2005: 83). The structure of state and business links in Latin America and the interaction of economical and political elites thus have a particular character, which is different from that of other continents.

With the globalization processes of the 1990s, transnational companies began to engage in Latin America but they pursued another strategy as in Asia. They tried to acquire big domestic enterprises and national banks. These acquisitions permitted them to remove competitors and to have access immediately to a "distribution network, local know-how and connections" (Cordey 2005: 122). The aim was "to improve their strategic position on national, regional and global markets" (122). Some business groups from the region managed to become regional transnational companies (TNCs), but most of the other TNCs were from the United States, Europe, and Japan. Local groups built joint ventures with triad TNCs. These big TNCs have a huge impact on the development of the economies, even if their investment has sometimes corresponded to a marginal role in their global strategies. Cordey argues that "to developing countries, they seem to remain with virtually no bargaining options and no alternatives but to open up their economies" (123). The transnational era of the Latin American economies began thus in the 1990s.

The result of this strategic alliance between political and business elites has been a wave of strikes and protests of the populations during the last decade. Some charismatic leaders such as Chávez have tried to introduce politics that favor groups that have become marginalized and impoverished in the preceding decades. Neo-liberal policies and indirect taxation had favored privileged groups, often small groups linked to the government, the presidents, some remaining domestic economic groups, and the TNCs. The populations of these countries have become skeptical in the presence of corruption and economic models favored by political elites.

This short overview may help to improve our understanding of social inequality and poverty that have resulted from these policies. This knowledge of processes that have taken place among the different elite groups permits us to better seize the dynamics of economic power strategies in different Latin American countries.[2]

COMPETITION IN ENTERPRISES IN DIFFERENT CIVILIZATIONS

The empirical contributions in this book revolve around the issue of competition in different civilizations (D'Iribarne 2003; 2004). Let us begin with the Chinese case. Chinese argue in terms of flows; they try to circulate capital as quickly as possible (Paulmier 2004: 185). The control of these flows is more important than the property of the capital (Wong 1997; Rocca 2006). The market is characterized by small enterprises that are very competitive. Markets are conquered progressively: First, according to the Chinese, they should be developed at the periphery before leaders try to have access to the core. According to this idea, Korean and Taiwanese groups have penetrated industries and high technology by conquering markets in Latin

America, Africa, and Asia (Paulmier 2004: 187). This sort of economy has favored the development of a merchant mentality looking for rapid profits. The enterprise has often been a family project, controlled by the family head and administered by children, nephews, or brothers-in-law. This sort of administration means small enterprises, financed by the family. Large groups and industrial firms have been state owned or state administered.

Japanese, Korean, and Chinese businessmen try to diversify their activities and their markets and to enlarge their economic possibilities. They demonstrate an economic mentality that is particularly adapted to capitalism (Huang 1998). One has only to think about the many small restaurants of these groups in Western towns. Asian cultures have thus been particularly well adapted to economic transformations.

When we think about Africa, the situation is different. The failure of many enterprises of the modern sector in African countries is caused by business systems that are not adapted to the social context. Their main characteristic is that they find it difficult to shape the link between the individual and the group (Henry 2004: 199). However, there are some examples of success. Some firms have invented books that describe in detail all procedures necessary for the functioning of enterprises. These books render objective the actions to be undertaken by economic actors and the staff. Another example that Henry (2004) evokes is software developed to control the economic process.

A different understanding of economic competition is that of Morocco (cf. Mezouar and Sémériva 2004). In this country, the behavior and attitudes of modern industrial economies have not been accepted. The life-world seems to be something rather malleable that can be interpreted by everybody according to his opinions. A further problem is that the direct and intermediate hierarchy has not been recognized and has been considered to have no legitimacy, while positive legal rights have characterized directors, and customary rights are used at the basis of society. Businesspeople have been marginalized and thus have decided to leave the country.

According to the socioanthropological tradition, in Africa, social facts cannot be reduced to individual phenomena. The rational economic actor of the Western culture seems to be particular to societies based on the market. There are scholars who underline that Western rationality is incongruent with African representations (cf. Engelhardt 1998; Latouche 1998). In most parts of the continent, an economic action is often secondary to exchange relations based on symbolic and social links. According to orthodox economical thinking, economic agents respond to prices and individual calculations. But in Africa, community and state pressures contribute to undermine rationalized development processes. Economic actions are here atypical, and that has led to opposition between the *Homo oeconomicus* and the *Homo africanus*. As Hugon underlines, Africans try to minimize risks that depend on social positions (Hugon 2006: 58). Under uncertain conditions, these actors prefer the short run and intergenerational investments. Furthermore, it is necessary to opt for the reversibility of decisions and to act according to current options. Insecurity and precarious situations let people select the short run and not the long run. In front of feeble states, social identities are forcibly based on community rules, even if these latter are also exposed to transformations.

There are some constant variables: Higher salaries may mean that African actors decide to work less, as they don't need more to survive. Insofar as salaries are often considered as absolutely necessary for monetary expenses (dowry, funerals, etc.), to work may signify for some people to accept an activity for a short time span. In Africa, economic exchange relations (e.g., gifts, reciprocal aid) influence labor relations. Therefore, social capital and social links are more important than the accumulation of goods. Despite widespread poverty, markets continue to be well furnished because of functioning distributive mechanisms, even if some actors are excluded from these community networks. These permit poor people to survive and permit elites to transfer capital outside their countries; the meanings of these distributive mechanisms are thus different and depend on social categories.

This signifies that African enterprises are influenced by microeconomic links based on community relations. Economic efficiency is not a priority, and entrepreneurial dynamics originating from the inside of African social systems are few. Characteristic dynamics of enterprises are linked to power relations and redistributive logics of social networks. Even if foreign enterprises underline elements such as profitability, they have to confront feeble states that are not capable of providing collective goods and services (e.g., infrastructure, energy). In Africa, public enterprises have become regulators of unemployment, as Hugon underlines (2006: 63–65), that means a feeble learning of characteristic elements of efficiency in the whole society.

The crisis of African economies during the last decades has thus led to their informality. Public jobs have become rare and the private economic sector has become more or less absent, so that the informal economy has continued to play an important role. Dominant criteria have been small units with feeble capital but where money has circulated, and goods and services have been provided. These organizations have not been characterized by salary relations but by community and power relations. Nowadays, most Africans have been influenced by this way of life permitting them to satisfy their basic needs: eating, housing, clothing, learning, caring, distracting, and so on. Informality has included female activities such as feeding and personal and material services, and male activities such as repairing, recycling of industrial goods, transports, producing, and transforming (Hugon 2006: 65).

Often, the head of the unit has been a young person; he/she has used some personal savings to create his/her business; he/she has made use of some simple technologies but has no staff. He/she has not benefited from any budget and has not distinguished between the productive and the domestic part of his/her business. If there has been some profit, the head of business has tried to diversify his/her activities. These informal activities seem to remain the most important economic pursuits in the near future, as they permit economic actors to survive. There may exist some enterprises functioning on different criteria, but the informal sector does not constitute, according to Hugon, the foundation of performing enterprises in Africa where the environment is characterized by feeble states and the predominance of community links.

How about Latin American societies? According to Inglehart (1998: 15), competition and economic success are not priorities of social actors in this region. A fundamental stability can be found that has been conceived as an obstacle to the development of differentiation and economic change. The upper classes have been interested in maintaining their fortune and have co-opted newly rich who have accepted their rules. These classes possess the potential to modernize the region but they have only been interested in its individual short-term use. The ethics of enterprises and savings have not been widespread and the determination to invest is lacking. Despite a more or less common history for centuries and a common geographic culture, tendencies to integrate several Latin American societies have been feeble. Economic, social, and political inequalities have been high and have continued to increase. Economic thoughts and actions have been introduced, but societal preconditions (an economic development based on agricultural produce) have been revealed to be insufficient. Instruction and performance have not been highly valued goods, while, at the same time, power and connections have determined economic and social positions. A group who favors modern economic values is still missing. Contrary to Asia, a reappraisal of traditional values and norms to strengthen development has barely been possible. Only in some larger countries of the region have enterprises existed that favored productivity; autochthonous enterprises that have been able to compete and to innovate are rather rare. The technical culture has been weak and economic training has been neglected. Because of the fact that cultural transfers from outside the region have been considered as uniform and powerful, intellectual elites have focused on processes of *self-finding,* of a denial of external influences. An alternative to the capitalism of the North seemed to be possible, with the state as the decisive factor. External reasons have been considered as causing regional and national underdevelopment (*dependencia*). The result of this denial of the economic development in the North has been a technical and industrial time lag that has prevented the formation of groups favoring industrial development. The recent political changes in some Latin American countries have demonstrated that their political and economical elites have only limited visions and strategies to change their societies. The political crises have shown that social and political pressure from below can oblige politicians and upper classes to change their societal projects. Impulses that come from other countries of the region or from the North seem to be necessary to implement social and economic transformations. It is only then that these societies will be ready to accept targets such as to change attitudes and consumption styles with corresponding economic, political, and social changes (Esser 2000).

CONCLUSION

It seems as if we are living today the creation of a world community that spans different world civilizations. In our contemporary world, there are groups of individuals who do not need to meet physically but who share common behaviors that define a sort of global culture. These people know that they belong to a common universe, that they form a group characterized by the same consciousness. Sociologists such as L. Sklair, M. Hartmann, and J. A. Scholte have studied these groups.

Civilization in the singular seems to be the culture of the present that has spread around the globe since the last quarter of the 20th century. This civilization is now underway. Networks of technoscience character-ize this global civilization, as Schaefer (2004: 79) argues. In this sense, globalization happens to cultural others and also to the core of the West, the American culture. The World Wide Web, human rights, world music, world markets, and the individualistic, capitalist way of life have spread widely and continue to do so. This is what is most characteristic of con-temporary globalization, a trend that appeals to many people. In this sense, one cultural model is being adopted, even if multiple cultures with alternative symbolic systems continue to exist that are opposed to a global civilization characterized by networks of technoscience. Local cultures are thus situated in a global civilization that encompasses large fractions of populations but continues to exclude whole groups of disadvantaged people. The theoretical discussion of these trends needs to be strength-ened by empirical case studies about regions from all over the world and about different societal structures, such as classes, families, and gender. This book presents such case studies, whose influence on further research is discussed in the concluding chapter.

Globalization may mean the triumph of market competition principles all over the world. Historical studies have shown that in former periods the state tried to organize and to rule societies, helping them to adapt to different economic structures. In our current world, transnational enter-prises try to avoid these organizational attempts of states and create a global economy where an absence of social rules related to competition can be found. Since the breakdown of the bipolar world order (East–West), financial crises and social upsets have shown that rules are neces-sary. Critical intellectuals and politicians begin to discuss these topics, even if governments that sustain global capitalism rarely follow them. Recent upsets in France (2005 and 2006) have shown that large soci-etal groups feel insecure when faced by global economic competition.

This book tries to shed light on these important issues by studying the transformations of socioeconomic practices in different world regions in an attempt to outline the character of the current global socioeconomic structure.

ACKNOWLEDGMENTS

I thank Nina Bandelj for very helpful critical comments on this chapter. Some parts of this chapter will appear in *The Encyclopedia of the Modern World* and are reprinted here by permission of Oxford University Press, Inc. Copyright 2008 by Oxford University Press, Inc.

NOTES

1. See for some more details on the history of globalization: Balachandran/ Subrahmanyam (2005).
2. Cordey (2005) analyzes in a case study the situation in Peru in order to concretize processes that he displayed in the other chapters of his thesis. As the cases of China and India are discussed in the conclusion and the chapters of Th. Pairault and F. Wherry in this book tackle Asian cases, we do not treat here the topic of globalization and Asia. The interested reader may find an economic analysis of Asian globalization in the book of Rajan (2003). Other parts of this introduction treat the understanding of socioeconomic practices in parts of Asia.

REFERENCES

Adda, Jacques. 2006. *La mondialisation de l'économie: Genèse et problèmes*, rev. 7th ed. Paris: La Découverte.

Ajayi, S. Ibi. 2003. "Globalisation and Africa." *Journal of African Economies* 12 (1): 120–150.

Akindele, S. T., T. O. Gidado, and O. R. Olaopo. 2002. "Globalisation, Its Implications and Consequences for Africa." *Globalization* 2 (1). http://globalization.icaap.org/content/v2.1/01_akindele_etal.html, accessed on December 30, 2006.

Arjomand, Saïd Amir, and Edward A. Tiryakian, eds. 2004. *Rethinking Civilizational Analysis*. Thousand Oaks, CA, London, New Delhi: Sage. Studies in International Sociology 52.

Aubert, Jean-Éric, and Josée Landrieu, eds. 2004. *Vers des civilisations mondialisées? De l'éthologie à la prospective*. Colloque de Cerisy: Éditions de l'Aube.

Balachandran, G., and Sanjay Subrahmanyam. 2005. "On the History of Globalization and India: Concepts, Measures and Debates." Pp. 17–46 in *Globalizing India: Perspectives from Below*, ed. Jackie Assayag and Christopher John Fuller. London: Anthem Press.

Baldwin, Richard E., and Philippe Martin. 1999. *Two Waves of Globalization: Superficial Similarities, Fundamental Differences*. Cambridge, MA: National Bureau of Economic Research Working Paper No. 6904.

Beaujard, Philippe. 2005. "The Indian Ocean in Eurasian and African World-Systems Before the Sixteenth Century." *Journal of World History* 16 (4): 411–465.

Blaney, David, and Naeem Inayatullah. 1998. "International Political Economy as a Culture of Competition." Pp. 61–88 in *Culture in World Politics*, ed. Dominique Jacquin-Berdal, Andrew Oros, and Marco Verweij. New York: St. Martin's Press.

Braudel, Fernand. 1998. *Grammaire des civilisations*. Paris: Bussière Camedan.

Brunel, Sylvie. 2005. *L'Afrique dans la mondialisation*. Paris: La Documentation française. Dossier 8048.

Chang, Ha-Joon. 2007. *The East Asian Development Experience. The Miracle, the Crisis and the Future*. London: Zed Books.

Conaghan, Catherine M., and James M. Malloy. 1994. *Unsettling Statecraft: Democracy and Neo-liberalism in the Central Andes*. Pittsburgh: University of Pittsburgh Press.

Cordey, Pierre-André. 2005. "Business and State Relations in Latin America: The Role of Transnational Corporations in Peru." PhD thesis, Fribourg, Switzerland.

D'Iribarne, Philippe. 2003. *Le Tiers Monde qui réussit*. Paris: Odile Jacob.

D'Iribarne, Philippe. 2004. "Mondialisation et maintien de la diversité des cultures au sein des enterprises." Pp. 171–180 in *Vers des civilisations mondialisées? De l'éthologie à la prospective*, ed. Jean-Éric Aubert and Josée Landrieu. Colloque de Cerisy: Éditions de l'Aube.

Engelhardt, Philippe. 1998. *L'Afrique miroir du monde?* Paris: Karthala.

Esser, Klaus. 2000. "Gehemmte Modernisierung in Lateinamerika." Pp. 260–295 in *Weltkulturen unter Globalisierungsdruck. Erfahrungen und Antworten aus den Kontinenten*, ed. Rainer Tetzlaff. Bonn: Dietz.

Evans, Peter. 1995. *Embedded Autonomy: States and Industrial Transformation*. Princeton, NJ: Princeton University Press.

Gibson, Nigel C. 2004. "Africa and Globalization: Marginalization and Resistance." *Journal of Asian and African Studies* 39 (1–2): 1–28.

Goldstein, Andrea, Nicolas Pinaud, Helmut Reisen, and Xiaobao Chen. 2006. *The Rise of China and India: What's in It for Africa?* Paris: OECD.

Grégoire, Emmanuel. 2002. "La difficile insertion de l'Afrique de l'Ouest dans la mondialisation." *Les Temps Modernes* 57 (620–621): 392–409.

Gruzinski, Serge. 2004. *Les quatre parties du monde: Histoire d'une mondialisation*. Paris: Éditions de la Martinière.

Henry, Alain. 2004. "Entreprises mondialisées en Afrique: Comportements et formes institutionnelles." Pp. 195–203 in *Vers des civilisations mondialisées? De l'éthologie à la prospective*, ed. Jean-Éric Aubert and Josée Landrieu. Colloque de Cerisy: Éditions de l'Aube.

Huang, Xiaoming. 1998. "What Is 'Chinese' About Chinese Civilization? Culture, Institutions and Globalization?" Pp. 218–240 in *Culture in World Politics*, ed. Dominique Jacquin-Berdal, Andrew Oros, and Marco Verweij. New York: St. Martin's Press.

Hugon, Philippe. 2006. *L'économie de l'Afrique*, 5th ed. La Découverte: Paris.

Inglehart, Ronald, Miguel E. Basáñez, Alejandro Menéndez Moreno. 1998. *Human Values and Beliefs: A Cross-cultural Sourcebook: Political, Religious, Sexual, and Economic Norms in 43 Societies; Findings from the 1990–1993 World Values Survey*. Ann Arbor: University of Michigan Press.

Jacquin-Berdal, Dominique, Andrew Oros, and Marco Verweij, eds. 1998a. *Culture in World Politics*. New York: St. Martin's Press.

Jacquin-Berdal, Dominique, Andrew Oros, and Marco Verweij. 1998b. "Culture in World Politics: an Introduction." Pp. 1–10 in *Culture in World Politics*, ed.

Dominique Jacquin-Berdal, Andrew Oros, and Marco Verweij. New York: St. Martin's Press.

Latouche, Serge. 1998. *L'Autre Afrique. Entre don et marché.* Paris: Albin Michel.

Mezouar, Abdelkébir, and Jean-Pierre Sémériva. 2004. "Entreprises et modernité dans les sociétés arabo-islamiques." Pp. 204–214 in *Vers des civilisations mondialisées? De l'éthologie à la prospective,* ed. Jean-Eric Aubert and Josée Landrieu. Colloque de Cerisy: Éditions de l'Aube.

Momayezi, Nasser. 2006. "Globalization: Impact on Development." Pp. 707–712 in *Encyclopedia of the Developing World,* Vol. 2, ed. Thomas M. Leonard. New York: Routledge.

Mozaffari, Mehdi, ed. 2002. *Globalization and Civilizations.* New York: Routledge.

Nederveen Pieterse, Jan. 2004. *Globalization & Culture. Global Mélange.* New York: Rowman & Littlefield.

Nicholas, Howard. 2005. *Forum 2005.* Special Issue of *Development and Change* 36 (6, November).

O'Rourke, Kevin H. 2002. "Europe and the causes of globalization: 1700–2000." Pp. 64–86 in *Europe and Globalization.* ed. Henryk Kierzkowski. London: Macmillan.

Paulmier, Thierry. 2004. "Métaphysique chinoise et mentalité économique." Pp. 181–194 in *Vers des civilisations mondialisées? De l'éthologie à la prospective,* ed. Jean-Éric Aubert and Josée Landrieu. Colloque de Cerisy: Éditions de l'Aube.

Poujol, Catherine. 2004. "Les nouveaux États d'Asie centrale face au processus de mondialisation." Pp. 143–158 in *Vers des civilisations mondialisées? De l'éthologie à la prospective,* ed. Jean-Éric Aubert and Josée Landrieu. Colloque de Cerisy: Éditions de l'Aube.

Rajan, Ramkishen S. 2003. *Economic Globalization and Asia. Essays on Finance, Trade, and Taxation.* Singapore: Institute of Policy Studies, World Scientific Publishing.

Rocca, Jean-Louis. 2006. *La condition chinoise: La mise au travail capitaliste à l'âge des réformes (1978–2004).* Paris: Karthala.

Rugumamu, Severine M. 2005. *Globalization Demystified. Africa's Possible Development Futures.* Dar es Salaam: Dar Es Salaam University Press.

Sanjuan, Thierry. 2004. "Refonder la mondialisation chinoise." Pp. 122–130 in *Vers des civilisations mondialisées? De l'éthologie à la prospective,* ed. Jean-Éric Aubert and Josée Landrieu. Colloque de Cerisy: Éditions de l'Aube.

Schaefer, Wolf. 2004. "Global Civilization and Local Cultures." Pp. 71–86 in *Rethinking Civilizational Analysis,* ed. Saïd Amir Arjomand and Edward A. Tiryakian. Thousand Oaks, CA: Sage. Studies in International Sociology 52.

Scholte, Jan Aart. 2005. *Globalization: A Critical Introduction,* 2nd ed. London: Macmillan.

Schuerkens, Ulrike, ed. 2004. *Global Forces and Local Life-Worlds: Social Transformations.* Thousands Oaks, CA, London, New Delhi: Sage. Studies in International Sociology 51.

Stiglitz, Joseph E. 2006. *Making Globalization Work.* New York: W. W. Norton.

Tetzlaff, Rainer, ed. 2000. *Weltkulturen unter Globalisierungsdruck. Erfahrungen und Antworten aus den Kontinenten.* Bonn: Dietz.

Williamson, Jeffrey G., and Kevin H. O'Rourke. 2002. "When Did Globalization Begin?" *European Review of Economic History* 6 (1): 23–50.

Wong, Roy Bin. 1997. *China Transformed: Historical Change and the Limits of European Experience.* New York: Cornell University Press.

2 Contradictions of Social Responsibility—(German) Business Elites and Globalization

Peter Imbusch

Business elites are facing criticism. There is increasingly frequent talk of social injustice in society and of business elites failing to fulfill their social responsibilities. The mood was expressed by Rolf Hochhuth in a recent drama, *McKinsey Is Coming* (Hochhuth 2003), where he points to Josef Ackermann—Chief Executive Officer of the Deutsche Bank—as a prime example of the moral erosion brought to the business community by globalization driven by profit maximization, shareholder value obligations, and the profit interests of anonymous shareholders. Hochhuth's indignation applies in particular to the high—and rising—salaries of top executives who make thousands redundant in order to bring their companies back to profitability. He considers this a sign of a dehumanization of business that is reflected in the breaking of social ties and in the collapse of human solidarities; it encourages a sort of "rogue capitalism" that will dispose of the bourgeois world together with its values. German Vice-Chancellor Franz Müntefering (SPD) took the same line as Hochhuth when he criticized the growing power of capital and the total economization of life, which in his eyes aids and abets shortsighted profit mentalities and loses sight of people on account of its quarterly success reports. He specifically attacked those individuals on the international financial markets who do not appear to be bound by any rules, setting upon companies like swarms of locusts before moving on. Complaining about the lack of morals of individual businessmen and criticizing their false concepts of freedom, Müntefering also promised a broad-based battle against this new form of capitalism.

"Locust capitalism," the craving for maximum shareholder value, "unpatriotic behavior"—there are abundant examples of this in the course of globalization. Executives announce high profits and mass dismissals in the same breath; they relocate production abroad, while simultaneously taking advantage of tax breaks; they hike up their salaries while levels of pay for the broad population have been stagnating or even declining for years. Not without reason did the legendary victory sign flashed by Josef Ackermann to the media before his appearance at the Mannesmann/Vodafone trial come to symbolize self-confident arrogance.

Opposed to this negative image, we find emphatic expressions on the part of business representatives with regard to corporate social responsibility and corporate citizenship, sustainable growth strategies, environmentally and socially acceptable rules, and the protection of stakeholder interests (Carroll 1999; Braun and Kromminga 2001; Wieland and Conradi 2002; Bohnet-Joschko and Schiereck 2002).[1] Business elites frequently proclaim themselves as socially responsible players. In recent years, even the World Economic Forum in Davos (Switzerland) has at times given the impression of being a philanthropists' club. Employers have always rejected their critics in this regard. The most vehemently disputed aspects of Hochhuth's play on the business world, for example, were the desire for revenge in analogy to Wilhelm Tell, the most famous figure from Switzerland, and the motifs of people violently taking the law into their own hands. It was called a "paragon of tastelessness" by the then president of the German Federation of Industries (BDI), Michael Rogowski, who also raised the question of whether the dramatist wanted to make murder an acceptable means of political dispute. Those who confuse the debate over executive salaries or jobs with class struggle, he claimed, had left the arena of common debate. The business world's response to Müntefering's "class struggle slogans" was likewise resolute. The latter failed to consider political and economic challenges, and the government had a poor grasp of business-related issues—this was essentially the unanimous opinion resounding from the business camp. BDI chief Ludolf von Wartenberg appealed to the Social Democrats (SPD) to return to their senses and work together with the business world on solutions to the crisis. Dieter Hundt, head of the BDA employers' federation, warned that calls for a boycott of particular companies would harm the very firms that are already facing economic difficulties. German Chamber of Industry and Commerce (DIHK) president Ludwig Georg Braun called for bold reforms for tomorrow instead of false ideologies from yesterday. At the same time, Karoline Beck of the Association of Young Employers (BJU) accused the Social Democrats of "political sloganeering" that was guaranteed to stir up debates on redistribution and envy.

These events lead right to the core of the question of corporate social responsibility. But what do they have to offer aside from superficial slights and pretty platitudes? What concrete ideas do business elites have about their social responsibility and how do they define their own role? Which social models do they represent? How and to what degree do business elites perceive social responsibility? These questions were the subject of a three-year research project that focused on the changes in social responsibility among business elites in Germany.[2]

I first describe the underlying problem before adding a number of brief explanations about the research project and its methods. I then examine the different definitions of social responsibility and introduce a few essential findings of the project. Thereafter I intend to examine the disparate practices of business elites on the front stage and on the back stage. I finish with a series of summarizing theses to illustrate the landmark changes that globalization has brought to business elites' understanding of responsibility.

DEFINING THE QUESTION

For about the last two decades, business elites in advanced industrial nations of Western Europe have favored a neo-liberal modernization project embedded in accelerated globalization trends. It essentially comprises measures serving liberalization, deregulation, denationalization, and corporate rationalization. These measures are legitimized by business leaders as a necessary means of maintaining profitability under globalized competition conditions and are in principle supported by most governments. The neo-liberal project and globalization then appear to be forces of circumstance ("Adapting to the laws of the market"; "There is no alternative"; "Globalization is not the problem but the solution") to which business leaders are just as subject as all other groups in society. Without them, Germany would face massive economic disadvantages and in the long term risk losing its industrial base.

Critics of this position claim that executives and business associations used globalization as a threat in order to justify far-reaching power shifts in society that result in social division and disintegration, exacerbate tension between and within countries, and undermine the traditional conditions of reproduction in political economies and nation–states. The elites are said to be blind to social issues and to exercise their power without responsibility, while the unlimited mobility of capital and the formation of global markets saw a dramatic decline in local and regional loyalties and in civil responsibility (Lasch 1995; Bourdieu 1998).

Managers and business leaders and their actions are coming under increasing criticism in the public eye—"business" is considered at least partly responsible for numerous problems, crises, and processes of disintegration. But what is the real picture as regards the social responsibility of employers and executives? And why should they assume social responsibility in the first place?

METHODOLOGICAL REFLECTION

Before I elaborate on these issues, I briefly introduce the research project "Business elites between globalization and social responsibility" funded by the Ministry of Education and Research (BMBF) and the methods it has incorporated.
The project centered on the following issues:

- How business elites see the relationship between business and society.
- How models for society represent business elites.
- How business elites define their own social responsibility.

- How business elites actually realize social responsibility.

In order to gain satisfactory answers to these questions as opposed to mere superficial findings, it was necessary to combine a variety of methods. First, we conducted a quantitative content analysis of two daily newspapers, *Frankfurter Allgemeine Zeitung* (FAZ) and the *Süddeutsche Zeitung* (SZ), covering several years in a period from the mid-1960s to 2002. The intention here was to determine which issues elites comment on in public and who speaks (and in what manner) about assuming responsibility within the sociopolitical debate.

Second, we assessed two journals published by business federations and selected corporate citizenship reports from the top fifty companies in order to gain an impression of the range of social commitment, concrete examples of taking responsibility, and resistance to allegedly illegitimate allocations of responsibility.

Third, we carried out problem-centered interviews with more than 50 representatives of business elites in accordance with a most-different sample. The aim was a concrete assessment of corporate concepts of responsibility in order to determine responsibilities and to get concrete examples in the representatives' own words.

The final part of our investigation comprised case studies that enabled us to expand on the insights gained within the scope of an initial exploration of material published by the media and business associations. The cases were selected using the method of theoretical sampling, while the categories themselves were determined inductively within the scope of the content analysis. The case studies cover selected examples of concrete responsibility.

The quantitative aspects of the analysis were designed to determine the absolute frequency of particular views; the qualitative aspects served to provide examples of particular views and findings and to shed light on more complex related factors. The combination of different methods made it possible to assess the validity of particular views and to check their reliability. For this reason, the scope of the analysis included not only documents published by the elites but also daily newspapers published in different years; interviews were therefore conducted not only with entrepreneurs, executives, and industry representatives, but with local experts as well. In examining the same subject with a variety of methods from different perspectives, we aimed to arrive at effective assessments and solid appraisals of social commitment among today's business elites. The results of the research project are included in the final report to the BMBF and in two publications containing the essential research results (Rucht, Imbusch, Alemann, and Galonska 2007; Imbusch and Rucht 2007a).

WHAT DOES SOCIAL RESPONSIBILITY MEAN?

Elites are by virtue of their position and/or function detached from their environment (Hradil and Imbusch 2003, 99–144; Hartmann 2004; Wasner

2004). They stand out through their influence on decision-making processes affecting society as a whole; they have access to power; and their power is largely institutionalized. However, who belongs to the business elites—aside from the group at the very top end comprising a few dozen "captains of industry" from the biggest corporations—is not clearly defined. Our study covered two groups: (a) top management at major companies and the owners of larger family businesses, and (b) leaders of business associations that were present in more than one federal state.

Social responsibility is far harder to define than elites or business elites. It is not at all necessary to share the positions of St. Gallen's business ethics theorist Peter Ulrich in order to assign responsibility to companies as "quasi-public institutions" or for this purpose to point to the German Constitution (*Grundgesetz*) and its stipulation of ownership-related social obligations. Even conventional elite theories portray employers and top executives as sociopolitical players; business activity is not neutral in social terms, and employers play a part in the shaping of society (Hoffmann-Lange 1992; Bürklin and Rebenstorf 1997). This gives rise to a social responsibility that goes beyond company interests. Another undisputed point is that the political spheres and the fields of action that can be shaped and influenced by employers and top executives in the course of globalization—understood in pragmatic terms as the global interlinking of economic and social activities (Beck 1997)—are growing, and these players are now established strategic/political forces at the international level. The privileged position of business elites leads to expectations that they should give something back to society (Lunau and Wettstein 2004). In addition, business elites themselves assume leadership in public debates, and they are frequently assigned a model status that assumes an obligation not only toward shareholders but also toward stakeholders, that is, those affected in the broadest sense by corporate decisions (Andrioff and McIntosh 2001).

The research project incorporated gradual forms of social responsibility. It is important to recognize that the term *responsibility* has recently been overused—especially in connection with the debates concerning corporate citizenship and corporate social responsibility; nearly everything that can be communicated in positive terms is rapidly remodeled as responsibility. In my opinion, sponsorship and other marketing measures that serve solely to promote an image or to advertise products cannot be considered a realization of social responsibility. Nor does social responsibility include the personal responsibility of top executives and employers for their immediate environment or the economic responsibility inevitably resulting from their professional role. The term *social responsibility* should only be applied where representatives of the business elites provide help that goes beyond their genuine obligations; that has a supportive or enhancing impact on society as a whole; that attempts to influence specific groups or areas of society; or that tackles such problems that lie beyond their immediate corporate horizons. The motives and interests can be very disparate. A minimum precondition for social responsibility, however, is the recognizable presence of an obvious benefit for other groups in society or the public at large in addition to any benefits for the company itself. This last point would at the same time be a benchmark for assessing whether and to what degree social responsibility is displayed.

For this reason, social responsibility should hereafter be generally understood as a position that is assigned to a businessperson or accepted and put into practice by these top executives themselves with the aim of improving the situation of disadvantaged social groups or of society as a whole (or at least trying to prevent conditions worsening). This kind of commitment normally involves money. Whether such funds are expended is ultimately down to the decision of the players—who will admittedly see themselves as being subjected to the expectations of their environment. Therefore one can identify three levels with regard to social responsibility: (1) There is an obvious obligation to assume responsibility that results from legislation or generally recognized standards of proper behavior; (2) assuming social responsibility comprises socially desirable actions that cannot be litigated but that, when neglected, can generate pressure of legitimacy; or (3) there are activities that exceed expectations and that are perceived as exemplary or selfless.

The various concepts of social responsibility among business players can be localized on a broad scale and differentiated along ideal-typical lines as follows:

Social responsibility in its narrowest sense involves focusing exclusively on commercial cost considerations. This involves the absolute rejection of any responsibility beyond the interests of the company and—in modern-day Manchester style—a focus on the unbridled generation of profits. The employees of a company are seen not as indispensable human capital but merely as a cost factor that can be rationalized at will. Seen from this perspective, ethics and a feeling of responsibility do not constitute economic categories, so responsibility is neither expected nor justified. This is reflected in the broad repertoire of defensive positions toward allocations of responsibility and corresponding patterns of legitimacy.

The free-market position, on the other hand, recognizes assumption of responsibility in the sense of successful business for the shareholders. This viewpoint envisages a convergence of commercial activity and responsibility in the sense of the commercially efficient management of a company within the context of a binding societal framework being seen as genuine proof of social responsibility. This shifts the focus onto the fulfillment of managerial tasks, the generation of income, and the provision of high-quality products. As Milton Friedman put it: "There is one and only one social responsibility of business—to use its resources and engage in activities designed to increase its profits" (Friedman 1962: 133). Further-reaching social commitment, meanwhile, is seen as extraneous to business and is declared to be a personal matter of employers and executives.

A third position with regard to social responsibility involves a fundamental recognition of the necessity of assuming social responsibility, although the latter is to varying degrees defined by economic pragmatism. It is emphasized, for example, that profits must first be generated before redistribution can be envisaged, or that social commitments are an "investment" in a particular social milieu, which then gives rise to win–win situations (Habisch, Meister, and Schmidpeter 2001). This is also the base for the very disparate views and concepts of corporate citizenship and corporate social responsibility. These range, as we know, from an intrinsic social responsibility (with the intention to adjust profits to outlays for social concerns) to moral responsibility in the sense of charity (giving without wanting to receive), to the principle of completely instrumental social investments (giving in the expectation of receiving).

Social responsibility in its broadest sense extends to far more than commercial considerations; it is not limited to observing norms and abiding under the law and does not allow responsibility to be lost in the anonymity of capital markets. Far more relevant is a strong orientation to stakeholders, a high level of sensitivity to social problems and increasing disintegration tendencies, and a considerable degree of self-reflection in business decisions with regard to the possible consequences of actions (sustainability, moral attitudes to responsibility etc.). Accordingly, corporate action is all the more obliged to assume social responsibility, even where this means concessions in terms of profit interests (Ulrich 1999, 2000).

In the case of business elites, finding a meaningful concept of social responsibility requires this responsibility to represent a range of actions that point beyond genuinely commercial activities and must as such be separated analytically from economic responsibility, especially from concern for the preservation of the company and all actions directly derived from this. In practice, however, making this distinction is not always easy, due to the many potential areas of overlapping for both aspects in the course of normal business activity. In principle, it means that the term can be applied to those positions and actions of business elites that do not inevitably result from commercial activities (e.g., the creation of jobs as a consequence of a commercially necessary investment)[3] and that instead require specific efforts, and possibly sacrifices as well. An example of this kind of effort is strict compliance with particular laws even where disregarding them would barely come to light but would involve economic advantages. A far more ambitious example of social responsibility could comprise a company renouncing highly profitable and by all means legal "business" because this would be associated with harming disadvantaged groups. In these and similar cases, the title "socially responsible behavior" assumes that ethical criteria (abiding to the law, consideration for disadvantaged groups, or the public good) outweigh the interest in competitive success and profit maximization. Here we are confronted with contradictory criteria and a decision in favor of social responsibility based on an ethical principle. There are also conceivable win–win situations in reality so that moral dictates and internal profit interests go hand in hand, meaning that social commitment at the same time brings economic advantages. The *"Unternehmen: Aktiv im Gemeinwesen"* ("Business: Active in the Community") network launched by business leaders in Frankfurt am Main, for example, proclaims: "Companies that are actively involved in the community are not only socially responsible but economically smart. They provide both meaning and benefits" (Frankfurter Aufruf 2003). Hans Michael Hölz, head of Corporate Citizenship & Sustainable Development at Deutsche Bank, put it in somewhat more generalized terms: "Today, socially responsible action is the prerequisite for being able to do business" (FAZ, January 3, 2005: 18).

SELECTED EMPIRICAL RESULTS

In recent decades, and more acutely in the last few years, Germany and other Western European countries have experienced a clear shift away from the traditional model of the national "Rhenanian capitalism" to the model of globalizing, neo-liberal capitalism (or "Anglo-Saxon capitalism"). At the same time, interventionist nation-states pursuing proactive economic policies have lost a lot of ground. Most governments see themselves in economic terms not as an authority that defines restrictions for commercial activity but rather as service providers that must optimize the conditions for global competition by way of greater flexibility, denationalization, deregulation, and tax cuts for business.

The transition from the "Rhenanian" to the "Anglo-Saxon" model of capitalism has had serious consequences, especially in terms of employment conditions and labor relations. What is for the great majority of the population a core area of society and has in Germany been a traditional cornerstone of social integration has recently experienced dramatic distortions whose implications also affect the middle classes (Boltanski and Chiapello 1999; Polterauer 2004; more generally cf. Sennett 2006). This involves not only an increase in precarious employment conditions but also escalating poverty, resulting in social exclusion, and a gradual polarization that gives rise to severe processes of disintegration (Castel 1995; Schultheis and Schulz 2005; Dörre et al. 2007). The new model is subject to criticism, not least due to these accompanying symptoms. This is evident in the analysis of daily newspapers and can also be inferred from a recent survey conducted in 20 countries for the World Economic Forum. Confidence in "global companies" is significantly lower than that in all other collective players (from "high" in the case of nongovernmental organizations [NGOs] to "low" in the case of national governments). And there are indications of a downward trend: "Trust in global companies is now at its lowest level since tracking began."[4]

What insights does the research project reveal with regard to the fundamental positions and attitudes of business elites, insofar as they are reflected in the mass media, in business industry journals, in keynote interviews, and in case studies on issues related to social responsibility? Here are a few selected findings (cf. also Schmucker 2005; Imbusch and Rucht 2007b).

Business Elites Have Very Disparate Views of Globalization

A closer look at the opinions expressed by the business world on globalization reveals that, in addition to the very wide range of views of globalization, there are divergent positions on the process of globalization. Those who unconditionally advocate the globalization process can be found in the Top 100 of German business, all of which have a considerable international dimension and are established leading players on world markets. For most of these companies, globalization is considered a natural form of internationalization, even if the executives stress that the costs and benefits of globalization could change in future. Accordingly, those in charge of these firms emphasize the "increased freedoms for the individual" and the potential for growth and profit for the company through free trade. For the majority of the companies, on the other hand, globalization is seen in rational terms as an inevitable consequence of worldwide market changes, a consequence that has to be dealt with by employers and managers in order to survive. It is repeatedly emphasized that there is no alternative to globalization, but that there is a need to shape it. Only a small number of companies and managers have a skeptical attitude to the extremely varied advantages and disadvantages associated with globalization. There is, however, point-blank rejection of the arguments and actions of alter-globalization movements such as Attac or opinions expressed by the World Social Forum (Imbusch 2007).

The Public Debate Over the Responsibility of the Business World Is Increasing

As time passes, the social responsibility of business elites is becoming increasingly prominent in the public debate. The same applies for the opinions of business elites as expressed in the media. Since the mid-1960s, corporate social responsibility has become an increasingly important issue. This trend is probably related to the fact that, in an era of accelerated globalization, the behavior of business leaders is inseparable from issues concerning society at large, while it is becoming increasingly clear that the commercially oriented decisions taken by business elites have far-reaching consequences for society. Although this was always the case to some extent, the consequences today—after the end of the era of full employment and widespread job security and after the end of the consensus over the "social principles of the market economy"—are far more negative, especially as the proposed formulas for resolving the crisis, if anything, appear to be exacerbating the problems. Accordingly, external assessments of business elites have likewise shifted from a slightly negative average rating in 1965 to progressively worse levels.

The Environment and the Labor Market Are the Prevailing Issues as Regards Corporate Social Responsibility

The period of analysis saw the clear emergence of two major issues in newspaper reports and within business associations. Problems related to employment and the environment are by far the most frequently covered in stories about corporate social responsibility, even if with fluctuating importance over the course of time. When it comes to the issue of employment, in particular, business elites emphasize that adapting to the conditions of globalized competition manifests itself in technological developments and technical revolutions but at the same time calls for institutional adjustments—that is, deregulating industrial relations and the labor markets—that more or less result as practical necessities. Critics, however, counter that this triggers a "race to the bottom" that would ultimately lead to conditions akin to early capitalism.

Business Elites Themselves Are Assigned a Prominent Role When It Comes to the Issue of Social Responsibility

The analysis of corporate social responsibility as reflected in the two daily newspapers under examination showed that business elites are the most frequently heard voices. They are responsible for around half of all opinions on the subject of responsibility. Representatives of the government, political parties, and the media represent the other half. Representatives of industry associations play a more significant role here than corporate spokesmen (71 percent to 29 percent). The category of industry associations is dominated by the Federation of German Industries (BDI) (12 percent each), the Confederation of German Employers Associations (BDA) (10 percent), and the German Chambers of Commerce and Industry (10 percent). These associations remain the spokespeople of the business community. A closer look, however, reveals significant differences in the positions of the individual associations. The positions assumed by the BDI, for example, are in general more radically free-market than those of the BDA. Another finding is that business elites generally tend to be mentioned within a context of problems and criticism rather than of success stories.

Expectations With Regard to the Assumption of Responsibility Change According to Political Climate

Political constellations also have an effect on external expectations concerning corporate responsibility; expectations are higher when the Social Democrats are in power than under conservative governments. Self-imposed commitment of business elites to socially responsible behavior, however, is greater under conservative governments than under the Social Democrats. This is clearly reflected in a comparison of the era of chancellor Helmut Kohl with that of chancellor Gerhard Schröder. Under conservative governments it is also easier to defend the position that assuming social responsibility is a natural result of the pursuit of commercial interests and as such also contributes to the common welfare. Business elites appear less defensive in conservative-led eras and can therefore play down the potential conflict between commercial efficiency and social responsibility. Under Social Democratic governments, however, employers and executives face far higher expectations. Business elites react in different ways to such external expectations as regards their social responsibility. Our research provides examples of a range of responses to the question of social responsibility, and these can be broken down into different types in an inductive process. The spectrum covers outright refusal of responsibility, various forms of quid pro quo activity, the exercise of coercion, and independent, proactive commitment. Over time, however, there is a growing willingness (rhetorically, at least) to assume social responsibility. Here we see major differences between small and medium-sized businesses on the one hand and major corporations on the other (Maaß and Clemens 2002). The latter, in particular, tend to be more eager to publicize their social commitment and responsibility so that their actions can be seen rather as a rewarding "investment" in a particular social milieu.

There Is a Huge Discrepancy Between How Employers and Managers Are Viewed by Themselves and the Views of Others

There has always been a huge discrepancy between how business elites are perceived by themselves and how they are viewed by others (Scheuch and Scheuch 2001; Hartmann 2002). Employers and executives prefer to see themselves as contributors and leaders whose innovation, dynamism, and expertise serve the common welfare. They attribute their success to their own efforts, to a high level of motivation, to hard work, and to their personality, which unites creativity, new ideas, loyalty, and integrity. Responsibility and a sense of duty rank high among individual values. High incomes are interpreted as a reflection of individual performance and a willingness to take responsibility; they reflect the significance of the position reached and at the same time symbolize the financial strength of the company. This very self-confident view of their own professional group, however, is increasingly at odds with public perceptions of business elites (Scheuch and Scheuch 1995; Hartmann 1996). The latter tend rather to be characterized by words such as "crooks," "greed," "mismanagement," "megalomania," and "unscrupulousness." It is as such not surprising that external assessments of business leaders' actions have become increasingly negative and deviate substantially from how business elites view themselves. For example, when asked in interviews whether they are portrayed fairly in the media, the response of business elites was overwhelmingly negative. A particular grievance among employers is the media's tendency to highlight specific cases of mismanagement or enrichment while seldom acknowledging the good work done by employers on a day-to-day basis or drawing attention to their useful functions in society. That said, a number of representatives—primarily from medium-sized firms but also from leading business federations—did emphasize that the negative portrayal was not solely the fault of biased journalists, but also a result of questionable behavior on the part of individual business leaders or entire companies. Within this context, the example most frequently cited by managers and industry representatives alike was the infamous Mannesmann/Vodafone case.[5] Isolated examples such as this are by no means typical, argue industry representatives, who say that the media does influence public opinion in general and fuel envy in particular.

Business Elites Call for Political and Social Reforms

Business elites emphasize the necessity of government reforms and claim that the welfare state is in need of "reorganization." For years now, representatives of the big employers' federations have in particular been calling for less government intervention and less regulation in connection with business activity. They want the state to limit its role—aside from its traditional sovereign activities (such as security)—to creating a "sensible" framework for free competition and otherwise not to be involved as an independent economic entity. The interviews revealed universal criticism not only of the hesitancy and slowness of reforms, but also of unions and labor movements deemed primarily or at least partly responsible for this. Their outdated slogans, unrealistic demands, and limited grasp of economic issues, say employers, impede progress toward preparing society for the future. Calls from business elites for reduced state involvement and their criticism of unions are based on the neo-liberal credo and/or arguments relating to practical necessities. Those who champion the neo-liberal credo are first and foremost those companies and sectors that are relatively strong competitors on the international market, while others often cling to open or hidden subsidies. The neo-liberal position also produces claims that a well-endowed welfare state paralyzes initiatives and individual motivation and therefore has to be cut back in times of global competition. Greater flexibility in employment conditions is likewise considered necessary in order to persevere in the face of global competition. A classic force-of-circumstance argument claims that "we" can no longer financially afford the welfare state in its current form due to demographic developments in the German society.

Recent Years Have Seen a Shift Among Employers and Top Executives Toward Increasingly Radical Free-Market Positions

We have recently seen a clear shift among business elites toward "more market." The analysis of industry and media reports and the interviews has confirmed a recent swing among employers and top executives toward free-market positions. Our survey analyzed positions on various issues and subject areas that produce five fundamental social conflicts that can be defined according to the following pairs: equality versus freedom, redistribution versus reward, collective versus individual responsibility, state versus market, and voluntary versus compulsory. One pole represents the Rhenanian capitalism and the welfare state, while the other corresponds more to the Anglo-Saxon style of capitalism with its heavily liberal orientation. In all cases, the balance has clearly shifted toward the liberal/free-market end of the scale. This applies least in the case of equality versus freedom, and most in the case of state versus market. This is also reflected in the predominant social values and the political instruments derived from them. What we can see is a shift from the concepts of solidarity and state responsibility to individual responsibility and market-oriented control. These were accompanied by extensive semantic shifts with regard to responsibility. Whatever the issue, we see a stronger propagation of individual responsibility and a stronger emphasis on the principle of reward for performance. Both aspects are at the same time merely the flip side of pruning government activity and reinforce individual freedom vis-à-vis the concept of equality. In terms of the central tension between welfare state and neo-liberal system, business elites today exhibit an unmistakable tendency toward the neo-liberal side. This has incorporated as well a change in the semantic content of corporate responsibility itself; the definition of responsibility is becoming increasingly narrow, first and foremost applying to the preservation of the company, then the workforce, and only then to the social milieu or specific society-related problems.

"Pressure" From Society Is Generally Necessary Before a Significant Degree of Responsibility Is Exhibited

The disparity in the constellations under which employers and executives assume social responsibility or responsibility in areas not directly connected to the company can be shown by several case studies (Imbusch and Rucht 2007a).[6] The scale of responsibility encompasses violating rules out of self-interest, defensiveness vis-à-vis responsibility, cooperation under pressure, indications on a willingness to assume responsibility, quid pro quo activities, substantial concessions, and proactive commitment for public welfare. An essential conclusion to be drawn from these studies is that the activities of companies have, on the one hand, been by and large issue specific; that is, they responded case by case with respect to particular responsibilities assigned to them by third parties. On the other hand, it was often only pressure from society that prompted companies to act in some way responsibly. This pressure can arise from a specific group or organization or, alternatively, from employees. It can also manifest itself in the form of a critical public opinion. In addition, the analysis of publications of industry associations and media reports shows that autonomous, proactive involvement is the exception, whereas there has been in recent years a significant increase in noncommitted signals and a restriction to symbolic actions.

The Relationship Between Globalization and Social Responsibility Is Complex

The research project produced clear evidence that globalization processes and competitive pressure, on the one hand, and social responsibility, on the other, are not necessarily mutually exclusive, and form instead a complex mutual relationship. This is not only caused by the business world having many different definitions of social responsibility. Another factor of equal importance is that big companies enjoy relatively stable budgets for social commitments and—especially at the international level—make mid- and long-term commitments that are—at least temporarily—protected against the vagaries of economic cycles. The earlier supposition that social responsibility among employers and management would erode in the process of globalization due to high competitive pressure and cost rationalization could not be verified. Big companies, in particular, act as strategic players that are confronted with different challenges on the global market and therefore consider obligations to accept corporate social responsibility indexes or the Global Compact initiative as competitive advantages to attain solid market expansion. Respecting these codes also promises considerable image-related benefits. One may even say that globalization obliges companies to portray themselves as "good citizens" and to assume an active role of social responsibility—at least rhetorically but also in real terms. However, there has been a serious shift in the semantic content of social responsibility.

There is a striking difference between corporate activity on the "front stage" and what happens on the "back stage" (Goffman 1959). Interestingly enough, the social involvement and the conspicuous demonstration of responsibility on the front stage correlates with a quite different policy on the back stage. It is at the back stage, where the enhanced power realized in the course of globalization is reflected in "subpolitics," that there are serious challenges to weak states.

INTERPRETATIVE PERSPECTIVES

The Front Stage: Social Responsibility as Part of Corporate Culture

The majority of companies in Germany are involved in some form of charity. The larger a company is, the greater in general will be its willingness to assume social responsibility. Most of the firms in the survey are involved in social activities. Only a small number of employers and managers refuse social activities, citing the strained economic situation or simple disinterest.

The forms of involvement are in some cases more visible, in others less conspicuous. Sometimes their involvement is made public, and in other cases it remains largely hidden. This applies both to large and small/medium-sized companies.

Larger companies, in particular, provide details of their activities and responsibilities in specially prepared company reports, in order to give them greater transparency. A report on social responsibility will typically say: "Social responsibility begins in the company. In the first place, it comprises securing the long-term existence of the company and generating jobs and value added. It is expressed in the development of environmental and resource-saving processes, in the quality of products and services, and in comprehensive and transparent public reports vis-à-vis the stakeholders" (Deutsche Bank 2003: 4). Not included in this narrow definition of responsibility is an additional range of activities that encompass more than immediate company-related factors: Donations and sponsorship, independent initiatives and projects, active involvement in national and transnational organizations, foundations and charities, and the voluntary work of employees are generally cited as expressions of social responsibility (Bertelsmann Foundation 2005). Though widely criticized, Deutsche Bank spends more money in absolute terms on cultural and social activities than any other company in Germany. Of the almost 70 million € budgeted for 2003, 35 percent was assigned to "Social Affairs," 35 percent to "Arts/Music," 25 percent to "Education and Science/Technology," and 5 percent to "Sustainability and Micro-Loans." Even if these outlays appear financially impressive, they only become meaningful in relation to the profits made (Fabisch 2004).

If we look beyond the immediate concern of the companies under analysis, we find the following picture: The commitment of small and medium-sized enterprises (SME, with less than 100 employees) is far greater than that of larger companies (with more than 100 employees). Although they make up only one-sixth of all contributions in this area, their spending for social activities as a proportion of their turnover is around four to five times higher than that of larger firms. For SMEs the average proportion of turnover is 0.24 percent, and for larger firms just 0.05 percent (IfM 2002; Dresewski 2004).

When we consider where and how employers and executives participate in social commitment, social issues are by far the most popular area (87 percent), followed by culture and education (76 percent), and sport (66 percent). Corporate commitment is less common in the areas of science/technology (42 percent) and the environment (31 percent). Traditional formats enjoy the greatest popularity. Four-fifths of all companies provide financial or material donations. Three quarters of the firms offer free services (apprenticeships, training courses, etc.). In many cases, employees (almost 50 percent of firms) and management (about 30 percent) are released from work in connection with corporate social responsibility (CSR) activities. In over half of the companies, executives themselves are committed on a voluntary basis (IfM 2002).

Given this significant degree of social commitment, employers and executives are unlikely to be accused of insufficient social responsibility or a complete lack of sensitivity for social problems. However, we have to assess the reasons why employers and executives try to find solutions to social problems, as well as the frequency and duration of these activities.

The empirical results show quite clearly that social commitment is not born from altruism and pure conviction. Instead, as surveys on corporate citizenship in Germany show (e.g., Westebbe and Logan 1995; Maaß and Clemens 2002; Seitz 2002), most major industrialists and top executives see their activities in terms of an investment in their social milieu. Thus they try to secure the foundations of their own survival and to accelerate expansion. According to these people, helping to reduce social problems and helping to develop their social environment are in the best interest of companies (Frankfurter Aufruf 2003).

If we then ask what companies expect from their social commitment, it becomes clear that three-quarters of companies consider the improvement of their public reputation a priority; their commitment serves first and foremost to improve their image. Secondary objectives are those concerning the workforce (the motivation and retention of employees, and an increase in employee satisfaction: 59 percent), customers and sales (product and corporate advertising, better relations with business partners, customer loyalty, enhancing sales channels: 53 percent), and the personal goals of management figures (personal interest in the relevant area: 47 percent). Ethical incentives, commitments without any strategic considerations, and the promise of at least indirect benefits are important for just a quarter of the companies.

The primary function of corporate social commitment is thus to win public exposure for the company's products and boost its image with an eye to the concerns of the community. In the case of larger companies and global players, these activities serve to complement other instruments related to communications and labor policy. They are an integral part of public relations and corporate policy (e.g., environmental reports, reports on corporate social responsibility and corporate citizenship, sustainability reports, etc.); (Daub et al. 2003; Schmidt and Beschorner 2005) and help to improve the image and corporate reputation, which is increasingly important in a global world (e.g., via participation in UN-led initiatives such as Global Compact). Within the context of the globalization process, the need to be perceived as not just successful but also socially responsible, businesses must also be seen in terms of integration in an evolving global society. As global politics become increasingly privatized (Brühl et al. 2001, 2004; Beck 2007; Aglietta and Rebéroux 2005), the new powerful centers that have a growing influence on the developments of a future multi-layered world society (following Münch 1998, 2001) are not democratically legitimized institutions. The declared intentions and the nonverifiable self-imposed obligations leave open to what extent employers and executives live up to their responsibility (Alfred Herrhausen-Gesellschaft 2004).

The Back Stage: Subpolitics and Its Accompanying Symptoms

In light of these facts, we cannot say that companies show no social commitment or do not at least exercise certain forms of social responsibility. Nevertheless, our analysis of corporate social responsibility has been concerned with what Goffman (1959) calls the "front stage." But there is also a "back stage." This centers on what Ulrich Beck summed up as "subpolitics," that is, that in the course of globalization the political agenda is defined not only by traditional political institutions but also by a variety of additional players who compete "to shape and persuade political power " (Beck 1993: 162). In recent decades, politics have begun to move outside formal areas of power and hierarchies, becoming a far-reaching "collateral consequence" of the uncoordinated actions of companies, commercial organizations, and international institutions (Beck 2002: 39).

What are the foundations of the power of business and how can business implement such subpolitical strategies? On the one hand, this power is based on the strength and importance of a company on the market place and on the awareness of being a recognized and important player in an evolving global society. This would be the positive economic side of their power.

On the other hand, it is based on the intimidating potential that results from economic globalization, that is, from the "orchestration of the threat" (Beck). Companies have more scope than ever for splitting their value-added activities and providing or buying products and services where conditions are most favorable. Currently, they are bound by hardly any political condition in their worldwide activities; they can choose alternative legal systems according to economic favors and thus circumvent the sovereign power of the nation–state (Engelhard and Hein 2001). Jobs and production sites are being relocated on a significant scale even by small and medium-sized firms to locations boasting greater cost-effectiveness, fewer employer stipulations, and minimal tax burdens (Wortmann 2003; Kabst 2004), meaning that the territorially rigid nation-states can be played off against each other. Given the variety of arguments, the looming power of business as such lies in not investing, taking jobs away, or not creating new jobs, paying no taxes, and thereby undermining the foundations of nation-based societies and politics. The power of enterprises is based on the "exit option" (Hirschman) vis-à-vis the nation–states. This seems to be the antidemocratic, questionable, and negative side of the economic power.

Four distinct areas can illustrate the far-reaching political consequences of subpolitics: the concept of state, political alignments, ways of life, and social inequality. For years, employers have been undermining the scope of government actions not only through their power to withdraw but also through a language style that attacks state intervention in society, urges the grinding down of government activity and the restriction of the latter to basic security-related functions, and propagates new, less extensive forms of state welfare. The objective here is not so much a kind of minimal state sovereignty according to the liberal "laissez-faire state" of the past, but the transformation of the state into a "global market state" or a "national competitive state." As a result, the role of the state as a counterbalance to a globalized world economy is replaced by its new role as an active player in the global economy, meaning that competition for business investment, the creation of competitive advantages, the removal of barriers to investment, general deregulation, and neo-liberal reformist policies now comprise the absolute agenda of state politics. Subpolitics means here that the state can no longer afford to disregard specific economic interests.

Economic globalization has triggered a crisis of the structures of the welfare state and the political players of the Keynesian postwar compromise. In the eyes of employers, unions are no longer partners but rather barriers to investment, insofar as they insist on pay increases, autonomous wage bargaining, agreements according to activities, and the right to strike, that is, the very same social achievements that conflict with the flexibility demanded by a globalizing business world. In the eyes of the business community, unions are frequently seen as relics from the past whose "politics of self-interest" gives them substantial blame for unemployment and other social problems. Their loss of power and influence is tangible at all levels, while employer federations have for some time now enjoyed the momentum as regards public opinion. Subpolitics of globalization means here that areas of social conflict with labor unions can be circumvented or negated by citing practical constraints and necessities. As a consequence, formerly legitimate interests can be disregarded as no longer relevant.

A further aspect of corporate social responsibility can be explicated in connection with the ways of life facilitated or advanced by globalization processes. While corporations turn their backs on the nation-state set-up through the relocation of production and jobs, management does the same by adopting specific customs and lifestyles that comprise a dismissal of the home country. Specifically, the cosmopolitan orientation of employers and executives means that global players have hardly any ties to a particular place. Zygmunt Bauman referred to how the conditions of a fast-changing modern society see the settled majority come under the control of a nomadic extraterritorial elite (Bauman 2000). The latter's mobility and lack of fixed domicile mean the loss of social ties and personal obligations toward particular production locations and their people. Their loyalty toward state bodies declines as globalization dissolves the nexus between above and below, between rich and poor, between globalization winners and globalization losers, ultimately leaving no more arenas of obligation in which balance and social justice could be contested (Beck 1997: 100–101, 166). The flip side of the coin are increasingly unstable ways of life that are characterized by general insecurity (Bauman 1999). The latter is the result of efforts on the part of industry to deregulate, to become more flexible, and to rationalize, and of the reduced scope for state action. The increase in atypical and temporary employment conditions, the working-poor syndromes, and ever widening holes in the social net mean that this insecurity is reflected among the concerned individuals in insufficient future sustainability, that is, an inability to plan ahead and take charge over the development of their lives (Bourdieu 1998; Sennett 1998). The zone of precariousness and vulnerability (Castel 1995) is expanding and leads to an erosion of the societal middle classes, where, even outside traditional problem groups, the feeling of being under threat of exclusion and an awareness of one's own potential superfluous character are growing. Subpolitics here comprises what referred to as the political economy of insecurity: rendering expensive tools of discipline not necessary by helping the market version of freedom to gain acceptance (Bauman 1999).

Last, but not least, the kind of social responsibility on the back stage is also evident in the very disparate but, as a whole, clearly expanding range of legitimizations of social inequality. There has been a significant increase in the latter over the last few decades at both the international and national level. Unemployment and poverty are becoming increasingly detached from traditional class and stratification structures and have affected the middle classes for a rather long time period. The process of individualization means that what people used to be able to deal with collectively by way of guaranteed solidarities is now experienced as one's personal fate and as individual failure—not least because the neo-liberal reforms are accompanied by an aggressive promotion of performance principles and a stronger emphasis on personal and individual responsibility. Society now follows new models of entrepreneurship, market/competition apotheoses, and success as opposed to performance (Barlösius 2001; Neckel 2001; Bröckling 2007). Elitist concepts and elite discourses have risen from the ashes. At the same time, welfare-state safety nets are discredited. Subpolitics in this context means the legitimization of social inequalities as natural and, in the case of dynamic liberal market economies, absolutely indispensable incentives. One can find a major shift in the semantics of justice, equality, and solidarity as well (Lessenich and Ostner 1998; Lessenich 2003).

LANDMARK CHANGE IN THE UNDERSTANDING OF RESPONSIBILITY OF BUSINESS LEADERS

Even if there was no sudden turning point, it is quite obvious that the end of the "Social Democratic century" (Ralf Dahrendorf) in Germany and comparable industrialized nations has shown signs of a profound change, with larger companies undergoing international operations and refocusing their approach on the issue of social responsibility. On the one hand, and further back in the past, companies did follow the imperative of profit maximization. Provision of social benefits and demonstration of responsibility were rarely based on corporate initiative—they were generally won by the efforts of the workforce, the unions, or an interventionist state. At the same time, the model and the very real figure of the caring employer always existed: the patriarch, the patron. He at least enjoyed respect and recognition within the middle classes and on a local basis—but to a lesser degree from his own workforce. During recent years, however, features such as "character" or "personality" became less significant in the self-image of business elites, triggering elements related to functional efficiency (Unger 2003).

Two other groups have once and for all superseded the traditional image of the employer. The first are investors, prototypically represented by the administrators of large hedge funds and the private equity departments of major banks, which are on a permanent lookout for the most lucrative forms of investment for their capital (Knorr-Cetina and Preda 2004; Windolf 2005). The other group comprises a younger generation of managers who perform specific tasks on a temporary basis. As financial returns have become ever more important and the expectations of shareholders have to be accounted on a quarterly basis (Identity Foundation n.d.-a, n.d.-b), the horizon of their action is becoming increasingly short-term. As the management of large firms is subject to a permanent process of evaluation, top executives are both a driving and a driven force on the increasingly globalized market.

Given this context, the approach of company executives toward the issue of social responsibility is generally different from the situation a few decades ago. In the heyday of the welfare state, social responsibility was seen as a moral obligation that meant on an individual level, for example, a willingness to pay substantial taxes and social contributions, and on the state level, caring about public goods and social welfare. The underlying principles were that (a) social responsibility was an obligation for all parties, but especially for the wealthy, and that (b) the underprivileged had a right to obtain transferred benefits. These assumptions were gradually undermined by the perception of social responsibility as an option for private individuals. This means that social responsibility has become a voluntary act for individuals, associations, and companies that may or may not be exercised—but not imposed by the force of law or binding obligations. This attitude signals a shift away from the European model of solidarity (based on mutual expectations and obligations) to the U.S. model of charity: solidarity based on pity and on the goodwill of those who give and the gratitude of those who take. This shift must at the same time be seen as connected to a change in the historical time period, that is, from the widespread legitimacy of social inequality to the specific emphasis on natural and individual inequalities by the elites.

Although their choice of words may vary, elites interpret responsibility in terms of purely tactical or strategic considerations with regard to external assessments of the company. The question of what society and its disadvantaged groups need most is overshadowed by the question of what kind of involvement is beneficial to the individual company, sector, or the business community as a whole. "Image construction" becomes prominent in its role as a competitive factor. In this context, one must consider the new concepts of corporate social responsibility—referred to as "a natural part of the historical development of corporate culture in Germany," as the leader of the BDA put it (Hundt n.d.: 4)—as well as corporate citizenship and participation in the Global Compact (Global Compact Office 2001; Whitehouse 2003; Christian Aid 2004). These concepts can be interpreted as a response to the growing criticism of corporate behavior.

Today's business elites represent significantly adjusted models of social development that are more closely oriented to the Anglo-Saxon form of a free-market economy than to the old Rhenanian model of capitalism. The harsher the market becomes, and the greater the prevalence of a lack of values and restraint (of which there are many different examples, from exorbitant management bonuses and severance packages to falsified accounts, fraudulent behavior, and improper conduct on the part of management and directors), the more employers have to do for their image. Saying this, the aim is not to disregard the beneficial social activities of companies but to put them in context. Linking up business objectives and public interest factors has in fact—on the surface, at least—become an expression of a well-considered strategy and an integral part of corporate culture (Kotler and Lee 2004).

CONCLUSION

Media analyses, interviews, and case studies on different aspects of social responsibility show that generalizations about specific sectors of business or "the business community" as a whole are problematic. Therefore, any summary of the findings presented would need to make more distinctions than the scope of a chapter allows. Approaches of social responsibility encompass outright rejection, noncommitted signals, quid pro quo activities, substantial concessions, and even wholly unsolicited proactive social commitment (Imbusch and Rucht 2007a, 9–30). Even when we assume that social responsibility is only indirectly connected to globalization, and that a systematic survey of empirical allocations of individual actions was not possible, there is a clear underlying trend. Citing increasing economic pressure from domestic and global competition, a clear majority of business elites refuse to assume social responsibility as an obligation. Notwithstanding those who claim social responsibility is unaffordable for economic reasons or is not their job, the majority of companies do acknowledge some kind of responsibility. This no longer has to do with the traditional concept of responsibility with its high degree of commitment, due to the fact that today responsibility is defined differently and is at best considered something to be performed on a voluntary basis. Under these circumstances, the interpretation of social responsibility can even be reconciled with the neo-liberal credo, and business leaders can portray specific painful measures or decisions as examples of social responsibility. They can thus consider the relocation of jobs, the search for a lean state, and the demands to scale down the welfare state and to break up outdated structures in the name of a more dynamic market economy in terms of responsibility. Here we have to deal with conflicting and clearly different concepts of responsibility. Returning to the case of the Deutsche Bank, we see what appears under the new conditions: huge profits, a return on investment of 26 percent, the promotion of Josef Ackermann from management spokesman to chief executive officer, a doubtful acquittal in the Mannesmann/Vodafone trial imposing a high fine on the accused, mass dismissals, and a full-hearted commitment to corporate social responsibility.

NOTES

1. It has now become almost impossible to keep track of the richness of such initiatives and associated services, events, brochures, and reports; the same applies to publications on the topic of corporate social responsibility. The subject has become a major "growth industry" in its own right having its own periodicals (e.g., the *Journal of Corporate Citizenship* and the *Forum Wirtschaftsethik*).
2. The reflections contained in this report go back to a research project that I conducted together with my colleague Dieter Rucht (Wissenschaftszentrum Berlin [WZB]): "Business elites between globalization pressure and social responsibility." (The translations from German into English in the article are mine.) Some of his thoughts were incorporated into this essay. Any mistakes are, of course, my sole responsibility. The Ministry of Education and Research (BMBF) supported the project from 2002 to 2005 as part of the Bielefeld (Germany) research project "Disintegration processes."
3. This is probably the predominant view within the business field. In a survey of companies, the most commonly cited associations with the term "corporate social responsibility" were "responsibility for employees" and "securing jobs" (38 percent each). Other aspects such as "showing ethical/moral values" (8 percent) and "taking democratic rights and duties seriously" (6 percent, however, scored only low proportions (Bertelsmann Foundation 2005: 6).
4. Cf. World Economic Forum, press release, December 15, 2005, www.weforum.org.
5. The case has become famous because of the takeover from the British Vodafone of the phone sector of the German enterprise Mannesmann. During the economic struggle, the share prices of Mannesmann rose excessively. The chairman of Mannesmann, Klaus Esser, received a gratification of several million Euros when he left the company. The supervisory board—including Josef Ackermann from the Deutsche Bank and members of the German unions—agreed on the payment. Inconsistencies and the high amount of the gratification caught the attention of German courts, which accused Esser and other leading personalities of fraudulent behavior and irregular advantages at the detriment of the company.

6. The case studies examined the following examples of different degrees of social responsibility: the Mannesmann/Vodafone case; the cigarette industry and its defensive battles; the compensation fund supported by the German industry for enforced labor during the Second World War; the German Corporate Governance codex; the gender-equality code of the German industry; a labor conflict at Volkswagen, which resulted in the model 5000x5000, granting working places for the acceptance of new wage structures; the introduction of the European Eco-Management and Audit Scheme (EMAS) as an environmental management system; the Boston Consulting Group's business@ school project; and the "shock advertising" of Benetton.

REFERENCES

Aglietta, Michel, and Antoine Rebéroux. 2005. *Corporate Governance Adrift. A Critique of Shareholder Value*. Cheltenham: Edward Elgar.
Alfred-Herrhausen-Gesellschaft. 2004. *Das Prinzip Partnerschaft. Neue Formen von Governance im 21. Jahrhundert*. München, Zürich: Pieper.
Andrioff, Jörg, and Malcolm McIntosh, eds. 2001. *Perspectives on Corporate Citizenship*. Sheffield: Greenleaf.
Barlösius, Eva. 2001. "Die Macht der Repräsentation." Pp. 181–203 in *Gesellschaftsbilder im Umbruch. Soziologische Perspektiven in Deutschland*, ed. Eva Barlösius, Hans-Peter Müller, and Steffen Sigmund. Opladen: Westdeutscher Verlag.
Bauman, Zygmunt. 1999. *In Search of Politics*. Cambridge: Polity Press.
Bauman, Zygmunt. 2000. *Liquid Modernity*. Cambridge: Polity Press.
Beck, Ulrich. 1993. *Die Erfindung des Politischen. Zu einer Theorie reflexiver Modernisierung*. Frankfurt a. M.: Suhrkamp.
Beck, Ulrich. 1997. *Was ist Globalisierung?* Frankfurt a. M.: Suhrkamp.
Beck, Ulrich. 2002. *Macht und Gegenmacht im globalen Zeitalter. Neue weltpolitische Ökonomie*. Frankfurt a. M.: Suhrkamp.
Beck, Ulrich. 2007. *Weltrisikogesellschaft*. Frankfurt a. M.: Suhrkamp.
Bertelsmann Foundation, ed. 2005. *Corporate Social Responsibility. A Survey of 500 Top German Companies*. Gütersloh: Bertelsmann.
Bohnet-Joschko, Sabine, and Dirk Schiereck, eds. 2002. *Socially Responsible Management. Impulses for Good Governance in a Changing World*. Marburg: Metropolis.
Boltanski, Luc, and Eve Chiapello. 1999. *Le nouvel ésprit du capitalisme*. Paris: Gallimard.
Bourdieu, Pierre. 1998. *Contre-feux*. Paris: Liber—Raisons d'agir.
Braun, Barbara, and Peter Kromminga, eds. 2001. *Soziale Verantwortung und wirtschaftlicher Nutzen. Konzepte und Instrumente zur Kommunikation und Bewertung von Corporate Citizenship und Corporate Social Responsibility*. Berlin: Unternehmen—Partner für die Jugend.
Bröckling, Ulrich. 2007. *Das unternehmerische Selbst. Soziologie einer Subjektivierungsform*. Frankfurt a. M.: Suhrkamp.
Brühl, Tanja, Tobias Debiel, Brigitte Hamm, Hartwig Hummel, and Jens Martens, eds. 2001. *Die Privatisierung der Weltpolitik. Entstaatlichung und Kommerzialisierung im Globalisierungsprozess*. Bonn: Dietz.
Brühl, Tanja, Heidi Feldt, Brigitte Hamm, Hartwig Hummel, and Jens Martens, eds. 2004. *Unternehmen in der Weltpolitik. Politiknetzwerke, Unternehmensregeln und die Zukunft des Multilateralismus*. Bonn: Dietz.
Bürklin, Wilhelm, and Hilke Rebenstorf. 1997. *Eliten in Deutschland. Rekrutierung und Integration*. Opladen: Leske & Budrich.

Caroll, Archie B. 1999. "Corporate Social Responsibility. Evolution of a Definitional Construct." *Business & Society* 38: 268–295.

Castel, Robert. 1995. *Les métamorphoses de la question sociale. Une chronique du salariat*. Paris: Arthème Fayard.

Christian Aid, ed. 2004. *Behind the Mask: The Real Face of Corporate Social Responsibility*. London: Christian Aid.

Daub, Claus-Heinrich, Rudolf Ergenzinger, Hector Schmassmann, and Marion Weik. 2003. *Nachhaltigkeitsberichte Schweizer Unternehmen*. Basel: Edition Gesowip.

Deutsche Bank. 2003. *Gesellschaftliche Verantwortung. Bericht 2003*. Frankfurt a. M.: Eigendruck.

Dörre, Klaus, Klaus Kraemer, and Frédéric Speidel. 2007. *Prekarität*. Wiesbaden: Verlag für Sozialwissenschaften.

Dresewski, Felix. 2004. *Corporate Citizenship. Ein Leitfaden für das soziale Engagement mittelständischer Unternehmen*. Berlin: Unternehmen—Partner für die Jugend.

Engelhard, Johann, and Silvia Hein. 2001. "Globale Unternehmungen." Pp. 27–48 in *Politik im 21. Jahrhundert*, ed. Claus Leggewie and Richard Münch. Frankfurt a. M.: Suhrkamp.

Fabisch, Nicole. 2004. *Soziales Engagement von Banken. Entwicklung eines adaptiven und innovativen Konzeptansatzes im Sinne des Corporate Citizenship von Banken in Deutschland*. München: Hampp.

Frankfurter Aufruf. 2003. *Unternehmen: Aktiv im Gemeinwesen—Der Frankfurter Aufruf*. Frankfurt a. M.: Eigendruck.

Friedman, Milton. 1962. *Capitalism and Freedom*. Chicago: University of Chicago Press.

Global Compact Office, ed. 2001. *The Global Compact. Corporate Leadership in the World Economy*. New York: United Nations.

Goffman, Erving. 1959. *The Presentation of Self in Everyday Life*. Harmondsworth: Anchor Books.

Habisch, André, Hans-Peter Meister, and René Schmidpeter. 2001. *Corporate Citizenship as Investing in Social Capital*. Berlin: Logos Verlag.

Hartmann, Michael. 1996. *Topmanager—Die Rekrutierung einer Elite*. Frankfurt a. M.: Campus.

Hartmann, Michael. 2002. *Der Mythos von den Leistungseliten. Spitzenkarrieren und soziale Herkunft in Wirtschaft, Politik, Justiz und Wissenschaft*. Frankfurt a. M.: Campus.

Hartmann, Michael. 2004. *Elitesoziologie. Eine Einführung*. Frankfurt a. M.: Campus.

Hochhuth, Rolf. 2003. *McKinsey kommt—Molières Tartuffe. Zwei Theaterstücke*. München: Deutscher Taschenbuch Verlag.

Hoffmann-Lange, Ursula. 1992. *Eliten, Macht und Konflikt in der Bundesrepublik*. Opladen: Leske & Budrich.

Hopkins, Michael. 2006. *Corporate Social Responsibility and International Development*. Cheltenham: Edward Elgar.

Hradil, Stefan and Peter Imbusch, eds. 2003. *Oberschichten—Eliten—Herrschende Klassen*. Opladen: Leske & Budrich.

Hundt, Dieter n.d. "Corporate Social Responsibility. Das gesellschaftliche Engagement von Unternehmern." P. 4 in *Betrifft: Bürgergesellschaft 18*. Bonn: Friedrich Ebert Stiftung—Arbeitskreis Bürgergesellschaft und aktivierender Staat.

Identity Foundation n.d.-a. *Quellen der Identität einer neuen Wirtschaftselite. Ein Soziogramm von Managern und Gründern der New Economy*. Düsseldorf: Selbstverlag.

Identity Foundation n.d.-b. *Quellen der Identität. Das Selbstverständnis der Top-Manager der Wirtschaft*. Düsseldorf: Selbstverlag.

Imbusch, Peter. 2007. "Wirtschaftseliten, Globalisierung und soziale Verantwortung." Pp. 199–214, in *Die Globalisierung und ihre Kritik(er)*, ed. Ivonne Bemerburg and Arne Niederbacher. Wiesbaden: Verlag für Sozialwissenschaften.

Imbusch, Peter, and Dieter Rucht, eds. 2007a. *Profit oder Gemeinwohl? Fallstudien zur gesellschaftlichen Verantwortung von Wirtschaftseliten.* Wiesbaden: Verlag für Sozialwissenschaften.

Imbusch, Peter, and Dieter Rucht. 2007b. "Wirtschaftseliten und ihre gesellschaftliche Verantwortung." *Aus Politik und Zeitgeschichte* 4–5: 3–10.

Institut für Mittelstandsforschung (IfM). 2002. *Corporate Citizenship. Das Unternehmen als "guter Bürger"—Kurzfassung.* Bonn: IfM.

Kabst, Rüdiger. 2004. *Internationalisierung mittelständischer Unternehmen.* München: Hampp.

Knorr Cetina, Karin, and Alex Preda, eds. 2004. *The Sociology of Financial Markets.* Oxford: Oxford University Press.

Kotler, Philip, and Nancy Lee. 2004. *Corporate Social Responsibility. Doing the Most Good for your Company and your Cause.* London: Wiley & Sons.

Lasch, Christopher. 1995. *The Revolt of the Elites and the Betrayal of Democracy.* New York: W. W. Norton.

Lessenich, Stephan, ed. 2003. *Wohlfahrtsstaatliche Grundbegriffe. Historische und aktuelle Diskurse.* Frankfurt a. M.: Campus.

Lessenich, Stephan, and Ilona Ostner, eds. 1998. *Welten des Wohlfahrtskapitalismus. Der Sozialstaat in vergleichender Perspektive.* Frankfurt a. M.: Campus.

Lunau, York, and Florian Wettstein. 2004. *Die soziale Verantwortung der Wirtschaft. Was Bürger von Unternehmen erwarten.* Bern: Haupt.

Maaß, Frank, and Reinhard Clemens. 2002. *Corporate Citizenship: Das Unternehmen als 'guter Bürger.'* Bonn: Institut für Mittelstandsforschung (IfM).

Münch, Richard. 1998. *Globale Dynamik, lokale Lebenswelten. Der schwierige Weg in die Weltgesellschaft.* Frankfurt a. M.: Suhrkamp.

Münch, Richard. 2001. *Offene Räume. Soziale Integration jenseits des Nationalstaats.* Frankfurt a. M.: Suhrkamp.

Neckel, Sighard. 2001. "Leistung und Erfolg. Die symbolische Ordnung der Marktgesellschaft." Pp. 245–265 in *Gesellschaftsbilder im Umbruch. Soziologische Perspektiven in Deutschland*, ed. Eva Barlösius, Hans-Peter Müller, and Sigmund Steffen. Opladen: Leske & Budrich.

Polterauer, Judith. 2004. *Gesellschaftliche Integration durch Corporate Citizenship?* Discussion Paper Non-Profit-Sector No. 24. Münster: Universität Münster.

Rucht, Dieter, Peter Imbusch, Annette von Alemann, and Christian Galonska. 2007. *Vom Paternalismus zur Imagepflege? Über die gesellschaftliche Verantwortung deutscher Wirtschaftseliten.* Wiesbaden: Verlag für Sozialwissenschaften (in press).

Scheuch, Erwin K., and Ute Scheuch. 1995. *Bürokraten in den Chefetagen. Deutsche Karrieren: Spitzenmanager und Politiker heute.* Reinbek: Rowohlt.

Scheuch, Erwin K., and Ute Scheuch. 2001. *Deutsche Pleiten. Manager im Größenwahn oder Der irrationale Faktor.* Berlin: Rowohlt.

Schmidt, Matthias, and Thomas Beschorner, eds. 2005. *Werte- und Reputationsmanagement.* München: Hampp.

Schmucker, Rolf. 2005. *Unternehmer und Politik. Homogenität und Fragmentierung unternehmerischer Diskurse in gesellschaftspolitischer Perspektive.* Münster: Lit-Verlag.

Schultheis, Frank, and Kristina Schulz, eds. 2005. *Gesellschaft mit begrenzter Haftung. Zumutungen und Leiden im deutschen Alltag.* Konstanz: Universitätsverlag Konstanz.

Seitz, Bernhard. 2002. *Corporate Citizenship. Rechte und Pflichten der Unternehmung im Zeitalter der Globalität.* Wiesbaden: Deutscher Universitätsverlag.

Sennett, Richard. 1998. *The Corrosion of Character.* New York: W. W. Norton.

Sennett, Richard. 2006. *The Culture of the New Capitalism.* New Haven CT: Yale University Press.

Ulrich, Peter. 1999. "Was ist 'gute' Unternehmensführung? Zur normativen Dimension der Shareholder-Stakeholder-Debatte." Pp. 27–52, in *Unternehmensethik und die Transformation des Wettbewerbs,* Festschrift für Horst Steinmann zum 65. Geburtstag, ed. Brij N. Kumar, Margit Osterloh, and Georg Schreyögg. Stuttgart: Schäffer-Poeschel Verlag.

Ulrich, Peter. 2000. *Republikanischer Liberalismus und Corporate Citizenship— Von der ökonomistischen Gemeinwohlfiktion zur republikanisch-ethischen Selbstbindung wirtschaftlicher Akteure.* Universität St. Gallen, Berichte des Instituts für Wirtschaftsethik No. 88, St. Gallen.

Unger, Stefan. 2003. "Die Wirtschaftselite als Persönlichkeit." Pp. 295–316, in *Die deutsche Wirtschaftselite im 20. Jahrhundert. Kontinuität und Mentalität,* ed. Volker Berghahn, Stefan Unger, and Dieter Ziegler. Essen: Klartext.

Wasner, Barbara. 2004. *Eliten in Europa. Einführung in Theorien, Konzepte und Befunde.* Wiesbaden: Verlag für Sozialwissenschaften.

Westebbe, Achim, and David Logan. 1995. *Corporate Citizenship. Unternehmen im gesellschaftlichen Dialog.* Wiesbaden: Westdeutscher Verlag.

Whitehouse, Lisa. 2003. "Corporate Social Responsibility, Corporate Citizenship and the Global Compact. A New Approach to Regulating Corporate Social Power?" *Global Social Policy* 3: 299–318.

Wieland, Josef, and Walter Conradi, eds. 2002. *Corporate Citizenship. Gesellschaftliches Engagement—unternehmerischer Nutzen.* Marburg: Metropolis.

Windolf, Paul, ed. 2005. *Finanzmarkt-Kapitalismus. Analysen zum Wandel von Produktionsregimen.* Wiesbaden: Verlag für Sozialwissenschaften.

Wortmann, Michael. 2003. *Strukturwandel und Globalisierung des deutschen Einzelhandels.* WZB-Discussion Paper, SP III 2003–202a, Berlin (Germany).

3 Negotiating Neo-Liberalism

Free-Market Reform in Central and Eastern Europe

Nina Bandelj

Scholars have claimed that the last two decades of the 20th century have seen a rise in market deregulation and economic liberalization on a global scale (e.g., Lash and Urry 1987; Albert 1993; Przeworski 1995; Campbell and Pedersen 2001). Although many welcome these developments as evidence that the market is finally freed to select out the most efficient policies (Posner 1986; Williamson 1990), others consider these changes as a result of a political project—neo-liberalism—promoted by international organizations and domestic political forces, like Reagan and Thatcher governments (Meyer et al. 1997; Gore 2000; Babb 2001; Campbell and Pedersen 2001; Carruthers et al. 2001; Brune et al. 2004; Henisz et al. 2005). But what drives the adoption of neo-liberal reforms?

The transformations after the fall of communist regimes in Central and Eastern Europe provide a particularly fruitful site to investigate the factors that lead some countries to embrace more widely and more deeply the neo-liberal economic policies than their counterparts. After denouncing socialist command economy as a legitimate institutional order, postcommunist governments chose the market system. To a significant degree, foreign neo-liberal economists and consultants who offered advice on how to best accomplish the market "transition" guided these decisions. More than fifteen years after 1989, most of the Central and Eastern European countries have firmly in place institutions that support market exchange and have substantially cut down the redistributive role of the state. However, the socioeconomic systems in these countries show sufficient variation to warrant an inquiry into the factors that determine the adoption of neo-liberal market reforms. Such an inquiry will also allow us to investigate the interactions between local life-worlds and the global economic modernity.

Although some countries in the region have adopted very extensive free-market reforms, including low flat tax rates, generous incentives for foreign direct investments, and cuts to social welfare systems, others have been able to maintain greater involvement of the state in the economy. What enables efforts to counter neo-liberalism in postsocialist states? I argue that economic policymaking is not driven by universally efficient outcomes but is embedded in external institutional pressures, and domestic legacies, culture, and politics. These social forces vary across individual countries and for various segments of reform, which leads to the divergence in the adoption of neo-liberalism in Central and Eastern Europe. Despite relatively uniform pressures from international financial organizations and the European Union, adoption of privatization, foreign direct investment (FDI) liberalization, reduction in taxing, and social spending have been shaped by institutional legacies and cultural framing of economic issues that shape the interests of governing elites as well as provide ideational and political resources to actors who resist reform. It remains to be seen, however, to what extent newly institutionalized democracies can carve distinct social-liberal paths to sustainable economic development in the era of neo-liberal global modernity.

In the following sections, I first review the literature on neo-liberalism, defining what it entails and how it spreads. Second, I put neo-liberalism in the context of postsocialist transformations. In the third section, I review how 10 Central and East European countries, all members of the European Union, adopted four neo-liberal reforms: (a) privatization, (b) FDI liberalization, (c) tax cuts, and (d) reductions in social spending. Finally, I summarize these changes for two very contrasting country cases to show the role of legacies, politics, and ideas in how Central and East European states negotiate neo-liberalism.

NEO-LIBERALISM

Although the words *neo-liberal* and *neo-liberalism* have recently been used very widely in the media and in policy and academic circles, it is important to define what we mean by them. I follow a definition of Campbell and Pedersen, who lay out the institutional, normative, and cognitive principles of the phenomenon. They argue that:

> [Neo-liberalism] includes formal institutions, such as minimalist welfare-state, taxation, and business-regulation programs; flexible labor markets and decentralized capital-labor relations unencumbered by strong unions and collective bargaining; and the absence of barriers to international capital mobility. It includes institutionalized normative principles favoring free-market solutions to economic problems, rather than bargaining or indicative planning, and a dedication to controlling inflation even at the expense of full employment. It includes institutionalized cognitive principles, notably a deep, taken-for-granted belief in neoclassical economics. (Campbell and Pedersen 2001, 5)

Indeed, many have spelled out that the key characteristic of the neo-liberal economic principles is the understanding that markets are "the most desirable mechanism for regulating both domestic and world economies"

(Fourcade-Gourinchas and Babb 2002, 533), which requires a reduction of "the role of politics and the state in the economy so that markets may function unhindered" (Henisz et al. 2005, 873). However, as we can see from the Campbell and Pedersen's definition just given, neo-liberal policies do encompass a wide range of policy domains, from welfare, taxation, and labor market regulation, to international capital mobility, as well as privatization.[1]

But where does neo-liberalism come from? As Fourcade-Gourinchas and Babb (2002) summarize, there are two different explanations to this question. On the one hand, proponents of free-markets argue that the recent recognition of the importance of neo-liberal policies is due to the fact that they actually work better than other kinds of, more state-focused, economic policies. On the other hand, critics argue that the rise of neo-liberalism is due to the increasing control of capital over labor, and the imposition of international agencies and financial institutions—often promoting neo-liberal development policies as "inevitable"—over domestic economic matters. Indeed, in their review of the International Monetary Fund (IMF) and the World Trade Organization (WTO), Babb and Chorev (2006: 2) note that these two organizations have played "a key role in imposing and maintaining" neo-liberal policies. Studies show that the IMF and World Bank loans increase the likelihood of durable policy reforms, such as the privatization of state-owned enterprises (Henisz et al. 2005). The WTO has also had an impact on massive reduction of tariffs (Chorev 2005), integral to neo-liberalism.

Indeed, we can trace the codification of the neo-liberal agenda by the international financial institutions in the practice to economic development known as the "Washington Consensus" (Williamson 1990, xiii). As Charles Gore summarized,

> In broad terms, this approach recommends that governments should reform their policies and, in particular: a) pursue macroeconomic stability by controlling inflation and reducing fiscal deficits; b) open their economies to the rest of the world through trade and capital account liberalization; and c) liberalize domestic product and factor markets through privatization and deregulation. Propagated through the stabilization and structural adjustment policies of the International Monetary Fund (IMF) and the World Bank, this has been the dominant approach to development from the early 1980s to the present. (Gore 2000: 789–790)

Consequently, one would expect that the incorporation into the activities of the international financial institutions would shape the adoption of neo-liberal reforms in any particular world region. In fact, economist John Williamson (1990, 1993), who coined the term "Washington Consensus," did so in an attempt to summarize policy reforms in Latin America, which, like other regions with the exception of some countries in East Asia, faced economic crises in the late 1970s and the early 1980s. The neo-liberal approach to handling the crisis was popularized by the example of Chile, which was the first nation in the world to implement a radical package of free-market reforms during the authoritarian government of General Augusto Pinochet (Fourcade-Gourinchas and Babb 2002: 542). Furthermore, neo-liberal reforms have also been very influential in the so-called market transition after the fall of the communist regimes in Central and Eastern Europe. I turn next to this topic.

THE NEO-LIBERAL SHOCK-THERAPY APPROACH TO POSTSOCIALIST TRANSFORMATIONS

The revolutionary acts in Central and Eastern Europe in 1989, and the subsequent collapse of communist regimes throughout the region, were followed by a myriad of challenges about how to transform socialist economies. During the late 1980s, the time of heightened adoption of neo-liberal policies elsewhere in the world, it is not surprising that an answer to the transformation question was provided by the international financial institutions and neo-liberal economists from the West. These argued for the necessity of rapid changes, "a shock therapy," "a big bang" approach, with the goal to quickly create markets by eliminating state command of the economy and supposed irrationalities of redistribution (Sachs 1989, 1993; Lipton and Sachs 1990a; Sachs and Lipton 1990b; Blanchard et al. 1991; Fischer and Gelb 1991; Aslund 1992, 1994, 1995; Blanchard et al. 1994). These observers emphasized that the most efficient way of economic organization is a self-regulated market. Socialist economies need to quickly create a private property rights regime, which can be effectively achieved by mass privatization. Prices and currency controls need to be released, state subsidies withdrawn and trade liberalized. This will give rise to a *depoliticized* economic system (Boycko et al. 1996) coordinated through market prices and competition with a clear incentive structure that will induce efficient corporate governance and rapid firm restructuring (Shleifer and Vishny 1994; Boycko et al. 1996).

By the mid 1990s, the proclaimed economic superiority of the shock-therapy transition won out among the international policy circles. As the then President of the International Monetary Fund, Michel Camdessus emphasized in a 1995 speech:

> First, and most important, the most appropriate course of action is to adopt a bold strategy. Many countries . . . have by now proven the feasibility of implementing policies of rapid—*and I stress rapid*—liberalization, stabilization and structural reform; and such policies have, indeed been shown to provide the key to successful transition and economic recovery—more so than a country's starting conditions, natural

resources, or external assistance. (quoted in Spicer et al. 2000, 631, emphasis added)

Underlying this shock therapy perspective is the assumption that laissez-faire free market is the best and most efficient way to organize contemporary capitalism, and that it is universally applicable. According to this discourse, once the inefficient state intervention is eliminated the invisible hand of the market will demonstrate its powers. Hence, the neo-liberal view of the postsocialist transformation was largely based on the understanding of history as a natural course of progression from one stage to another, whereby socialism is only a slight detour before Central and Eastern Europe (finally) reaches capitalism. Capitalism, like the one proven to work in the West, is considered as a clear destination, or an endpoint of the transition journey. Hence, to achieve market transition in Central and Eastern Europe, the reformers were advised to take advantage of the "great void [that] opened up" (Aslund 1992: 16) and rely on a market blueprint proven to work in the Western capitalism. As the shock therapy approach proscribed, old institutions of command economy should be erased, private property rights should be put in place, and—voilà—markets would emerge that would allocate resources efficiently.

From a policy standpoint, neo-liberalists feared that a more gradual negotiated reform process would require the inclusion of a plurality of interests springing up in the newly democratizing states, and would therefore likely lead to a political stalemate on economic reforms (Lipton and Sachs 1990: 297). In addition, gradualism would continue to maintain the inefficient state sector (Frydman and Rapaczynski 1993: 202). Moreover, gradualism would likely give rise to "spontaneous privatization" whereby insiders (managers or state bureaucrats) would appropriate formerly state-owned assets for personal gain (Boycko, Shleifer, and Vishny 1995; Kaufman and Siegelbaum 1997). For all these reasons, neo-liberalists held that market transition in Central and Eastern Europe should be accomplished quickly via mass privatization and stabilization, which might, like the shock therapy, hurt in the short term but would undoubtedly provide beneficial results not long after.

Indeed, the neo-liberal approach has held a wide appeal to the postcommunist governments. "After communist regimes in Eastern Europe collapsed in 1989, the new postcommunist governments have embarked, at various speeds, on neo-liberal economic reforms designed to bring about rapid liberalization, macroeconomic restructuring, and, ultimately, privatization" (Bockman and Eyal 2002: 310). While socialism was a closed system that shied from international interactions, as soon as the Iron Curtain was lifted, Central and Eastern European countries opened up to international influences, including the neo-liberal policy prescriptions, promoted and advocated by international organizations, like the International Monetary Fund (IMF), the World Bank, the European Bank for Restructuring and

Development (EBRD), and the Organization for Economic Cooperation and Development (OECD).

This means that immediately after 1989 postsocialist states sought membership in these international organizations and that they applied for loans from the IMF. Taking these loans imposed a set of common standards and obligations in line with the association's philosophy of liberal economic development. As Table 1 shows, all postsocialist countries, except Slovenia, were bound by the IMF loans for most or even the whole of the first decade after 1989. In addition, signing Article VIII of the IMF Agreement, which all countries, including Slovenia, accomplished between 1994 and 1998, meant that members agreed not to "impose restrictions on the making of payments and transfers for current international transactions" and thus liberalization to cross-national financial flows (IMF 2005: 1).

Moreover, immediately following the regime changes in Central and Eastern Europe, the postcommunist states began with the integration into the European Union (EU). To affirm their desire to integrate into the European Union, in December 1991 Poland and Hungary were the first among the postsocialist states to sign the so-called Europe Agreements. Marking the beginning of a country's path toward EU integration, the Europe Agreements provided a bilateral institutional framework between EU member states and postsocialist countries, covering trade-related issues, political dialogue, legal harmonization, and other areas of cooperation, including industry, environment, transport, and customs. These EU Agreements were quite neo-liberal in nature, as they required the abolition of most tariffs and the adaptation of the regulatory framework to EU rules (Meyer 1998). Following Poland and Hungary, Romania and Bulgaria signed the Agreement in spring 1993. The Czech Republic and Slovakia, after the dissolution of the federal state, each separately signed the agreement in October 1993. The three Baltic states followed in June 1995 and Slovenia in June 1996.

The signing of the Europe Agreements was followed by years of the EU accession process, in which Central and East European applicants had to adapt their institutional frameworks to the *acquis communautaire*, the common European legislation. This process was successfully completed by 2005 for eight of the postsocialist countries, Czech Republic, Estonia, Hungary, Latvia, Lithuania, Poland, Slovakia, and Slovenia, who joined the EU in May 2004, and by 2006 for Bulgaria and Romania, who joined in January 2007. Table 1 summarizes the integration of Central and Eastern Europe in international institutions.

Why could links to international organizations have an important impact on the domestic policy choices of Central and East European countries? I would argue that this is because these links have consequences for the distribution of political power. Decision making at the level of the nation-state can be substantially constrained because of its integration into transnational structures. It is not that any integration into transnational structures is directly linked to the loss of state power, but the coercive power of these

Table 1. Integration of Central and Eastern Europe Into International Institutions

Country	Europe Agreement signed	Application for EU membership	Accession to EU	IMF loans	IMF Article VIII	GATT/WTO membership	OECD membership
Bulgaria	March 1993	December 1995	January 2007	1991–2000	September 1998	December 1996	No
Czech R.	October 1993	January 1996	May 2004	1991–1994	October 1995	January 1995	1995
Estonia	June 1995	November 1995	May 2004	1991–2000	August 1994	November 1999	No
Hungary	December 1991	March 1994	May 2004	1990–1994 1996–1998	January 1996	January 1995	1996
Latvia	June 1995	October 1995	May 2004	1992–2000	June 1994	February 1999	No
Lithuania	June 1995	December 1995	May 2004	1992–2000	May 1994	May 2001	No
Poland	December 1991	April 1994	May 2004	1990–1996	June 1995	July 1995	1996
Romania	February 1993	June 1995	January 2007	1991–2000	March 1998	January 1995	No
Slovakia	October 1993	June 1995	May 2004	1991–1992 1994–1996	October 1995	January 1995	2000
Slovenia	June 1996	June 1996	May 2004	none	September 1995	July 1995	No

Sources: EU (2005) and IMF (2005); for IMF loans, Vreeland (2002); for OECD membership, OECD (2006).

structures is more evident for those states, which come from the periphery, and cannot assert their interests as vehemently as core states can. Because postsocialist states were emerging back to the world system scene from the periphery, they were structurally in rather weak positions to negotiate with international institutions. Particularly clear is the case of IMF loans. As it is stated on the IMF's web site, "an IMF loan is usually provided under an 'arrangement,' which stipulates the specific policies and measures a country has agreed to implement in order to resolve its balance of payments problem" (IMF 2006). Should countries stray, the IMF exerts pressure to put them back on (the neo-liberal) track. For instance, like a scolding parent,

"IMF *warned* Romania that progress in disinflation and consolidation of the external position will require wage and financial discipline in the state-owned enterprises, continued fiscal consolidation, and prudent monetary policy" (EBRD 2001, emphasis added). Clearly, countries bound by IMF loans are also tied to the institution's prescriptions for economic development.

However, it is important to acknowledge that the role of neo-liberalism on developments in postsocialist Europe is not just a manifestation of an imbalance of power and thus externally imposed pressure. Sociologists Johanna Bockman and Gil Eyal (2002) propose that neo-liberalism's success in East Europe is in large part due to transnational dialogues between American and East European economists in which neo-liberal ideas were worked out already during socialism. For instance, to facilitate this dialogue, the Ford Foundation had established exchange during the Cold War with Poland (signed in 1957), Yugoslavia (1959), Hungary (1962), Romania (1965), Czechoslovakia (1968), and Bulgaria (1968). Participants in such dialogues were economists who later championed neo-liberal reforms in their home countries, like Václau Klaus from the Czech Republic or Leszek Balcerowicz from Poland. Therefore, ideological predispositions of domestic decision makers have clearly been important. Moreover, even in terms of international pressures, domestic actors and their interests have channeled these forces. For all these domestic ideological and political reasons, we should see differences in the way in which individual postsocialist countries embark on neo-liberal development paths.

Expected variability in adoption is also likely because, after all, neo-liberalism is not a natural response to postsocialist transformations. In particular, evolutionary economists, political scientists, and sociologists countered neo-liberalist proscriptions because they presupposed that, in principle, the paths after the fall of communist regimes were multiple and uncertain, and that initial conditions—in sharp contrast to what the then IMF president Camdessus claimed in the quote provided earlier—did matter (Murrell 1992, 1993; Poznanski 1993; Stark 1992, 1996; Grabher and Stark 1997; Spicer, McDermott, and Kogut 2000). These observers argued that social change in Central and Eastern Europe was not about a "transition" to market but a *transformation* of social, political, economic, and cultural circumstances that configured a socialist system. Social change should be seen "not as a transition from one order to another but as transformation—rearrangements, reconfigurations, and recombinations that yield new interweavings of the multiple social logics that are a modern society" (Stark and Bruszt 1998: 7). Based on this perspective, also known as "path-dependency," structures inherited from before and during the socialist period have influenced transformation processes (Seleny 1991; Stark 1992; Szelényi and Kostello 1996; Stark and Bruszt 1998). Therefore, we could expect that the economic policies adopted after 1989 would be shaped by the institutional legacies of the socialist system. This should be particularly evident for the reform of the postsocialist welfare states. Since socialism instituted the Marxist–Leninist ideology of social equality (Kornai 1992), among other privileged goals of socialism, these collectivist tendencies would also shape public opinions about valued goals in the postsocialist period. For those reformers that have responded to public opinion, the cuts to the welfare state and to social provisions have not been so easily executed, even if these actors themselves have been champions of neo-liberal reforms.

Overall, economic policymaking and, in particular, the adoption of neo-liberal reforms in Central and Eastern Europe are embedded in international pressures, domestic discourses and politics, and institutionalized legacies of the socialist system. These elements have led countries to embrace more or less neo-liberalism as a development policy. Moreover, different policy areas can be linked to different interests and legacies. Hence, there are differences not only across countries but also across policy domains within individual countries. For this reason, I present economic reforms in 10 countries of Central and Eastern Europe along four distinct policy domains that pertain to the core agenda of the "Washington consensus": (a) privatization, (b) FDI liberalization, (c) tax reform, and (d) social policy reform. I discuss each of these areas separately in the next sections. The summary is provided in Table 2.

PRIVATIZATION

Privatization of state-owned enterprises was one of the first items on the postsocialist transformation agenda. But it was not straightforward how to best achieve privatization and how quickly it should be done. The advocates of the shock-therapy approach agreed that rapid mass privatization would allow for the most economically optimal solution. Such privatization would involve distribution of vouchers (quasi company shares) to the population. Then via auctions, voucher holders (individuals or investment funds) would invest these "shares" into specific firms, which would thus become joint-stock companies with individual owners. Subsequently, these owners could struck efficient bargains and further exchange shares at will, which would lead to eventual consolidation of shares by strategic investors willing to engage in firm restructuring, contributing to overall improved economic performance (Shleifer and Vishny 1994; Boycko et al. 1995).

It is important to note that mass privatization was not advocated only on economic grounds. The major problem, as David Lipton and Jeffrey Sachs saw it, is that

> the real risk in Eastern Europe is not that the privatization process will be less than optimal, but that it will be paralyzed entirely. We believe that unless hundreds of large firms in each country are brought quickly into the privatization process, the political battle over privatization will

Table 2. Neo-Liberal Reform Indicators for Central and Eastern Europe

	Bulgaria	Czech Republic	Estonia	Hungary	Latvia	Lithuania	Poland	Romania	Slovakia	Slovenia
Private-sector share in GDP 2002 (percent) [a]	75	80	80	80	70	75	75	65	80	65
Mass privatization (25 percent of LSE in 2 years) [b]	no	yes	no	no	yes	yes	no	yes	no	no
FDI Stock 2003 (percent GDP) [c]	25	50	79	58	32	27	27	23	36	16
Government expenditures 2003 (percent GDP) [d]	38.4	44.1	36	46.9	35.4	31.5	44.8	32.3	39.2	48.2
Expenditure on health and education 2002 (percent GDP) [d]	6.8	11.3	10.7	11.2	9.1	10	10.3	6.2	7.7	12.5
Unionization Rate (estimated percent) [e]	30	30	15	20	30	15	15	50	40	41.3
Income Tax 2005 (percent) (W-Europe average 44 percent)	29	32	26	38	25	33	40	16 [g]	19	50
Corporate Tax 2005 (percent% percent) (Western Europe average 31 percent)	19.5	28	0	16	15	15	19	16 [g]	19	25
Flat tax rate 2005 (yes or no)	no	no	yes	no	yes	yes	no	yes	yes	no

(continued)

Table 2. Neo-Liberal Reform Indicators for Central and Eastern Europe (Continued)

	Bulgaria	Czech Republic	Estonia	Hungary	Latvia	Lithuania	Poland	Romania	Slovakia	Slovenia
Gross National Income per capita 2003 (US$ purchasing power parity)[d]	7,140	15,600	12,680	13,840	10,210	11,390	11,210	7,140	13,440	19,100
Real GDP 2005 (1989 = 100)[d]	93.4	119.5	120	124.2	96.9	95.3	146.8	105.1	124.9	135.2

[a] EBRD (2004).
[b] King and Hamm (2006), LSE = large state-enterprises.
[c] UNCTAD (2006).
[d] TRANSMONEE (2006).
[e] Data from: Lado (2002); all figures are estimates except for Slovenia; the figures refer to the years from 1999 to 2001.
[f] Euractiv (2006).
[g] EIU (2006).

soon lead to stalemate in the entire process. (Lipton and Sachs 1990: 297–298)

In practice, postsocialist countries did not uniformly follow the neo-liberal mass privatization prescriptions. Given the initial wide support of mass privatization programs among the international policy elites (Spicer et al. 2000), this strategy was widely contemplated (and perhaps even planned), but it was not implemented across the Central and East European region. Even if we define mass privatization quite conservatively as a program that covered at least 25 percent of all large state-owned enterprises over a period of two years, then mass privatization happened in the Czech Republic, Latvia, Lithuania, and Romania, but not in Bulgaria, Estonia, Hungary, Poland, Slovakia, and Slovenia (King and Hamm 2006).

The diversity was also large in terms of specific strategies that countries chose to create private property rights. Each country selected a unique combination of different policies that could be broadly characterized as voucher privatization, direct sales, or management/employee buy-outs (EBRD 2001). In the end, individual Central and East European countries more or less quickly implemented different combinations of these strategies (Dallago et al. 1992; Earle et al. 1993), leading to a more or less extensive reduction of the state sector.

For instance, the privatization in the Czech Republic was relatively fast and extensive. The allocation of property rights in this country was achieved largely by the distribution of vouchers to citizens over the age of eighteen, for which they were asked to pay a nominal fee. Each person could receive vouchers equal to 1000 investment points and could then exchange these points for shares in the enterprises offered for sale in auctions or invest them in investment privatization funds (Hanousek and Kroch 1998). The voucher privatization happened in two rounds, the first in 1992 and the second in 1994. By 1995, only 10 percent of all large and medium-sized enterprises were still counted as entirely state-owned in the Czech Republic, while this figure was 22 percent in Hungary and 54 percent in Poland (World Bank 1995). Not surprisingly, then, the Czech privatization "has been widely heralded as one of the most impressive accomplishments in the economic transformations of the formerly communist countries" (Svejnar and Singer 1994: 43). This result was largely due to the leadership of Václav Klaus, the Czech Prime Minister and neo-liberal economist, who held a firm hand over the privatization process and whose goal was to "privatize quickly and with determination" (Turek 1993: 266). By 1995, private-sector share in GDP was already at 70 percent, the highest among the Central and East European countries. By 2000, this number increased to 80 percent, reaching top regional levels.

In contrast, Slovenia adopted a gradualist approach to privatization designed by a group of domestic academic economists who largely rejected the advice of Western experts advocating a shock-therapy approach. As

Mencinger (2004: 77) reported, Slovenia considered two alternative strategies of privatization. One advocated by the majority of Slovenian academic economists was "decentralized, gradual and commercial privatization, which the government would only monitor; the other [codified in a Jeffrey Sachs-Peterle-Umek Act] advocated massive and speedy privatization administered by the government and relying on the free distribution of enterprise shares [via vouchers]" (Mencinger 2004: 77). After long negotiations in the parliament, the Ownership Transformation Act was passed in November 1992, which "combined the decentralization, gradualism, and diversity of privatization methods of the first approach with the free distribution of vouchers called for under the second" (Mencinger 2004: 77). Hence, most Slovenian companies were privatized through the free distribution of vouchers (called ownership certificates) to citizens who could then exchange these for shares in the privatizing company, either directly or through privatization in investment funds. Twenty percent of the shares of each company that was being privatized was allocated to the quasi-governmental funds (Simoneti, Rojec, and Gregorič 2004: 231). In addition, Slovenian privatization policy privileged management and employee buyouts, whereby management and employees were encouraged to invest their ownership certificates in the companies they worked for. This not only maintained insider control but limited privatizations to foreign owners (Simoneti, Rojec, and Gregorič 2004). Overall, the process of privatization in Slovenia has been slow. The private sector accounted for 50 percent of the economy in 1995, which was below the regional average. By 2000, this figure was at 65 percent, still below the regional average, and unfinished privatization business remained in banks, utilities, and other large state firms.

In Poland, the initial package of reforms was designed by a team of economists and neo-liberal foreign advisors, including Jeffrey Sachs, led by Leszek Balcerowicz, Polish finance minister during the Solidarity government in 1990, as part and parcel of the famous "shock therapy" approach to the Polish transformation (Sachs 1989; Frydman and Rapacynski 1994). These reforms included two separate laws: the Office of the Ministry of Ownership Act, and the Privatization of State-Owned Enterprises Act that defined several principal privatization strategies: sales to foreign investors, initial offerings on the newly organized stock exchange, and the management and employee takeover of firms through leasing or outright ownership. The privatization was to be "accomplished quickly," in line with the shock therapy approach (Frydman and Rapaczynski 1994: 14). However, the process was mostly handled by regional "voivodship" (county) offices, and not by the central privatization ministry. In addition, firm privatizations needed to be approved by the firm's managers and employees. This favored a decentralized process, which contributed to the fact that the Polish privatization was much slower than expected. By the end of 1996, only about 20 percent, out of a designated total of 8,853 enterprises, were privatized (Graybow et al. 1998).

Although announced much earlier, during the initial shock therapy package of reforms, the mass privatization was launched only in 1996 and was based on giving citizens vouchers, which represented an ownership stake in fifteen National Investment Funds, run by state-selected foreign and local management groups. The vouchers went on sale in November 1995 for a nominal amount of 20 zloty (approximately US $7). By the end of the distribution in November 1996, 90 percent of Poles had participated in this voucher program (Graybow et al. 1998).

The Law on Commercialization and Privatization of State-Owned Enterprises, in effect from January 1997, reshaped Polish privatization policy. The State Treasury, which assumed control of privatization in August 1996, now had the power to privatize firms without requiring the consent of the firm's insiders as previously practiced. At the same time, employees of a privatized firm were given the right to acquire 15 percent of that firm's shares for free. In 1995, an estimated 60 percent of gross domestic product (GDP) was produced by the private sector, and by 2000 this number was at 70 percent, the regional average.

While countries clearly chose among the multitude of privatization possibilities, the choices they made were not random. As Stark and Bruszt (1998) convincingly argue, privatization choices depended on ways of extrication from the communist system. For example, the strategies adopted in Poland reflected that the regime change resulted from negotiations between the old and the new elite; in Hungary, that the end of communism was marked by political party competition; and in Czechoslovakia, that the Communist leaders capitulated. Privatization strategies also depended on the type of socialism. For example, unlike other states, Slovenia, a part of the former Yugoslavia, where socialism was based on workers' self-management, implemented management and employee buyouts as their primary privatization strategies. Because the Yugoslav self-management system privileged a decentralized control of workers' councils, decisions to allow firm insiders, workers and managers, to acquire ownership stakes of the property, seem largely consistent with the spirit of self-management (Bandelj 2007).

Overall, privatization in Central and Eastern Europe has been a complex process, captured well by Janusz Lewandowski, Polish Privatization Minister, who characterized privatization as a process where "someone who doesn't know who the real owner is and doesn't know what it is really worth sells it to someone who doesn't have any money" (quoted in Verdery 2003: 1). More importantly, the complexity and uncertainty implicated in the privatization process highlight that the act of privatization is not an objective economic process whereby the one right solution is clearly obvious. Rather, privatization as a process is an economic policy idea diffused across national borders as part of neo-liberal reforms. Empirically examining what determines whether a country launches a privatization program, Kogut and MacPherson (2003) found that the rapid and widespread adoption has a lot to do with the number of U.S.-trained and particularly Chicago-trained economists in a country of adoption, showing the role of ideas and not only objective economic conditions on adoption of economic policy. Moreover, in their recent study of the worldwide diffusion of neo-liberal market reforms in the infrastructure sectors, including telecommunication and electricity privatizations, Henisz, Zelner, and Guillén (2005: 871) find robust evidence that countries implement these reforms not only because of domestic economic and political factors but also because of "international pressures of coercion, normative emulation and competitive mimicry." For instance, whether a country decides to privatize its telecommunications or energy sectors significantly depends on this country's exposure to multilateral lenders like the World Bank and the International Monetary Fund (who espouse the neo-liberal credo) and the competition with and imitation of peer countries.

LIBERALIZATION TO FOREIGN DIRECT INVESTMENT

Conceptualizing market transition in postsocialism as "capitalism without capitalists," Eyal, Szelenyi, and Townsley (1998) emphasized that socialism didn't create propertied classes that could easily acquire assets available for sale during privatization. In fact, in many countries foreign investors played a very important role in this process, and the majority of FDI entering Central and Eastern Europe in the first decade after the fall of the communist regimes has been privatization related, with the exception of the Czech Republic, which has been able to attract some sizable greenfield investment (Czechinvest 2005).

Moreover, in many cases the postsocialist elites embraced FDI as a transition strategy because powerful transnational organizations and prominent economic advisors have been advocating FDI as a catalyst in the transition and a panacea that would help reverse the substantial drops in economic welfare that happened in these countries immediately after the collapse of communism (Schmidt 1995). Therefore, consistent with the spirit of neo-liberalism, many postsocialist governments have used FDI as an economic development strategy and have put in place provisions to attract foreign capital. The United Nations Conference on Trade and Development (UNCTAD) collects information on FDI and compiles country reports.[2] In these reports it is written, for instance, that "Bulgarian government is increasingly liberalizing its foreign investment regime," that Hungary and Romania have in place "various types of incentives" for FDI, that Latvian government provides "tax exemptions as an incentive," and that the Slovakian one offers "corporate tax holidays" (UNCTAD 2006). These notes point to the increasingly liberal FDI policies adopted across the Central and East European region.

Nevertheless, it is also important to consider that there may be discrepancies between the formal policy and informal legitimacy granted to the entry of foreign capital. Many observers have argued that early decisions related to FDI in Central and East European countries have been plagued by fears of losing control and surrendering national economic (and political) sovereignty. For states that had emerged from decades-long foreign occupation by the Soviet rule, allowing domestic assets to be acquired by foreigners has been a particularly sensitive issue. This is how economist Hans-Werner Sinn and colleagues understood the "surprisingly low demand for FDI" and the "mixed feelings in [Central and East European countries] about the role of FDI" (Sinn et al. 1997: 182). Seven years after 1989, these authors reported that

> [Central and East European countries] fear that FDI makes a country vulnerable to foreign influence, a partial loss of sovereignty, and that national treasures are sold at low sale prices to the west. . . . Polish privatization minister Gruszecki warned against giving foreigners too much preference in the privatization process; former prime minister Pawlak argued that he had tried his utmost to prevent foreign investors taking over Polish companies. Polish trade unions accuse foreign investors of employing "slave labor" and taking away the "family silver." (Sinn et al. 1997: 182)

As Bandelj (2007) has shown, the actual penetration of FDI into individual postsocialist countries is strongly linked to the efforts of postsocialist states to legitimize FDI *practice* and not only institute appropriate *policy*. Hence, some states, like Hungary, Estonia, and the Czech Republic, established early state FDI agencies (that worked hard to promote the country as an investment location) and began selling their strategic state monopolies in the banking and telecommunication sectors to foreigners already in the beginning years of the postsocialist transformation. For instance, a consortium of Finish and Swedish corporations acquired Estonian Eesti Telekom in 1992 and a consortium of Deutsche Telekom and an American company acquired a significant share of the Hungarian Matav Telecommunications in 1993. (As Table 2 shows, Hungary and Estonia rank among the countries with the most inward FDI.)

Other postsocialist states, like Slovenia and Romania, have been the more protectionist ones. In Slovenia, the sale of the first strategic monopoly to foreigners only happened in 2001 when the Belgian KBC Bank acquired one-third of the largest Slovenian bank, Ljubljanska Banka. According to Bandelj (2007), whether postsocialist states legitimized FDI as a desirable economic development strategy—and therefore embraced a particular aspect of neo-liberalism—depended not so much on the actual economic conditions (e.g., budget deficits, external debt, GDP decline) but on (a) international pressures, especially the European Union integration process, and mimicking behavior of other postsocialist states, (b) political power and a pro-reform orientation of the elites, and (c) the prevalence of the nationalist protectionist discourse.

Hence, as Table 3 displays, in several postsocialist European countries, notably Estonia, Hungary, and the Czech Republic, foreign investors have penetrated the postsocialist economies so deeply that they may rightfully be considered as a large constituency of the new postsocialist elite in these countries (Eyal et al. 1998; King and Szelenyi 2005). In contrast, Slovenia's FDI stock has been low, as have those of Romania and Poland, compared to other postsocialist states.

Despite individual country differences, it is important to remember that, on average, European postsocialist economies have liberalized their borders quite substantially to foreign capital. In 2004, the average proportion of FDI stock in GDP for the 10 countries examined here was 39 percent, which is almost twice as much as the average for the developed countries. This share is also much higher than in most of the developing countries, and actually substantially larger than in China, one of the main recipients of FDI today, where this figure was 15 percent in 2004. Hence, to a significant extent, all postsocialist countries have legitimated liberalization to foreign capital flows, advocated as one of the key neo-liberal reforms.

TAX POLICY REFORM

Pereira and colleagues (1993) as well as Lavigne (1995) report that the international financial institutions and the European Union pressured postsocialist countries to adopt neo-liberal fiscal policies. According to Campbell (2001: 113, emphasis in original), "international lending agencies, particularly the IMF, tried to *coerce* these governments into pursuing neo-liberal policies by demanding balanced reductions in taxes and spending as a quid pro quo for financial assistance." Campbell compared Hungary, the Czech Republic, and Poland in terms of their spending and tax policies as of 1995. He observed that the pressure to pursue neo-liberal fiscal reform in Hungary at the beginning of the transition was substantial because policymakers viewed compliance as necessary to appease western (IMF) creditors.[3] In the Czech Republic, the first postcommunist leaders were intellectually committed to the neo-liberal approach, especially Václav Klaus, as were his counterparts in Poland, where the American advisors to the first postcommunist Polish government legitimated the neo-liberal approach. However, due to political party fragmentation in Hungary and the strength of union opposition in Poland, these two countries loosened their fiscal reforms over the years while the Czech Republic was able to keep on track of a tighter fiscal policy (Campbell 2001).

Still, the Czech efforts were pale in comparison to Estonia, the most liberal postsocialist country in terms of its tax regime. In particular, as Feldmann (2003) reports, Estonia adopted unilateral free-trade abolishing tariffs on all imports, including agricultural goods, as part of a package of radical market-oriented reforms immediately after the fall of communism and

Table 3. Penetration of FDI into Central and Eastern Europe

	1990	2000	2003	2004
Bulgaria	<1	18	25	32
Czech Republic	4	39	50	53
Estonia	–––	51	79	85
Hungary	2	49	58	61
Latvia	–––	29	32	33
Lithuania	–––	21	28	29
Poland	<1	21	27	25
Romania	–––	18	23	25
Slovakia	<1	18	37	35
Slovenia	4	15	16	15
Average for preceding 10 above	2	28	37	39
World	8	18	22	22
European Union	11	26	33	32
Developed economies	8	16	21	21
Developing economies	10	26	26	26
USA	7	12	13	13
China	6	18	16	15
Japan	<1	1	2	2

Note. Source: UNCTAD (2006). Numbers refer to the FDI stock as percent share in GDP in a particular country. Regional definitions follow UNCTAD as follows: developed economies include Western Europe, North America, Australia, Israel, Japan, Malta, and New Zealand; developing economies include Africa, East, South and Southeast Asia (excluding Japan), West Asia (excluding Israel), Central Asia, Latin America and the Caribbean, and the Pacific (excluding Australia and New Zealand).

the regaining of sovereignty from the Soviet Union. According to Feldmann (2003: 523):

> Import quotas inherited from Soviet central planning were removed in 1991–1992, but without introducing tariffs other than on a handful of goods (and even these were phased out in 1997). In 1991 more than 200 goods were covered by import quotas or licenses and by the beginning of 1993 only five of them were still in force (all abolished by 1995). The average weighted tariff was 1.4 percent in 1993 and went down to

zero in 1997. The most remarkable feature of trade policy reform was that no tariffs were levied on agricultural goods. With one brief exception—tariffs against grain imports from Russia were in place for three months in 1993—there was unilateral free trade in agriculture through the 1990s.

In explaining these policy choices, Feldmann noted that several factors were relevant but, interestingly, he did not privilege the role of international organizations in this process. Rather, according to Feldmann, the decided tariff policy was due to the initial economic crisis, a deeply discredited former Soviet regime, weak interest groups, and a neo-liberal consensus among the new elites in postcommunist Estonia. All these elements were necessary for the free tariff system to be enacted, and neither condition was sufficient on its own. To be precise, most postsocialist countries faced severe economic crises right after the collapse of communist regimes, and in many countries interest groups were also weak. What might have been rather unique in Estonia, Feldmann (2003: 525) acknowledged, was "the strength of ideas conducive to liberalization-economic liberalism" shared by the ruling elite in this country.

Consistent with the ultraliberal tariff policy, Estonia also introduced a flat-rate income tax in 1995. More recently, Slovakia has also adopted a flat tax rate of 19 percent as part and parcel of its fiscal reforms of 2004. Moore (2005: 3) reports that these reforms have been undertaken in a context of a need for medium-fiscal consolidation and the plan to meet the European Union Maastricht fiscal deficit criterion of 3 percent of GDP. Moreover, the whole Slovakian 2003 tax reform has conformed to the core IMF recommendations on tax system design (Moore 2005: 5). Hence, this reform has to be viewed in the context of Slovakia's international linkages.

Moreover, these recent neo-liberal reforms in Slovakia were possible because of the political circumstances in the country. After the breakup of Czechoslovakia, the illiberal nationalist Mečiar government, in power from 1992 to 1998, significantly stalled market and democratic reforms in Slovakia. The European Union even threatened exclusion from accession by not placing Slovakia among the top five judged on accession readiness in 1997, arguing that the country had moved away from democratic politics under Mečiar's government (Mannin 1999). In 1998, Mečiar was defeated and the opposition, headed by Mikuláš Dzurinda, took over and started to bring Slovakia back on track for the European Union accession negotiations. However, it was really during Dzurinda's second term, starting in 2002, that this center-right reformer implemented major free-market policies, vastly surpassing the emerging liberal market orientations in its postsocialist peers like the Czech Republic, Hungary, Poland, and Slovenia, all countries evaluated until this period as more successful in the transition process. The reforms adopted by the Dzurinda government included sharp cuts in taxes from 38 percent for individuals and 25 percent for corporations to a flat tax rate of 19 percent across the board, 10-year tax holidays and subsidies for strategic investments that encouraged employee retraining and job creation, introduction of flexible working hours, and a fundamental restructuring of the health care and social welfare, cutting benefits by half.

How were these changes, likened to Slovakia's second revolution (Butora et al. 1999), possible? According to O'Dwyer and Kovalcik (2007), they were possible because of the radical shift in power, going from one extreme to another, from the autocratic nationalist protectionist Mečiar government to the neoliberal Dzurinda government. But they were also possible because the Dzurinda government dismissed unions as partners in reforms, ending an officially recognized tripartite bargaining system in place since 1989, and disregarded negative public opinion that accompanied reforms.

A flat tax rate was also put on the reform agenda in Slovenia by the new center-right government that was installed after the 2004 elections. Already during their electoral campaign in September 2004, then leader of the opposition and subsequently Slovenian Prime Minister Janez Janša put the flat tax rate on the agenda. The Janša government actually paid a visit to Slovakia, heralded as a prime example of the successful tax reform. As Vukovic (2006) reported, Janša argued that the flat tax rate would increase the efficiency of the tax system, make it more transparent, and boost the national economy. After taking office, the new government established a council of economic advisors to prepare the economic reforms, including the flat tax rate proposal. The council was chaired by a young U.S.-educated economist Mićo Mrkaić, known to the public for his controversial editorials in the *Finance* Magazine, advocating neo-liberal reforms.

However, the relatively strong Slovenian trade unions, most likely the strongest in the postsocialist region (Feldmann 2006), raised their voices against the flat tax rate proposal, arguing that it would increase the differences between rich and poor. Moreover, they argued that lower state revenues would additionally hit the poor, as the government would be forced to cut back on social services.

The media also focused most critically on the flat tax rate reform proposal. The public was sympathetic to the arguments by the labor unions because the majority harbored socialist convictions that increasing social inequality and poverty was bad. In addition, the economic situation in Slovenia was relatively comfortable; the country had just entered the European Union, and was realistically preparing to enter the European Monetary Union. People wondered why any changes to the current system were necessary. Mass demonstrations in November 2005 organized by the trade unions against the flat tax rate proposal rested on these ideas.

In the meanwhile, Mrkaić resigned from his post as the leader of the Slovenian Economic Reform council, as did, after a very short term, his successor and professional colleague, another young neo-liberal economist, Jože P. Damijan. In light of these circumstances, Prime Minister "Janša was forced to save face and uphold his credentials as a reformer" (Vukovic 2006: 1).

Consequently, in August 2005, when his Finance Minister Andrej Bajuk unveiled the tax reform, it was not a surprise that "Mr Bajuk . . . chose to ditch the more radical tax reform proposals and opted instead to flatten the tax scale at the margins" (Vukovic 2006: 1).

SOCIAL POLICY REFORM

By eliminating the role of the state in the economy, neo-liberal reform packages also required lower social provisions. However, according to Orenstein and Haas (2002: 6), "East-Central European states maintained a high commitment to welfare spending that actually grew as a percentage of gross domestic product (GDP), which was at the same time falling in absolute levels in line with declines in GDP [due to post-1989 economic crises]." Indeed, the adoption of low social provisions was the hardest among all neo-liberal reforms proposed, largely due to the socialist legacies of a very generous welfare state and its ideological underpinnings in social equality. Even though inequalities were not completely eliminated during socialism, they were substantially smaller than for any other world region at a comparable level of economic development (Boswell and Chase-Dunn 2000; Heyns 2005).

Economic crises that followed the fall of communist regimes certainly created social costs, in particular the rise of unemployment and poverty (Milanovic 1998). However, the cuts to social provisions were not widespread. Not that the neo-liberally minded leaders in postsocialist states did not try to do so. For instance, in the early Polish reform days, the adoption of stringent fiscal policies was met with widespread disapproval. After embracing the Balcerowicz shock therapy approach in Poland, the cutting of many social programs and enterprise subsidies led to social unrest. As Campbell summarizes:

> A number of strikes and lockouts skyrocketed from 250 to 7,443 per year and the number of workers involved annually more than tripled to 383,200. Most of these involved demands for higher wages or continued enterprise subsidies to preserve jobs and social programs. These efforts were successful. . . . [C]ollective action had undermined the sustained and full implementation of the neoliberal plan. Policymakers had ignored IMF conditionality requirements and succumbed to public pressure for more spending. (2001: 116–117)

Also in Hungary, the Bokros package of 1995 tackled the generous welfare system, a reform effort supported by the IMF (Bokros and Suranyi 1996: 38). However, the proposed change in the structure of family allowances, providing that families with incomes in the top 10 percent be excluded from eligibility, and paid maternity leaves be eliminated altogether, resulted in widespread protests. The matter also reached the Constitutional Court, which ruled that the immediate suspension of maternity leave would violate the rights of women who were pregnant. The 1998–2002 Fidesz government led by Viktor Orban fully reinstated the maternity leave program (Szikra 2005). Likewise, Václau Klaus in the Czech Republic tried to reform the welfare state by privatizing health insurance but was not successful, due to electoral and interest group pressures to maintain generous welfare entitlements (Orenstein 2001).

However, the social provisions reform did make strides along the neo-liberal lines during the 2002 Dzurinda government in Slovakia. Much like the way it handled tax reforms, despite resistance from both labor and business in the tripartite council, the government passed a fundamental overhaul of the pay-as-you-go pension system in 2003 (Moore 2005). Hence, by disregarding labor and public opinion, in its pension reform, Slovakia did depart from the socialist legacy of welfare state, which has otherwise showed remarkable resilience across the postsocialist region.

NEGOTIATING NEO-LIBERALISM

From the ten postsocialist countries covered in this chapter, Estonia and Slovenia provide a very effective comparison that allows us to summarize why some countries embraced neo-liberalism more than others. This comparison elucidates how negotiating neo-liberalism in postsocialism has depended on socialist legacies, ideological convictions of governing parties, and the strength of other interest groups, in particular labor.

Two of the smallest countries in Central and Eastern Europe, Estonia and Slovenia, with 1.4 and 1.9 million inhabitants, respectively, actually have much in common. Both countries, after a long period of communist rule and redistributive economies, emerged as independent states in 1991 out of large federal and multiethnic states, the Soviet Union and Yugoslavia, respectively. Both were highly developed compared to the federation average and also instrumental in starting the processes of disintegration of these federations. Both states were among the first to successfully complete the EU negotiations (Feldmann 2006).

However, despite these similarities the two countries took very different approaches to market transition. Estonia embarked on an expedient neo-liberal market reform program, whereas Slovenia chose to implement more gradual and selective reforms. Estonia was eager to liberalize its Soviet-style economy and opened itself to foreign investment. During privatization, it relied on direct sales through auctions to outside bidders with a very liberal foreign direct investment regime. The country also adopted a unilateral free trade regime with zero tariffs across the board, making it one of the most open economies in the world, on pair with Hong Kong and Singapore (Feldmann and Sally 2002). Slovenia, on the other hand, was part of former

Yugoslavia where the command economy was less centralized, more highly integrated into the West, and organized by workers self-management. This type of socialism left a mark on the preferred method of privatization in Slovenia, that is, management and employee buyouts, thus greatly limiting the involvement of foreign investors. None of the political interest groups consolidating at the beginning of the Slovenian postsocialist transformation were strongly neo-liberal, in contrast to Estonia, where neo-liberal policy ideas predominated. This is the reason why Slovenia decided to privatize in a more gradual manner, forgoing mass privatization. As a consequence, by 2000, almost one-half of all employed were still in the public sector, while in Estonia only one-quarter were employed in the public sector. The private-sector contribution in Slovenia in 2002 was at 65 percent, below the regional average, and in Estonia, it was 80 percent, above the regional average. Moreover, labor was much stronger and better institutionalized in Slovenia than in Estonia. For instance, in 2000, unionization rate in Slovenia was about 40 percent, whereas less than 15 percent of the Estonian workforce was unionized. The flat tax rate of 25 percent was adopted without major obstacles in Estonia in 1995, with zero tax on reinvested earnings for corporate profits. In contrast, in Slovenia the flat tax rate proposal was adamantly opposed by the labor unions and disapproved by the general public. Overall, Slovenia has maintained high taxes. In 2005, the income tax rate was the highest in the postsocialist region (50 percent), while the corporate tax (25 percent) was among the highest compared to its peer countries, which largely embraced neo-liberal fiscal policies.

As for the role of FDI, among the ten countries included in this study, Estonia and Slovenia stand at two exact opposite ends of a continuum, with the highest and the lowest levels of relative FDI stock, respectively. By 2004, Slovenia's accumulated FDI stock amounted to only 15 percent of GDP, whereas in Estonia this share was 85 percent. This has largely been influenced by the institutionalization and legitimization of FDI as a development strategy in Estonia, whereby the country started selling strategic monopolies to foreigners early on and quickly established a professional FDI agency to promote and attract FDI into Estonia. In contrast, a nationalist protectionist discourse was prevalent in Slovenia, coupled with the preference to insiders in the privatization process, due to the socialist self-management legacy. This led to a few active efforts to promote FDI into Slovenia, despite the fact that, due to international pressures, the official FDI policy has been significantly liberalized over recent years (Bandelj 2004).

Social provisions have been the elements of the reform where Estonia and Slovenia do not differ starkly. As Table 2 shows, although government expenditures have been somewhat higher in Slovenia (as we would expect for a country that embraced neo-liberalism less enthusiastically), they have not been minimalist in Estonia. Considering the spending on health and education, with about 11 percent and 12.5 percent in Estonia and Slovenia, respectively, these rather generous social expenditures carry the legacies of the socialist welfare state in both countries. It seems that social provisions in Central and Eastern Europe can be drastically reformed only if a neo-liberal ruling elite vehemently disregards the prevalent socially minded public sentiments, a measure that has recently occurred in Slovakia. About seventeen years after the fall of the communist regimes, some of the postsocialist institutions are rather weakly developed. Hence, we can expect them to still undergo changes in the future.

CONCLUSION

This chapter has examined the adoption of neo-liberal reforms in ten countries of Central and Eastern Europe after the collapse of the communist regimes. Neo-liberalism was the prevalent development ideology advocated by international organizations in the period of postsocialist transformations. But why did some countries manage to resist jumping onto the neo-liberal bandwagon, and why were there differences across different policy domains such as privatization, foreign direct investment liberalization, tax policy, and social spending?

The fact that we can observe cross-country and cross-domain variation points to the weakness of the argument that neo-liberalism has simply been the result of free-market behaviors that spontaneously emerge after the inefficient control of the party-state in the economy has disappeared. Nor could neo-liberalism in Central and Eastern Europe be understood as a simple reaction to the widespread promotion of neo-liberal policy by international institutions and Western economic advisors who advocated a shock therapy approach to postsocialist reforms. Although international pressures certainly played an important role, at the global as well as the European level, the actual policy outcomes were negotiated domestically. Hence, the differences across countries should be understood as embedded in socialist legacies, and shaped by domestic political forces. Most clearly, neo-liberalism has been adopted where neo-liberally minded reformers took hold—like early reformers in Estonia, or Václav Klaus in the Czech Republic, or Mikuláš Dzurinda in Slovakia—and where these reformers did not ignore resistance from popular movements and/or labor unions in favor of a greater role of the state in the economy.

Considering that the liberal market orientation is supported by the European Union, and more widely by the powerful international financial organizations, resistance to neo-liberal policies may be harder than their adoption. Hence, it is an empirical question whether the young postsocialist democracies will be able to pursue developments in line with the more coordinated rather than liberal market variety of capitalism (Hall and Soskice 2001). What seems to be more obvious is the fact that the economic policy choices will not follow some universal efficiency principles. If this analysis permits any indication, future policy choices and implementations will happen in the historical context of institutions, and will depend on the convictions of the domestic economic elites about desirable development strategies, balancing simultaneously other domestic political interests and international pressures.

NOTES

1. As regards privatization, Henisz, Zelner, and Guillen investigated the reform of state-owned enterprises in the telecommunication and energy sectors on a global scale and found that dozens of countries adopted such reforms between the 1980s and 1999. For instance, in the 1980s they could only find 10 countries reforming their telecommunications sectors and 44 their electricity sector, but these figures increased to 124 and 94 by the end of 1999 (2005: 873).
2. Country profiles are available online at http://www.unctad.org.
3. Hungary as well as Poland had accumulated substantial foreign debts by 1989.

REFERENCES

Albert, Michel. 1993. *Capitalism vs. Capitalism*. New York: Four Walls Eight Windows.

Aslund, Anders. 1992. *Post-Communist Economic Revolutions: How Big a Bang?* Washington, DC: Center for Strategic and International Studies.

Aslund, Anders. 1994. "Lessons of the First Four Years of Systemic Change in Eastern Europe." *Journal of Comparative Economics* 19 (1): 22–38.

Aslund, Anders. 1995. *How Russia Became a Market Economy*. Washington, DC: Brookings Institution Press.

Babb, Sarah. 2001. *Managing Mexico: Economists from Nationalism to Neo-Liberalism*. Princeton, NJ: Princeton University Press.

Babb, Sarah, and Nitsan Chorev. 2006. "The Globalization of Economic Governance: The IMF and the WTO in Historical Perspective." Paper presented at the Annual American Sociological Association Meetings, Montreal, Canada.

Bandelj, Nina. 2004. "Negotiating Global, Regional, and National Forces: Foreign Investment in Slovenia." *East European Politics and Societies* 18 (3): 455–480.

Bandelj, Nina. 2007. "And the Last Shall be First: Party System Institutionalization and Second-Generation Economic Reform in Postcommunist Europe." *Studies in Comparative International Development* 41: 3-26.

Blanchard, Oliver, Rudiger Dornbusch, Paul Krugman, Richard Layard, and Lawrence Summers. 1991. *Reform in Eastern Europe*. Cambridge, MA: Cambridge University Press.

Blanchard, Oliver, Kenneth A. Froot, and Jeffrey D. Sachs. 1994. *The Transition in Eastern Europe*. Chicago: University of Chicago Press.

Bockman, Johanna, and Gil Eyal. 2002. "Eastern Europe as a Laboratory for Economic Knowledge: The Transnational Roots of Neoliberalism." *American Journal of Sociology* 108 (2): 310–352.

Bokros, Lajos, and Gyorgy Suranyi. 1996. "Letter to Michel Camdessus (February 2)." In *Hungary: Request for Stand-By Arrangement*. EBS/96/18 (February 5). Washington, DC: International Monetary Fund.

Boswell, Terry, and Christopher Chase-Dunn. 2000. *The Spiral of Capitalism and Socialism: Toward Global Democracy.* London: Lynne Rienner.

Boycko, Maxim, Andrei Shleifer, and Robert Vishny. 1995. *Privatizing Russia.* Cambridge, MA: MIT Press.

Boycko, Maxim, Andrei Shleifer, and Robert W. Vishny. 1996. "A Theory of Privatisation." *Economic Journal* 106 (435): 309–319.

Brune, Nancy, Geoffrey Garrett, and Bruce Kogut. 2004. "The International Monetary Fund and the Global Spread of Privatization." IMF Staff Papers, vol. 51, no. 2, http://www.imf.org/External/Pubs/FT/staffp/2004/02/brune.htm, accessed December 12, 2006.

Bútora, Martin, Grigorij Mesežnikov, Zora Bútorová, and Sharon Fisher. 1999. *The 1998 Parliamentary Elections and Democratic Rebirth in Slovakia.* Bratislava: Institute for Public Affairs.

Campbell, John L. 2001. "Convergence or Divergence? Globalization, Neo-liberalism and Fiscal Policy in Post-communist Europe." Pp. 107–139 in *Globalization and the European Political Economy,* ed. Steven Weber. New York: Columbia University Press.

Campbell, John L., and Ove K. Pedersen, eds. 2001. *The Rise of Neoliberalism and Institutional Analysis.* Princeton, NJ: Princeton University Press.

Carruthers, Bruce G., Sarah L. Babb, and Terence C. Halliday. 2001. "Institutionalizing Markets, or the Market for Institutions? Central Banks, Bankruptcy Law, and the Globalization of Financial Markets." Pp. 94–126 in *The Rise of Neoliberalism and the Institutional Analysis,* ed. John Campbell and Ove Pedersen. Princeton, NJ: Princeton University Press.

Chorev, Nitsan. 2005. "The Institutional Project of Neo-liberal Globalism: The Case of the WTO." *Theory and Society* 34 (33): 317–355.

CzechInvest. 2005. "Annual Report 2004." http://www.czechinvest.org/web/pwci.nsf/dwnl/B35DEBE63465BD52C1256EEB00326DC7/$File/annual%20report%202004.pdf, accessed March 25, 2005.

Dallago, Bruno, Gianmaria Ajani, and Bruno Grancelli. 1992. *Privatization and Entrepreneurship in Postsocialist Countries: Economy, Law, and Society.* New York: St. Martin's Press.

Earle, John S., Roman Frydman, and Andrzej Rapaczynski. 1993. *Privatization in the Transition to a Market Economy: Studies of Preconditions and Policies in Eastern Europe.* New York: St. Martin's Press.

European Bank for Restructuring and Development. 2001. *Investment Profile.* London: EBRD. http://www.ebrd.com/about/index.htm, accessed April 15, 2003.

European Bank for Restructuring and Development. 2004. *Transition Report 2003.* London: EBRD.

European Union. 2005. "Europa: The European Union On-line." Accessed June 5, 2005 (http://europa.eu.int).

Economist Intelligence Unit (EIU). 2006. "Romania Factsheet 2005." http://www.economist.com/countries/Romania/profile.cfm?folder=Profile-FactSheet, accessed December 12, 2006.

Euractiv. 2006. "Flat Tax: Economic Panacea or Pandora?" http://www.euractiv.com/Article?tcmuri=tcm:29-134426-16&type=News, accessed December 12, 2006.

Eyal, Gil, Ivan Szelényi, and Eleanor Townsley. 1998. *Making Capitalism Without Capitalists.* New York: Verso.

Feldmann, Magnus. 2003. "Free Trade in the 1990s: Understanding Estonian Exceptionalism." *Demokratizatsiya* 11 (4): 517–533.

Feldmann, Magnus. 2006. "Emerging Varieties of Capitalism in Transition Countries: Industrial Relations and Wage Bargaining in Estonia and Slovenia." *Comparative Political Studies* 39 (7): 826–854.

Feldmann, Magnus, and Razeen Sally. 2002. "From the Soviet Union to the European Union: Estonian Trade Policy, 1991–2000." *The World Economy* 25 (1): 79–106.

Fischer, Stanley, and Allan Gelb. 1991. "The Process of Socialist Economic Transformation." *Journal of Economic Perspectives* 5 (4): 91–106.

Fourcade-Gourinchas, Marion, and Sarah Babb. "The Rebirth of the Liberal Creed: Paths to Neoliberalism in Four Countries." *American Journal of Sociology* 108 (3): 533–579.

Frydman, Roman, and Andrzej Rapaczynski. 1994. *Privatization in Eastern Europe: Is the State Withering Away?* Budapest: CEU Press.

Gore, Charles. 2000. "The Rise and Fall of Washington Consensus as a Paradigm for Developing Countries." *World Development* 28 (5): 789–804.

Grabher, Gernot, and David Stark. 1997. "Organizing Diversity: Evolutionary Theory, Network Analysis and Post-socialism." *Regional Studies* 31 (5): 533–544.

Graybow, Charles, Adrian Karatnycky, and Alexander Motyl. 1998. *Nations in Transit—1998: Civil Society, Democracy and Markets in East Central Europe and the Newly Independent States.* London: Transaction.

Hall, Peter, and David Soskice. 2001. *Varieties of Capitalism: The Institutional Foundations of Comparative Advantage.* Oxford: Oxford University Press.

Hanousek, Jan, and Eugene Kroch. 1998. "The Two Waves of Voucher Privatization in the Czech Republic: A Model of Learning in Sequential Bidding." *Applied Economics* 30 (1): 133–143.

Henisz, Witold J., Bennet A. Zelner, and Mauro Guillén. 2005. "World-Wide Diffusion of Market-Oriented Infrastructure Reform, 1977–1999." *American Sociological Review* 70 (6): 871–897.

Heyns, Barbara. 2005. "Emerging Inequalities in Central and Eastern Europe." *Annual Review of Sociology* 31: 163–197.

International Monetary Fund. 2005. "Articles of Agreement of the International Monetary Fund: Article VII—General Obligations of Members." http://www.imf.org/external/pubs/ft/aa/aa08.htm, accessed June 18, 2005.

International Monetary Fund. 2006. "The Process of IMF Lending." http://www.imf.org/external/np/exr/facts/howlend.htm (accessed March 20, 2006).

Kaufman, Daniel, and Paul Siegelbaum. 1997. "Privatization and Corruption in Transition Economies." *Journal of International Affairs* 50 (2): 419–458.

King, Lawrence, and Ivan Szelényi. 2005. "Post-Communist Economic Systems." Pp. 205–232 in *The Handbook of Economic Sociology: Second Edition*, ed. Neil J. Smelser and Richard Swedberg. Princeton, NJ: Princeton University Press.

King, Lawrence, and Patrick Hamm. 2006. "The Governance Grenade: Mass Privatization, State Capacity, and Economic Development in Post-communist and Reforming Communist Societies." Paper presented at the American Sociological Association Meeting, Montreal, Canada.

Kogut, Bruce, and J. Muir Macpherson. 2003. "The Decision to Privatize as an Economic Policy Idea: Epistemic Communities, Palace Wars and Diffusion." Paper presented at the conference: The International Diffusion of Political and Economic Liberalization, Harvard University, 3–4 October.

Kornai, János. 1992. *Socialist System: Political Economy of Communism.* Princeton, NJ: Princeton University Press, and Oxford: Oxford University Press.

Lado, Maria. 2002. "Industrial Relations in the Candidate Countries." *European Industrial Relations Observatory On-line.* http://www.eiro.eurofound.ie/2002/07/study/TN0207102Fa.html, accessed April 5, 2003.

Lash, Scott, and John Urry. 1987. *The End of Organized Capitalism.* Madison: University of Wisconsin Press.

Lavigne, Marie. 1995. *The Economics of Transition: From Socialist Economy to Market Economy.* New York: St. Martin's Press.

Lipton, David and Jeffrey Sachs. 1990. "Privatization in Eastern Europe: The Case of Poland. *Brookings Papers on Economic Activity* 2 (Spring): 293–341.

Mannin, Mike. 1999. *Pushing Back the Boundaries: The European Union and Central and Eastern Europe.* Manchester: Manchester University Press.

Mencinger, Jože. 2004. "Transition to a National and a Market Economy: A Gradualist Approach." Pp. 67–82 in *Slovenia: From Yugoslavia to the European Union*, ed. Mojmir Mrak, Matija Rojec, and Carlos Silva-Jáuregui. Washington, DC: The World Bank.

Meyer, John W., John Boli, Thomas George, and Francisco Ramirez. 1997. "World Society and the Nation-State." *American Journal of Sociology* 103 (1): 144–181.

Meyer, Klaus. 1998. *Direct Investment in Economies in Transition.* Aldenhot Northampton, MA: Edward Elgar.

Milanovic, Branko. 1998. *Income, Inequality and Poverty During the Transition From Planned to Market Economy.* Washington, DC: World Bank.

Moore, David. 2005. "Slovakia's Tax and Welfare Reforms." *International Monetary Fund Working Paper* WP/05/133. Washington, DC: International Monetary Fund.

Murrell, Peter. 1992. "Conservative Political Philosophy and the Strategy of Economic Transition." *East European Politics and Societies* 6 (1): 3–16.

Murrell, Peter. 1993. "Evolutionary and Radical Approaches to Economic Reform." Pp. 215–231 in *Stabilization and Privatization in Poland: An Economic Evaluation of the Shock Therapy Program*, ed. Kazimierz Z. Poznanski. Boston: Kluwer.

O'Dwyer, Connor, and Branislav Kovalcik. 2007. And the Last Shall be First: Party System Institutionalization and Second-Generation Economic Reform in Postcommunist Europe." *Studies in Comparative International Development* 41: 3–26.

Orenstein, Mitchell A. 2001. *Out of the Red: Building Capitalism and Democracy in Postcommunist Europe.* Ann Arbor: University of Michigan Press.

Orenstein, Mitchell A., and Martine R. Haas. 2002. "Globalization and the Development of Welfare States in Central and Eastern Europe." BCSIA Working Paper. John F. Kennedy School of Government, Harvard University, Boston.

Organization for Economic Cooperation and Development. 2006. "Membership." http://www.oecd.org/countrieslist/0,3025,en_33873108_33844430_1_1_1_1_1,00.html, accessed December 12, 2006.

Pereira, Luiz, Carlos Bresser, Jose Maria Maravall, and Adam Przeworski. 1993. *Economic Reforms in New Democracies: A Social-Democratic Approach.* New York: Cambridge University Press.

Posner, Richard. 1986. *Economic Analysis of Law*, 3rd ed. Boston: Little Brown.

Poznanski, Kazimierz Z. 1993. "An Interpretation of Communist Decay: The Role of Evolutionary Mechanisms." *Communist and Post-Communist Studies* 26 (1): 3–24.

Przeworski, Adam. 1995. *Sustainable Democracy.* New York: Cambridge University Press.

Sachs, Jeffrey. 1989. "My Plan for Poland." *International Economics* 3 (6): 24–29.

Sachs, Jeffrey. 1993. *Restructuring Poland's Jump to the Market Economy.* Boston: MIT Press.

Sachs, Jeffrey, and David Lipton. 1990. "Poland's Economic Reform." *Foreign Affairs* 69 (Summer): 47–66.

Schmidt, Klaus-Dieter. 1995. "Foreign Direct Investment in Eastern Europe: State-of-the-art and Prospects." Pp. 268–289 in *Transforming Economies and European Integration*, ed. Rumen Dobrinsky and Michael Landesmann. Aldershot, UK: Edward Elgar.

Seleny, Anna. 1991. "Hidden Enterprise and Property Rights Reform in Socialist Hungary." *Law and Policy* 13 (2): 149–169.
Shleifer, Andrei, and Robert Vishny. 1994. "Privatization in Russia: First Steps." Pp. 137–164 in *The Transition in Eastern Europe*, Volume 2: *Restructuring*, ed. Oliver Blanchard, Kenneth Froot, and Jeffrey Sachs. Chicago: University of Chicago Press.
Simoneti, Marko, Matija Rojec, and Aleksandra Gregorič. 2004. "Privatization, Restructuring, and Corporate Governance of the Enterprise Sector." Pp. 224–243 in *Slovenia: From Yugoslavia to the European Union*, ed. Mojmir Mrak, Matija Rojec, and Carlos Silva-Jáuregui. Washington, DC: The World Bank.
Sinn, Hans-Werner, Alfons J. Weichenrieder, Bruno S. Frey, and Ailsa A. Röell. 1997. "Foreign Direct Investment, Political Resentment and the Privatization Process in Eastern Europe." *Economic Policy* 12 (24): 177–210.
Spicer, Andrew, Gerald McDermott, and Bruce Kogut. 2000. "Entrepreneurship and Privatization in Central Europe: The Tenuous Balance Between Destruction and Creation." *Academy of Management Review* 25 (3): 630–649.
Stark, David. 1992. "Path Dependence and Privatization Strategies in East Central Europe." *East European Societies and Politics* 6 (1): 17–54.
Stark, David. 1996. "Recombinant Property in East European Capitalism." *American Journal of Sociology* 101 (4): 993–1027.
Stark, David, and László Bruszt. 1998. *Postsocialist Pathways: Transforming Politics and Property in East Central Europe*. Cambridge, MA: Cambridge University Press.
Svejnar, Jan, and Miroslav Singer. 1994. "Using Vouchers to Privatize an Economy: The Czech and the Slovak Case." *Economics of Transition* 2 (1): 43–69.
Szelényi, Ivan, and Eric Kostello. 1996. "The Market Transition Debate: Toward a Synthesis?" *American Journal of Sociology* 101 (4): 1082–1096.
Szikra, Dorottya. 2005. "Hungarian Family and Child Support in the Light of its Historical Development." Paper presented at the Conference on "Fighting Poverty and Reforming Social Security: What Can Post-Soviet States Learn from the New Democracies of Central Europe?" Woodrow Wilson International Center for Scholars, Washington, DC (June 10).
TRANSMONEE. 2006. "UNICEF Innocenti Research Centre." http://www.unicef-icdc.org/resources/transmonee.html, accessed April 20, 2006.
Turek, Otakar. 1994. "Interconnection Between Macroeconomic Policies and Privatisation: The Case of the Czech Republic." Pp. 265–278 in *Privatisation in the Transition Process, Recent Experiences in Eastern Europe*, ed. Yilmaz Akyuz, Detlef Kotte, Andras Koves, and Laszlo Szamuely. Geneva: United Nations.
UNCTAD. 2006. "World Investment Report: Search by Country/Economy." http://www.unctad.org/Templates/Page.asp?intItemID=3198&lang=1, accessed March 20, 2005.
Verdery, Katherine. 2003. *The Vanishing Hectare: Property and Value in Postsocialist Transylvania*. Ithaca, NY: Cornell University Press.
Vreeland, James. 2002. *The IMF and Economic Development*. Cambridge: Cambridge University Press.
Vukovic, Marko. 2006. "The Tax Reform: Finally Flattened." *Slovenia Times* December 1: 1–2.
Williamson, John. 1990. *Latin American Adjustment: How Much Has Happened?* Washington, DC: Institute for International Economics.
Williamson, John. 1993. "Democracy and the Washington Consensus." *World Development* 21 (8): 1329–1336.
World Bank. 1995. *World Development Report*. Oxford: Oxford University Press.

4 Mobilizing International Auditing Standards in Arenas of Political and Economic Change in Post-Soviet Russia

Andrea Mennicken

Since the late 1990s, auditing standards, in particular International Standards on Auditing, have come to assume a key position in current debates about the development of auditing in Russia. For auditors, regulators, academics, and other parties involved in the production and consumption of audits, it has become almost impossible to think of good auditing as independent from internationally oriented standards. These standards are presented as solutions to problems of audit quality assurance, as a means to enhance the professional qualification of auditors, as an instrument for the management of public mistrust, and as a tool to deal with issues of cost-effectiveness and the internal organization of audit work. The standards are promoted as a regulatory device that can be employed to facilitate the development of the emerging audit profession, and to accelerate Russia's integration into the West. This chapter is devoted to a detailed empirical examination of the conditions that made possible the rise in the popularity and perceived indispensability of the standards. The collapse of the Soviet Union initiated a new era in the understanding and management of Russia's economy and society. In 1991, Russia, together with other Eastern European and former Soviet states, made a radical break with socialist modes of government. The roles of government had been called into question and, as a consequence, spheres of state action and nonaction became renegotiated. Processes of reform were initiated, aimed at the liberalization of economic activities, the freeing of prices, the introduction of private property, and the establishment of more pluralistic, democratic forms of governance.

At the heart of the envisaged economic transformation processes stood the market. Post-Soviet reality became defined in terms of market-oriented development and Western-oriented notions of progress. Especially in the early years, between 1990 and 1992, transformation policies became grounded in beliefs that processes of radical marketization, liberalization, and privatization could transform Russia's highly bureaucratized, static economic system into a dynamic, competitive capitalist economy (Boycko et al. 1995; Sachs and Warner 1995; Åslund et al. 1996; Gaidar 2003).

The creation of new market-oriented political and economic structures relied to a large extent on the imitation and transplantation of Western patterns. The supposedly successful capitalist societies of Western Europe and the United States became important reference points for what postcommunist Russian society aspired to become (Pickles and Smith 1998; Lane 2002b). Against the background of a dismantled Soviet state apparatus of control, Western auditing came to be regarded as a possible mechanism for redefining the regulatory roles of the state, and accelerating processes of market-oriented modernization (cf. e.g., Danilevskii 1994; Boycko et al. 1995; World Bank 1996). For example, in a statement published by the Russian accounting journal *Bukhgalterskii uchet* [The Bookkeeper's Account] in 1991 we can read:

> Completely new forms of control should accompany the market economy; one form of those [new controls, A.M.] is auditing. . . . In developed countries, audit services make up one of the strands of big business. A thoughtful adoption of auditing services in our country could have a huge social and organizational impact on the improvement of the management of industry in our developing market economy. . . . It is necessary to learn quickly and intensively more about western audit expertise. (Erzhanov and Erzhanov 1991: 37)

In another issue, also from 1991, it is stated:

> The presence of enterprises and organizations with different forms of property and financing urgently require the foundation of self-financing [khozraschetny] control organs; i.e. audit services. The development of a web of auditing firms can lay down the beginning of a genuine establishment of economic principles of financial control. (Danilevskii 1991: 6)

A central role in the formation and redefinition of Russian audit practices was played, and is still played, by the International Standards on Auditing (ISAs). Government officials as well as audit professionals began to promote the standards as a device that should help make abstract programs of audit reform tangible and manageable. The ISAs were appealed to as a way of helping to create a regulatory space through which auditing, and Russia's economy, could be organized according to Western constructs of a global market economy. But what are the conditions facilitating, and the problems accompanying, the promotion of international auditing standards as accelerators of governmental reform and economic development? The following study seeks to shed more light onto the mechanisms, strategies, and political activities underlying the incorporation of Western auditing models and international standards into programs of market-oriented governmental reform.

The analysis is methodologically grounded in participant observation methods, archival research, and in-depth interviewing. The fieldwork for this study was carried out in Moscow during 2001 and 2002, over a total period of twenty-one weeks. During the stays in the field, altogether, forty-eight semistructured interviews were conducted with former Soviet financial inspectors, Russian auditors, government officials, representatives of new professional associations, academics, and Western consultants. For the interviews, people were mainly selected who played key roles in the dissemination and/or application of international auditing standards. The fieldwork for this study was carried out in Moscow: the financial, regulatory, and political heart of the Russian Federation. Participant observations were carried out in the international audit department of a leading Russian audit firm, a European Union (EU)-funded Tacis audit reform project, and the International Center for Accounting Reform (ICAR). The observations and interviews were complemented with an analysis of legal, professional, and academic texts.

Throughout the chapter, the search for new post-Soviet mechanisms of market-oriented governance is conceptualized as a two-edged process. To understand the dynamics of post-Soviet transition, it is argued, local constructions of new forms of regulation, such as auditing, have to be analyzed side by side with global representations of appropriate economic governance. These representations are, at least to a great extent, produced and circulated by multilateral financial agencies, international professional accounting associations, multinational corporations, and consultancy firms. Considering the multiplicity of agencies involved in the re-regulation of Russian government, it is further stressed that market-oriented development should be analyzed as a less coherent totality than is often assumed. Following Foucault's (1981/1991: 76–79) accentuation of the polymorphous nature of objects and processes often treated as homogeneous, a view is proposed that treats ideas of neo-liberalism and market development as a loose conglomeration of different institutions, ideas, calculative instruments, and policy prescriptions from which actors pick and choose depending on prevailing political, economic, social, and historical conditions.

From this it also follows that we need to look beyond the inherent instrumentality of the standards if we are to explain fully the sudden rise in popularity of them. Studies of standardization in other areas have shown that approaches couched wholly in terms of—always externally ascribed—technical effectiveness and operational superiority run the risk of confusing normative claims with explanation (cf. Brunsson 1998; Brunsson and Jacobsson 2000; Power 2002). The ascribed and the actual functionality of standards can be easily conflated, leaving neglected questions about the actual working, and about limits of processes of standardization. To avoid such pitfalls, this chapter emphasizes the constructed nature of the indispensability and functionality attached to standards. A body of literature is utilized that stresses the constructed nature of means–ends relations, and focuses on the processes that result in the production of indispensability.

A core concept in this context is the notion of problematization (cf. Callon 1980; Callon et al. 1986; Latour 1987; Miller 1991; Robson 1994). The concept of problematization was initially developed and employed by sociologists and anthropologists devoted to the study of science and technology (e.g. Callon et al. 1986; Latour 1987). A few years later, sociologically oriented accounting researchers took up the concept, primarily, for the study of accounting change (e.g., Miller 1991; Robson 1991; Miller and O'Leary 1993). Studies that use the notion of problematization assume that the existence and relevance of some practice or technology cannot be sufficiently explained by reference to their ultimate function (Robson 1991). The notion of problematization refers to the strategies and activities by which something, for example, an accounting technology or regulatory instruments such as professional standards, are mobilized and rendered indispensable. The concept implies that a problem is neither fixed nor independent of its contexts.

To enhance the importance and inevitability of a certain technology or regulatory instrument, it is crucial to endow them with wider significance. This can be achieved by linking them to a chain of problematizations that go beyond the immediate context of a particular organization or a local problem.

The positioning of tools, technologies, or regulatory devices, such as auditing standards, in a wider chain of problematization involves, to a large extent, the work of translation and representation. Representation, in this context, refers to the vocabularies, arguments, and rationales through which certain techniques and instruments are bestowed with meaning and related to a wider problem-set. The notion of translation is used to denote the processes whereby disparate and sometimes opposed sets of concerns and interests are restated and transferred into a more or less coherent and unitary set of proposals and instruments (Callon 1980, 1986; Latour 1987; Robson 1991). It is argued that in Russia auditing standards have come to be so important because they make it possible for auditors, regulators, and other parties concerned to create a platform through which wider reform demands, business interests, professionalizing strategies, and other concerns can be articulated, operationalized, concentrated, and negotiated. It is further pointed out that the standards are able to serve as the focus of such varied attention not so much because of some inherent, preset problem-solving capacity, but because of their ambiguity and conceptual openness.

Although International Standards on Auditing make reference to concrete audit techniques, for example, with respect to sampling or testing procedures, they do not entail very precise definitions of the objectives and outcomes of an audit. Nor are they related to any specific notion of accountability. ISAs are aimed at being broad enough so that they can be linked up to a variety of different accounting and auditing contexts:

> Within each country, local regulations govern, to a greater or lesser degree, the practices followed in the auditing of financial or other information. . . . National standards on auditing and related services published in many countries differ in form and content. IAPC [International Audit Practices Committee, now International Audit and Assurance Standards Board (IAASB), A.M.] takes cognizance of such documents and differences and, in the light of such knowledge, issues ISAs, which are intended for international acceptance. (International Federation of Accountants [IFAC] 2001, 92)

To be applicable to a variety of different situations, ISAs necessarily have to maintain a level of abstraction that can only be made concrete by the users themselves. The text of the standards is formulated in an abstract manner, so that it can embrace a variety of meanings and interpretations and thereby make the standards attractive to a wide range of people and institutions. One example of the conceptual indistinctiveness and abstract nature of the standards is provided by those sections of the standards that define the objective and principles governing an audit. In ISA 200, for example, it is stated that:

> the objective of an audit of financial statements is to enable the auditor to express an opinion whether the financial statements are prepared, in all material respects, in accordance with an identified financial reporting framework. (IFAC 2001: 148)

The standard further says:

> An audit in accordance with ISAs is designed to provide reasonable assurance that the financial statements taken as a whole are free from material misstatement. (IFAC 2001: 149)

Neither the notion of "material misstatement" nor the idea of "reasonable assurance" is defined in more concrete, substantive terms. It is left open to the judgment of the auditor, regulator, and the wider context to define and negotiate the meaning of these terms.

To depict the various mechanisms, agencies, and arguments through which the agenda of international audit standardization has been formed and promoted in Russia, this chapter considers the rise and spread of audit standards in three different arenas. These are the arenas of professionalizing strategies, national macroeconomic management, and global economic governance. According to Burchell et al. (1985: 390), an arena is defined by a specific field of operations and relations that constitute a recognized area of institutional life. An arena is composed of "certain institutions, economic and administrative processes, bodies of knowledge, systems of norms and measurement, and classification techniques" (Burchell et al. 1985: 400). Interrelated arenas make up an "accounting constellation" (Burchell et al. 1985). The linkages and interactions that exist between arenas and their actors respectively form an accounting constellation, according to Burchell et al.

For the purposes of this chapter, the notions of arena and accounting constellation are considered useful for two particular reasons. First, they draw our attention to the wider context that shapes and promotes processes of audit standardization. They help us locate the emergence and spread of audit standardization in a multifaceted web of intersecting problems, ideas, know-how, and events that go beyond the interests and survival strategies of a single organization. The study of an accounting constellation makes it possible to see that accounting, auditing, and standardization practices are deeply entwined in issues and events that are of wider social, economic, and political concern. Second, the notion points to the historical contingency of processes of audit standardization. The kinds of linkages that are formed between certain calculative technologies, audit concepts, standardizing agencies, and wider social, political, and economic contexts are largely dependent on the specific historical situation surrounding standardizing activities. One cannot understand the emergence of a specific accounting constellation—or, in our case, the agenda of audit standardization—without reference to the specific historical events and crises that accompany these developments, be it in a facilitating or a constraining way.

The arenas described next constitute three distinct areas of institutional life. Activities within each arena are organized around certain core operations. For the arena of the emerging Russian auditing profession, for example, these consist of the performance of external controls of financial reporting systems. Within the arena of macroeconomic management, Russian government agencies are mainly concerned with the drafting and implementation of new rules and reform programs to manage political and economic transition. And within the arena of global economic governance, multilateral agencies, such as the International Monetary Fund (IMF), the Organization for Economic Cooperation and Development (OECD), the World Trade Organization (WTO), and the World Bank, want to contribute to the creation of an international regulatory framework for global economic operations. The actors in the three arenas are acting in a phase of systemic change and regulatory uncertainties, where boundaries are unsettled, and new identities still have to be created. The following sections describe how these three arenas, and their actors and agencies, are involved in the setting and promotion of agendas of audit standardization and, on the other hand, how the audit standards themselves are implicated in the creation and facilitation of the different arenas.

STANDARDS AND STRATEGIES OF PROFESSIONALIZING

Within the newly emerging Russian auditing profession, debates on audit standardization started in the early 1990s. These debates took place against the background of high institutional uncertainty, which, inter alia, expressed itself in professional disorientation and public mistrust, particularly regarding the entrepreneurs that populated the new audit market. The breakdown of the Soviet system had led to the dissolution of many infrastructures, institutions, and beliefs. Old patterns of social, political, and economic order had been delegitimized and disrupted, and new structures of political and economic government still had to be built. Against the background of these developments, auditing was put forward as a mechanism to advance the adoption of a new capitalist order, but neither the new auditors nor the government agencies that had supported the development of the auditing business knew what they had let themselves in for. Especially in the early years, that is, between 1987 and 1993, audit objectives and audit functions were still largely undefined, and the boundaries between practices of socialist inspection and capitalist auditing appeared to be extremely blurred. The new Russian auditors had been confronted with the task of establishing a new, Western practice without knowing what auditing meant. It was during these times that international auditing standards first attracted the attention of the core of a new group aspiring to be professionals.

The debate on audit standardization was particularly pushed by a small number of influential Russian audit firms mainly located in Moscow and some of their big international counterparts who had just begun to operate in the Russian audit market. Involved in the initiation of debates on audit standardization were, inter alia, the Russian audit firms Rufaudit, Rusaudit, FBK, and UNICON; the international firms Ernst and Young, Deloitte and Touche, PricewaterhouseCoopers, Arthur Andersen, KPMG, PKF, and BDO, and the professional associations Union of Professional Audit Organizations (SPAO, operating today under the name of IPAR, which stands for Institute of Professional Auditors in Russia) and the Russian Collegium of Auditors (RCA). IPAR and the RCA were the first professional associations that explicitly adopted ISAs as their major methodological and normative working basis, and prepared initial Russian translations of the international auditing standards. Russian audit firms such as Rusaudit, Rufaudit, UNICON, and FBK began in the early 1990s with the creation of departments for international audit methodology and standards, and organized internal seminars about international accounting and audit standards. The audit firm FBK even founded its own publishing company—FBK Press—in order to actively participate in the publishing of books and journals devoted to the promulgation of so-called Western audit approaches based on international standards.

In the absence of national auditing standards and regulations, most of the Western firms also referred to international audit standards in their work and audit reports. To Russian firms that either tried to model themselves on their international counterparts or were aiming for membership within one of the big international auditing networks (e.g., the networks of PKF or BDO International), this gave further input to the adoption and propagation of the international standards.

The organizing themes underlying debates about audit standardization initiated by auditors and their professional associations were, and still are, above all, those of professionalizing and entrepreneurial development. Auditing standards, in particular international standards, were introduced as a means of creating a jurisdiction of professionalism that could help ground, protect, and represent a realm of new capitalist expertise. In particular, agendas of audit standardization entered and shaped debates about Russian audit development and professionalizing in three key ways.

First, the standards were introduced as a framework to aid the structuring and systematization of audit work. They were seen as a device with which to imagine the unknown. Especially in the early 1990s, when methodological learning materials, such as audit textbooks or audit manuals, were not easily available and training programs still had to be developed, international auditing standards constituted a valuable source for those auditors who were looking for some official, generally recognized guidance in their work. The collapse of the old regime had led to a regulatory vacuum in the area of financial control. The international standards, laid down in a 700-page long book, were seen as something that could fill this vacuum. They constituted something tangible, readily available, and internationally validated that auditors could refer to in their work. The standards thus became treated as a blueprint that helped translate abstract ideas of auditing into a manageable process of formalized organization.

Second, the standards were discussed as a mechanism within which professionalism could be articulated and demonstrated. They constituted, and still constitute, an important device of professional representation and symbolic distinction. A senior auditor of a leading Russian audit firm, for example, comments on this aspect:

> For our firm ISAs are important, because they enhance our prestige. If a firm offers services in accordance with international standards, I think that this is an entry to a more, well, to a higher level. The business reputation of the firm will be much higher and valuable.

The standards make it possible for the auditors to differentiate themselves from the past, and to define and communicate a new identity. Audit standards are seen as a mechanism for demarcating new territories of professionalism and underlining claims of autonomy and independence. The standards are put forward as a vehicle to represent and certify audit work. They shall provide auditors with a repertoire of terms, rules, and new images that they can employ to draw, at least rhetorically, a distinction between themselves, the detested state inspectors, and so-called quack auditors, often referred to as "black auditors"[1] [*chornye auditory*], who frequently sign audit reports without leaving behind any traceable checks, for example, in the form of audit documentation. A declared commitment to and knowledge of the standards is put forward as a sign of professional expertise and quality. Thereby, so it is hoped, the standards can be employed to enhance the public standing and external legitimacy of the profession.

Third, the standards came to be seen as a means that could help individual professionals, audit firms, and professional associations seeking international recognition to connect themselves to the Western world of auditing. As a Russian partner of a big international audit firm puts it: "(International auditing standards) are important, because they allow you to show that auditing develops in a direction that follows a Western understanding."

A British Chartered Accountant, leading an internationally funded center for accounting and audit reform in Moscow, states:

> For the Russian auditing profession, I think that many of the firms and the professionals involved feel that if they want to have international recognition of their work, they have to have the capacity to do it to international standards. They know that if the Big Five and some of the small international firms do auditing, automatically that is recognized internationally; that is acceptable. I think they feel that if they produce a report that says Russian national standards that won't work, however competent, proper and compliant with everything, that would not be recognized. And they recognize that if they are able to have a capacity to produce international-audit-standards work, then they stand a chance of being able to compete with international areas.

The standards are perceived as a device through which Russia's auditing profession can be organized into, and transformed according to, international constructs of global audit professionalism. An important aspect in this context is the fact that the standards already enjoy worldwide acknowledgement. The international acceptability of the standards and their application in many other countries reinforce beliefs that the standards constitute a trustworthy, workable measure to identify professional quality and expertise. This is especially relevant for those firms that want to offer audit services in accordance with, and acceptance of, the West. The major dream that motivates the promulgation and adoption of the standards in this context is that of international competitiveness. The incorporation of internationally accepted standards should enable the indigenous firms to attract international clients, and at least in part to counter the dominance of Western firms.

What lies beneath most of the rationales and arguments previously presented is the assumption that auditing should constitute something contextually invariable, measurable, and externally assessable. The Deputy Director of a big indigenous audit firm notes in this respect: "Everything that concerns auditing . . . well, that doesn't have any national cores. That is a technology, a science . . . you have plans."

Debates on audit standardization are driven by appeals to international conformity, comparability, and consistency. As the comment of the Director of Audit Methodology at another big Russian audit firm illustrates, agendas of audit standardization are seen as a vehicle to reach professionalism through international similarity:

> The word "audit" should mean the same in Russia as in the West, such as is it the case with the Big Mac at McDonald's. At McDonald's, no matter whether you go to the Place "Than-Na Men" in Peking, to the Arbat in Moscow or to somewhere in Boston—a Big Mac should be of the same quality; the rolls should be the same, the meat, it all should just be the same. And therefore, I think that for us [the international auditing standards] are very important.[2]

Professional expertise is here conceptualized in terms of its objectivity, technical neutrality, and structural uniformity. It is regarded as something contextually independent that needs to be internationally communicable, comparable, and measurable (Porter 1992). Elements of variability and subjectivity are called into question. Audit quality is associated with ideals of conformity and procedural consistency. Expertise is discussed as something that should be largely independent from individual judgment and, instead, be rooted in mechanisms of formalization and codification.

To obtain a fuller understanding of the conditions enabling such views of "professionalizing through standardization," it is important to understand that the profession was not the only locale where agendas of audit standardization were developed and put forward. Governmental institutions also constituted an important arena for the promulgation of processes of audit standardization, through the incorporation of the standards in regulatory frameworks and wider programs of reform and socio-economic development. It is to this second arena that we now turn.

SPURRING MACROECONOMIC DEVELOPMENT

Parallel to the emerging audit profession, the Russian government, in particular the Ministry of Finance and the Ministry of Economic Development and Trade, began to put the adoption of international auditing standards on its reform agendas. These developments were inextricably linked to the dissolution and reorientation of the state apparatus of financial control. Audit standards were discussed as a means of enhancing governmental control and of inducing higher degrees of transparency in the activities of the profession. Instead of professional institutes, the Ministry of Finance was, and still is, mainly responsible for the control of audit business conduct and the issuance of professional licenses. In this context, agendas of audit standardization were promoted as a tool through which state authorities could regain their regulatory grip on audit activities and establish new centers of market-friendly, neo-liberal control. The standards came to be seen as a device that could help state authorities in the governance and consolidation of audit activities. The standards should guide state authorities, especially the Ministry of Finance, in the establishment of a system of external control and thereby contribute to the stabilization and legitimacy of the developing audit business. With the introduction of internationally recognized performance measures, it was further hoped that the variety within, and public confusion about, the profession could be reduced and, in turn, progress in the government-led transition from inspection to auditing would be achieved.

Such hopes and concerns were articulated in close connection to wider debates on market-oriented forms of government and socioeconomic development. The collapse of the Soviet system of command and control had led to a fundamental reconceptualization of the roles and objectives of macroeconomic management, and a search for new mechanisms of government that would be more suitable for the envisaged market oriented economy. Socialist forms of rule, at least in the eyes of the reformers, had to be replaced with new market-oriented modes of government. The search for these new mechanisms of government was and still is to a large extent driven by the desire to bring Russia closer to the West and to participate, side by side with other influential nation states and particularly the then G7 nations, in the conduct of world politics and global capitalism.

Within governmental documents, explicit reference to international accounting and auditing standards began to be made in the late 1980s and early 1990s. On October 19, 1990, for example, the Supreme Council of the Soviet Union adopted a resolution about "Basic directions of the stabilization of the national economy and the transition towards a market economy." Among other things, the document discussed the importance of a fundamental accounting and audit reform. The existing system of financial reporting was declared to be outdated and in need of reform, in order to enable it to become more suited to market economic structures. It was hoped that this could be achieved through the introduction of international standards, especially international accounting standards. Two years later, after the collapse of the Soviet Union on October 23, 1992, the Supreme Council of the Russian Federation endorsed a similar program, namely, the "Program for the transition of the Russian Federation to international practices in accounting and statistics." This program also underlined the importance of international standards and the development of a unified methodological audit and accounting framework to advance the creation of a new, market-oriented system of financial control.

Subsequent to the issuing of these programs in 1993, the Scientific Financial Research Institute of the Ministry of Finance (NIFI) began with the drafting of a first set of ten Russian auditing standards, which, to a large extent, followed the structure and content of the international auditing standards issued by the International Federation of Accountants (Danilevskii 1994: 119).[3] One year later, the development of the standards was delegated to the Presidential Auditing Commission. The commission was founded in February 1994, following a presidential decree (Danilevskii 1994: 31). The major aim of the commission was to spur the development of a regulatory framework for the newly emerging auditing business. Aleksashenko, at that time chairman of the commission, wrote in the preface to the publication of the draft standards:

> The absence of [a system of] legal regulation of auditing [leads to] a confusion of audit activities with inspections of financial-economic activities and makes the establishment of market relations in our country difficult. The organization and methods of auditing in Russia should be developed on the basis of the expertise formed by world practice. . . . All aspects of auditing, the rights and obligations of auditors and enterprises using their services should be comprehended in the same manner [*odnoznachno*]. Auditing standards shall regulate the interrelations between audit firms, enterprises, tax, and other authorities that control the lawfulness of the activities of enterprises; and shall also be taken into account in arbitration processes. . . . The list of necessary auditing standards for the Russian Federation was prepared in accordance with the recommendations of the International Auditing Practices Committee of the International Federation of Accountants. . . . With their help the auditor will be able to decide about necessary measures and depth of audit controls, as well as methods of expediency. (Aleksashenko in Danilevskii 1994: 3–4)

Two years later, in 1996, the commission officially adopted a first set of eleven auditing standards. These standards included revised versions of the draft standards and a couple of new standards dealing with matters of audit planning, sampling, and documentation. Between 1998 and 2000, the development of the standards was further advanced by the adopted government program entitled "Program for action for the period 1998–1999 with regard to the conduct of audits of financial statements of economic entities in accordance with international standards" (Krikunov 2000, 2001a). In 1999, consistent with this program, another set of fourteen standards was approved. By 2000, the number of audit standards had reached thirty-nine in total, the amount prescribed by the program.

Until 2001, the auditing standards were not compulsory. Although adopted by a governmental regulatory body, the standards did not enjoy a legal, mandatory status. This was changed in August 2001, when the government approved a new Federal Audit Law. Subsequent to the issuing of the new law, the old audit standards began to be replaced step by step by the new standards. The major aim of this undertaking was to move the Russian audit standards closer to the terminology, wording, and structure of the standards issued by the IFAC. The reworking of the standards was undertaken in close cooperation with the audit profession. For example, the Russian audit firm FBK, in connection with an EU-funded Tacis project, undertook the major bulk of work involved in redrafting the first twelve standards. These new standards follow largely the official, IFAC-endorsed Russian translation of International Standards on Auditing that had been prepared under the leadership of the International Center for Accounting Reform in Moscow (ICAR) and published in 2000. Krikunov, who was between 2001 and 2004 the head of the State Department for the organization of auditing activities, welcomed the issuing of the new standards as "an important step in the development of Russian auditing" (Krikunov 2001b).

Parallel to these developments, agendas of international audit standardization became incorporated in wider reform plans that were drafted to outline and orchestrate long-term macroeconomic development. Of particular relevance in this context is the "Gref Program," issued by the Ministry of Economic Development and Trade, and the economic development policy letters of the Ministry of Finance.[4] These texts present ISAs as one component in a series of new, Western infrastructural elements that are intended to help rebuild Russia's shattered economy and accelerate its adaptation to the international world of capitalism. In conjunction with other instruments of financial and macroeconomic governance and other standardization mechanisms, the Gref Program introduced ISAs as a measure that could be employed to "improve competitiveness, transparency and accountability," "enhance the development of the private sector," "encourage foreign investment," and "achieve efficient protection of ownership rights." Similar statements can also be found in the Letter of Development Policy for the Third Structural Adjustment Loan that was issued by the Russian government on July 17, 1998. Here it is stated on page 2 that:

> The structural [reform] measures [to which audit standards also belong, A.M.] are designed to: (i) improve the competitiveness, transparency and accountability of infrastructure monopolies; (ii) enhance the development of the private sector; (iii) liberalize international trade and encourage foreign direct investment; (iv) enhance fiscal management; and (v) reform the financial sector.

With respect to matters of accounting and auditing reform, the letter states on page 9: "The overarching goal [is] to achieve substantial progress in implementing financial accounting, auditing standards, and practices, in line with international principles."

Such statements echo wider debates on regulatory effectiveness and market development. The standards were able to attract the attention of the government against the background of the growing problematic of the cumbersome nature of the Russian state bureaucracy and its traditional system of command and control. To achieve economic modernization, the Gref Program recommended, first of all, the "reduction of the administrative regulation of economic activities" (Gref Program 2001: 85). In the name of deregulation, the number of state organs involved in economic regulation should be significantly reduced and the "representation of the interests of citizens and organizations on federal and local levels" improved, "for example, through the mechanism of self-regulating professional associations" (Gref Program 2001: 87). On page 71, the program states: "The government should find an optimal balance with regard to its relations with private entrepreneurship—step by step it should withdraw from practices of unnecessary intervention in business affairs."

Such proposals were preceded and stimulated by earlier reform programs of economic liberalization and privatization. These programs had placed considerable emphasis on state independence, competition, and the economic market as coordinator and driver of economic activity. It was assumed that market order and economic development would come about as a result of the de-monopolization of state power and the marketization of economic relations (Blanchard et al. 1993; Åslund 1995; Boycko et al. 1995; Lane 2002a). For example, Boycko et al. (1995: 126), who between 1991 and 1992 had advised the Russian government in matters of economic reform, stated in their evaluation of the Russian privatization process:

> To stimulate restructuring, free-market reformers must pursue efforts to take the remaining control rights away from politicians and allocate them to private agents who have the corresponding cash flow rights. At the same time, they must continue efforts to reallocate control rights from managers to outside investors.

However, a desire to spur Russia's macroeconomic development was not the only rationale underlying the production and dissemination of such statements. The Russian government, at that time, also drew much attention to neo-liberal standardization and deregulation programs because of their prominence within wider inter- and supranational debates about regulatory appropriateness. The international acceptance and Western promotion of standardization agendas turned them into an important device through which Russian state agencies could demonstrate their willingness to reform. With the adoption of internationally acknowledged instruments of regulation, the Russian government could signal regulatory progressiveness, communicate international conformity, and, subsequently, enhance its legitimacy and right to existence. Multilateral agencies, such as the OECD, WTO, World Bank, IMF, and, last but not least, IFAC (which was and is responsible for the issuing of the standards), played an important role in the international positioning and spread of the standards.[5] It is to these institutions of global economic governance that we now turn.

THE ARENA OF GLOBAL ECONOMIC GOVERNANCE

To accelerate the transfer of economic knowledge, and to accelerate the country's reintegration into the worlds of transnational business and international politics, the Russian government together with representatives of the emerging audit profession sought to build cooperations with Western agencies and governments at an early stage. Within the sphere of accounting and auditing, projects of international cooperation and knowledge exchange were established with the governments of Sweden, France, Britain, and the United States. In addition, the Ministry of Finance became the beneficiary of several EU-funded Tacis accounting and audit reform projects, and the recipient of World Bank and IMF aid for the development of new economic infrastructures.[6]

Since 1993, the European Union had launched five projects dealing with accounting and audit reform in Russia, of which the two latest audit reform projects were started in 2000 and 2004 and finished in 2002 and 2006. The main objective of both projects was to assist the Russian government, auditors, and professional associations in the development and application of a regulatory framework for auditing based on international standards. As stated in the project announcement of the project that was started in 2000, the overall aim of the project was

> to promote the recovery of the Russian economy by improving the quality of corporate governance and management, and by stimulating the flow of foreign and domestic investment into enterprises. The specific aim of the project is to develop an effective and appropriate regulatory framework for the auditing system, and to implement new auditing standards.[7]

The audit and accounting reform projects were embedded in wider EU initiatives of private sector developments. The reform of auditing was seen as contributing to the development of the market infrastructure:

> A coherent and clear auditing system is one of the pillars of modern economies. It promotes transparency, exercises discipline on management and allows trust to be built among economic operators. . . . The integration of internationally recognized auditing standards into the Russian environment is an important step in Russia's transformation into a market economy and an absolute requirement for the creation of a favorable climate for international investment.[8]

Parallel to the EU Tacis projects, the World Bank began to promulgate international auditing standards through the issuing of structural adjustment loans. The development of the Russian "Program for action for the period 1998–1999 with regard to the conduct of audits and accounts of economic entities in accordance with international standards," for example, was issued in conjunction with Russia's application for a structural adjustment loan (Voronov et al. 1999). The spread of international audit standardization agendas was further stimulated by Russia's application for WTO membership. The American Chamber of Commerce wrote in this respect in a "White Paper on Standardization, Certification and Licensing in the Russian Federation" from June 1996:

> The establishment of a coherent system of standardization, certification, and licensing is essential to both Russian economic development and integration into world markets. Compliance with international standards is also a vital component of Russia's potential membership in the World Trade Organization.

The OECD contributed to the spread of the standards through the foundation of a regional federation of accounting and audit associations in the Commonwealth of Independent States (CIS) to foster the adaptation of the East-European and EastAsian economies to international accounting and auditing standards.[9] The European Bank for Reconstruction and Development (EBRD) stated in its "Strategy for the Russian Federation" (2000, 4):

> The Bank's key strategic objectives [for the financial sector] are to promote competition and more effective corporate governance and to reduce the level of politicization of the financial sector. . . . The Bank will, above all, seek to establish and demonstrate high standards of business conduct.[10]

In this context, International Standards on Auditing are seen as contributing to the establishment of these standards of business conduct. Agendas of international audit standardization were further supported by the Intergovernmental Working Group of Experts on International Standards of Accounting and Reporting (ISAR) of the United Nations Conference on Trade and Development (UNCTAD).[11] As stated in its mission, inter alia, ISAR's mandate is to "promote increased transparency and financial disclosure by encouraging the use of internationally recognized accounting and auditing standards and improved corporate governance."[12]

International auditing standards have also been promoted here as a means to support institutional capacity building and enhance Russia's development prospects.

Another important locale through which Western agencies promulgated agendas of audit standardization in Russia was constituted by ICAR, the International Center for Accounting Reform, in Moscow. ICAR was set up in 1998 with the objective of providing the Russian government and other concerned entities with guidance in the transition towards international accounting and auditing standards.[13] ICAR attempted to assist Russian auditors in the adoption of international standards through

> the reworking of the normative base for the reform of the accounting and auditing systems, the preparation of practical instructions for the application of the reform and the development of training materials and re-training courses for practicing accountants.[14]

In October 2000, ICAR released the first official, IFAC-endorsed Russian translation of international auditing standards that the center disseminated in seminars, conferences, and through its newsletters. Four years after its foundation, ICAR had developed into a lively contact point and information center for accountants, auditors, regulators, and other parties concerned who wanted to learn more about Western forms of business conduct, accounting, and audit work. In this context, international accounting and auditing standards came to be promoted as regulatory devices that could help establish new forms of capitalist expertise and, thereby, stimulate market-based economic reform.

Most of the activities of the already mentioned Western organizations were not solely driven by regional development concerns. Wider debates about global economic governance and international stability constituted important triggers for their involvement in the promulgation of international standardization agendas in Russia, and still do so. In view of an increasing internationalization of economic processes and markets, national regimes of regulation came to be questioned. Events such as the Mexican (1994–1995) and Southeast Asian (1998) financial crises and the collapse of the Barings bank led to serious doubts about the regulatory capacities of state-bound regimes of command and control. Against the background of these doubts, demands for more internationalization and decentralization of regulatory regimes grew in popularity and influence. In this context, international standards, including international auditing standards, were introduced as a new source and technique of regulation that would be able to overcome the boundaries of state control, facilitate economic coordination, and contribute to the integration and stabilization of international trade and commerce.

A significant increase in attempts to internationalize and privatize economic governance regimes can be observed since the mid 1990s. Within the context of auditing and accounting, in 1997 for example, the International Federation of Accountants, in cooperation with the World Bank and other international financial institutions, created the International Forum for Accountancy Development (IFAD).[15] IFAD's work focused on a so-called improvement of accounting and auditing practices in developing and transitional economies. Regarding the regulation of auditing, IFAD's declared vision was:

> For all general purpose, financial statements are to be audited in com-
> pliance with a single worldwide framework of auditing standards that
> provides users with assurance regarding the results, financial position,
> and changes in the financial position of entities.[16]

The establishment of IFAD was stimulated by criticism of the then president
of the World Bank, James Wolfensohn, who in 1997 said that the profession was not doing enough to enhance accounting capacity and capabilities
in developing and emerging nations. These allegations were premised, at
least in part, on the assumption that the Mexican and East Asian financial
crises were sparked off by the low quality and high variability of international financial reporting practices.

In reaction to these criticisms, the then president of IFAC, Frank Hard-
ing, suggested that the expertise of the accounting profession and the financial resources of the World Bank, as well as other international financial
institutions, should be harnessed to develop transnational partnerships in
order to increase the quality and uniformity of international accounting and
auditing practices. In this context, international auditing and accounting
standards were put forward as a mechanism that should help achieve these
goals. Two years later, IFAD, together with IFAC, supported the creation
of the Financial Stability Forum (FSF), which was founded with the aim of
"promoting international financial stability through information exchange
and international cooperation in financial supervision and surveillance."[17]

The Financial Stability Forum was established in order to bring together
national authorities, in particular, the G7, international financial institutions, sector-specific international regulators, and committees of central
bank experts. In accordance with its mission, the forum seeks to "coordi-
nate the efforts of these various bodies in order to promote international
financial stability, improve the functioning of markets, and reduce systemic
risk."[18]

To accelerate the internationalization of local regimes of financial regulation, the Financial Stability Forum established a Task Force to address
the implementation of standards. The Task Force identified twelve groups
of key standards that should be used to promote international financial
stability and capital market development. Among those standards are the
International Standards on Auditing. The forum issued its compendium
of standards as a "common reference point for the various economic and
financial standards that are internationally accepted as relevant to sound,
stable, and well-functioning financial systems."[19]

It is still too early to assess the long-term consequences of these and
other international standardization attempts. However, what can be said at
this stage is that all these initiatives contributed to the creation of a realm
of "regulatory appropriateness" (March and Olsen 1989), in which international standards, including auditing standards, became a central element.
Especially for developing and transitional economies seeking transnational

investment and political acceptance, adherence to international standards came to be seen as a crucial factor for the establishment of international recognition and legitimacy.

But processes aimed at international standardization are not a one-way process of change. As this chapter has shown for the case of post-Soviet Russia, the rise and spread of international auditing standardization agendas are grounded in a multiplicity of diverse aspirations, hopes, fears, and struggles. Hence, instead of presuming the superiority of Western modernization schemes, we have to ask how these schemes are produced, diffused, and played out. This chapter has tried to make a first step in that direction and open up for investigation the diverse rationales, individual aspirations, and organizational constellations by which post-Soviet audit modernization processes became constituted and acted upon.

CONCLUSION

The rise of international auditing standards in post-Soviet Russia cannot be understood without reference to the wider institutional contexts, political activities, rationales, and agencies involved in the development and promulgation of the standards. A range of factors, not just immediate concerns about audit quality, contributed to the rise of ISAs in Russia. Among these factors are professionalizing strategies, concerns about macroeconomic development, and the problematic of international financial stability. The analysis of the promulgation of the standards in three different institutional arenas—the professionalizing of audit, macroeconomic development, and global economic governance—showed that an understanding of the dynamics of international standardization requires paying attention to multiple, differing types of actors and agencies. Professional groups, national and international audit firms, state agencies, multilateral organizations, financial intermediaries, and educational units all contributed to this process. International auditing standards were made indispensable not so much on the grounds of their inherent functionality. Rather, it was the involvement of the standards in wider discourses on regulatory appropriateness and economic development that provided them with significance and indispensability. In this context, it has further been shown that most of the roles and rationales ascribed to the standards had been articulated at a distance from actual audit practices. The standards were endowed with significance not in reflection of their actual working, but in view of wider demands for international conformity and legitimacy. The standards were used to define a new governmental identity and to concretize capitalist reform requests. They became attached to neo-liberal dreams of control and economic prosperity.

Of course, from this position it is still a long way to their incorporation into day-to-day audit activities. International auditing standards evoke ideas of similarity and comparability that make them attractive in particular to actors situated at the peripheries of global capitalism. But we have to be careful not to overestimate the actual homogenizing and connecting potential of the standards. International standards, including international auditing standards, do not automatically constitute a universal yardstick against which different economic and regulatory practices can be measured and compared. Whether or not international auditing standards arrive at a certain place, and whether or not they are "successfully" translated, are always prone to debate. The outcome depends on the viewpoints of the actors, as well as on the local circumstances where the standards are supposed to take root. To paraphrase Clifford (1997: 8–9), one cannot avoid the global reach of Western institutions and capital markets, but global determination works through as well as against local differences. To understand how processes of international audit standardization work, we have to pay closer attention to the linkages and webs of interaction through which attempts are made to translate the rules into possibilities for regulatory and professional action. This chapter has sought to contribute to our understanding of the complex "constellation" (Burchell et al. 1985) of different agencies, rationales, and political strategies influencing the ways in which international auditing standards are used and acted upon in post-Soviet regulatory and economic activity.

ACKNOWLEDGMENTS

This study was financially supported by the Department of Accounting and Finance at the London School of Economics and Political Science (LSE), the Centre for Analysis of Risk and Regulation (CARR, also based at LSE), the British Economic and Social Research Council (Award R42200034280), and a fellowship from the Clifford Barclay Scholarship Fund. The support of these institutions and foundations is gratefully acknowledged. I also thank Peter Miller, Mike Power, Richard Macve, and Anthony Hopwood for their comments on earlier drafts of this chapter.

NOTES

1. In Moscow, the term "black auditors" has become widely used among regulators and professionals for describing auditors who are formally qualified but pursue audit activities in an unethical manner, for example, by providing clean audit reports without backing these up with detailed checks. The word *black* in this context is used to denote the shady, illegal nature of the activities of these professionals.
2. It should be noted that the interviewee, in this context, does not refer to McDonald's in an ironic sense. Especially at the beginning of the Russian reform process, McDonald's was advanced as a symbol of Western liberalism and market-oriented development: values to which many of the new Russian entrepreneurs aspired. Nevertheless, it is obvious that the inter-

viewee did not know the efforts of the plant to adapt this product to local standards. Thus a Big Mac is not the same in Moscow and Beijing, as local tastes influence the final product.

3. Similar to their international counterparts, the Russian draft standards included standards on the basic principles of auditing, the goals and scope of financial audits, the formulation and conclusion of an audit engagement, audit evidence, fraud and error, the use of the work of an expert, information for management, audit reports, and the audit of post-balance sheet events.

4. The Russian Ministry of Economic Development and Trade issued the Gref Program for the first time in 2001. It is a 250-page document that sets out a strategic program of social and economic policy for 2001–2010. The economic development policy letters of the Ministry of Finance were produced in connection with the Structural Adjustment Programs of macroeconomic reforms of the World Bank.

5. IFAC began with the issuing of International Standards on Auditing in 1979. The International Congress of Accountants established IFAC with the objective of creating a globally operating, unified accountancy profession with harmonized accounting and auditing practices (Institut der Wirtschaftsprüfer 1978).

6. It is important to note that international cooperation was not completely voluntary; institutional pressures exercised by the West, for example, through multilateral agencies such as the World Bank, IMF, OECD, and WTO also drove the search for cooperation. In the eyes of many Russian reformers, after the collapse of the Soviet system, there was no other choice than to adapt to the West through the incorporation of internationally accepted regulatory structures and economic policies.

7. Cf. EU project announcement from January 2000, Ref. No. SCR-E/110158/C/CS/RU, page 2.

8. Cf. EU project announcement from January 2000, Ref. No. SCR-E/110158/C/CS/RU, page 1.

9. In June 1999, the OECD, in cooperation with the U.S. Agency for International Development USAID), helped constitute the Regional Federation of Accountants and Auditors–Eurasia, a regional federation of CIS accounting and audit associations. The federation was founded to "develop and strengthen the accounting and audit profession through their respective associations, integrate the profession into and create linkages with the international community, and develop sustainable self-regulatory organizations in the region." See www.oecd.org/document/12/0,2340,en_2649_201185_2379468_1_1_1_1,00.html. The web site was accessed in December 2006.

10. The EBRD "Strategy for the Russian Federation" from the year 2000 was downloaded from the bank's web site in November 2000.

11. ISAR was created by an ECOSOC resolution in 1982 and is serviced by the United Nations Conference on Trade and Development.

12. This quote was taken from ISAR's mission statement, which is published on its web site. See www.unctad.org/Templates/Page.asp?intItemID=2905&lang=1. The web site was accessed in August 2006.

13. The founders of ICAR were the EBRD, the American Chamber of Commerce, the German Business Association, the Foreign Investment Advisory Council, and the Russian Institute of Professional Accountants. The task of ICAR was further supported by USAID, the UK Department for International Development (DFID), and the European Tacis Program.

14. Cf. www.amcham.ru/amcham/biznes/account.htm. The web site was accessed in October 2003.

15. IFAD was dissolved in 2002 when it had completed its work with the publication of "GAAP Convergence 2002," focusing on the worldwide movement toward convergence with IFRS. See www.iasplus.com/resource/ifad.htm for more information. The web site was accessed in December 2006.
16. Cf. www.ifad.net/content/shared/shared_f_aboutifad_visi.htm. The web site was accessed in May 2002. See also www.iasplus.com/resource/ifad.htm. This web site was accessed in December 2006.
17. Cf. http://www.fsforum.org/home/home.html. The web site was accessed in December 2006.
18. Cf. http://www.fsforum.org/home/home.html. The web site was accessed in December 2006.
19. Cf. Issues Paper of the Task Force on Implementation of Standards that was presented at the meeting of the Financial Stability Forum, March 25–26, 2000. Cf. www.fsforum.org/publications/Issues_Paper_Standards00.pdf. The web site was accessed in December 2006.

REFERENCES

American Chamber of Commerce. 1996. "White Paper on Standardization, Certification and Licensing in the Russian Federation." White Paper issued by the American Chamber of Commerce in Russia, Moscow.
Åslund, Anders. 1995. *The Politics of Economic Reforms: Remaining Tasks.* Stockholm: Stockholm Institute of East-European Economies (SIEEE).
Åslund, Anders, Peter Boone, Simon Johnson, Stanley Fischer, and Barry W. Ickes. 1996. "How to Stabilize: Lessons from Post-Communist Countries." *Brookings Papers on Economic Activity* 1: 217–314.
Blanchard, Olivier, Maxim Boycko, Marek Dabrowski, Rudiger Dornbusch, Richard Layard, and Andrei Shleifer. 1993. *Post-Communist Reform: Pain and Progress.* Cambridge, MA: MIT Press.
Boycko, Maxim, Andrei Shleifer, and Robert Vishny. 1995. *Privatizing Russia.* Cambridge, MA: MIT Press.
Brunsson, Nils. 1998. *A World of Standards as a Social Form.* Stockholm: SCORE Working Paper.
Brunsson, Nils, and Bengt Jacobsson, eds. 2000. *A World of Standards.* Oxford: Oxford University Press.
Burchell, Stuart, Colin Clubb, and Anthony G. Hopwood. 1985. "Accounting in Its Social Context: Towards a History of Value Added in the United Kingdom." *Accounting, Organizations and Society* 10 (4): 381–413.
Callon, Michel. 1980. "Struggles and Negotiations to Define What Is Problematic and What Is Not: The Socio-Logic of Translation." Pp. 197–219 in *The Social Process of Scientific Investigation (Sociology of the Sciences Yearbook),* ed. Karin Knorr, Roger Krohn, and Richard Whitley. Dordrecht: Reidel.
Callon, Michael. 1986. "Some Elements of a Sociology of Translation: Domestication of the Scallops and the Fishermen of St Brieuc Bay." Pp. 196–233 in *Power, Action and Belief,* ed. John Law. London: Routledge and Kegan Paul.
Callon, Michel, John Law, and Arie Rip eds. 1986. *Mapping the Dynamics of Science and Technology.* London: Macmillan Press.
Clifford, James. 1997. *Routes: Travel and Translation in the Late Twentieth Century.* Cambridge, MA: Harvard University Press.
Danilevskii, Iurii A. 1991. "Finansovyi kontrol' i audit: problemy stanovleniia [Financial Control and Audit: Problems of Formation]." *Bukhgalterskii uchet* [The Bookkeeper's Account] 55 (3): 3–9.

Danilevskii, Iurii A. 1994. *Audit v Rossii* [Auditing in Russia]. Moscow: Kontakt.

Erzhanov, M. S. and A. B. Erzhanov. 1991. "Auditorskii kontrol' deiatel'nosti sovmestnykh predpriiatii [Audit Control Activities of Joint Ventures]." *Bukhgalterskii uchet* [The Bookkeeper's Account] 55 (1): 37–40.

European Bank for Reconstruction and Development. 2000. "Strategy for the Russian Federation." Document of the European Bank for Reconstruction and Development, http://www.ebrd.com/about/strategy/country/russia/strategy.pdf, accessed April 17, 2001.

Financial Stability Forum. 2006. "The Financial Stability Forum," http://www.fsforum.org/home/home.html, accessed December 4, 2006.

Financial Stability Forum. 2006. "Issues Paper of the Task Force on Implementation of Standards (March 2000)," http://www.fsforum.org/publications/Issues_Paper_Standards00.pdf, accessed December 4, 2006.

Foucault, Michel. 1981/1991. "Questions of Method." Pp. 73–86 in *The Foucault Effect: Studies in Governmentality*, ed. Graham Burchell, Colin Gordon, and Peter Miller. London: Harvester Wheatsheaf.

Gaidar, Yegor. 2003. *State and Evolution: Russia's Search for a Free Market*. Seattle: University of Washington Press.

Gref Program. 2001. "Osnovnye napravleniia sotsial'no-ekonomicheskogo razvitiia rossiiskoi federatsii na dolgosrochnuiu perspektivu [Basic Directions of Socio-Economic Development in the Russian Federation in the Long Term]." White Paper issued by the Russian Ministry of Economic Development and Trade, http://www.economy.gov.ru/wps/portal/economica/social/progsocrazvit, accessed March 29, 2002.

IAS Plus by Deloitte. 2006. "International Forum for Accountancy Development (IFAD)," http://www.iasplus.com/resource/ifad.htm#gaap2002, accessed December 3, 2006.

ICAR. 2003. "Mission Statement," http://www.amcham.ru/amcham/biznes/account.htm, accessed October 4, 2003.

IFAC. 2001. *Handbook of Auditing and Ethics Pronouncements*. New York: IFAC.

IFAD. 2002. "About the International Forum of Accountancy Development," http://www.ifad.net/content/shared/shared_f_aboutifad_visi.htm, accessed May 10, 2002.

Institut der Wirtschaftsprüfer. 1978. *Accounting and Auditing in One World*. Munich: IdW-Verlag.

Krikunov, Andrei V. 2000. *Opyt razvitiia i regulirovaniia auditorskoi deiatel'nosti: Na Primere Shvetsii i Rossii* [The Experience of the Development and Regulation of Auditing: The Cases of Sweden and Russia]. St. Petersburg: Iuridicheskii Tsentr Press.

Krikunov, Andrei V. 2001a. "Organizatsiia rossiiskogo audita: itogi i perspektivy [The Organization of Russian Auditing: Results and Perspectives]." *Auditorskie Vedomosti* [Auditing News] 5 (2): 13–24.

Krikunov, Andrei V. 2001b. "Vazhny etap razvitiia rossiiskogo audita [An Important Stage in Russian Audit Development]." *Auditorskie Vedomosti* [Auditing News] 5 (11): 7–18.

Lane, David, ed. 2002a. *The Legacy of State Socialism and the Future of Transformation*. Lanham, MD: Rowman and Littlefield.

Lane, David. 2002b. "Trajectories of Transformation: Theories, Legacies, and Outcomes." Pp. 3–30 in *The Legacy of State Socialism and the Future of Transformation*, ed. David Lane. Lanham, MD: Rowman and Littlefield.

Latour, Bruno. 1987. *Science in Action: How to Follow Scientists and Engineers Through Society*. Cambridge, MA: Harvard University Press.

March, James G., and Johan P. Olsen. 1989. *Rediscovering Institutions: The Organizational Basis of Politics.* New York: The Free Press.

Miller, Peter. 1991. "Accounting Innovation Beyond the Enterprise: Problematizing Investment Decisions and Programming Economic Growth in the U.K. in the 1960s." *Accounting, Organizations and Society* 16 (8): 733–762.

Organization for Economic Cooperation and Development. n.d. "The Regional Federation of Accoutants and Auditors," www.oecd.org/document/12/0,2340,en_2649_201185_2379468_1_1_1_1,00.html, accessed December 2, 2006.

Pickles, John, and Adrian Smith, eds. 1998. *Theorising Transition: The Political Economy of Post-Communist Transformations.* New York: Routledge.

Porter, Theodore M. 1992. "Objectivity as Standardization: The Rhetoric of Impersonality in Measurement, Statistics, and Cost-Benefit Analyses." *Annals of Scholarship* 9 (1/2): 19–59.

Power, Michael. 2002. "Standardization and the Regulation of Management Control Practices." *Soziale Systeme* 8 (2): 191–204.

Robson, Keith. 1991. "On the Arenas of Accounting Change: The Process of Translation." *Accounting, Organizations and Society* 16 (5/6): 547–570.

Robson, Keith. 1994. "Inflation Accounting and Action at a Distance: The Sandilands Episode." *Accounting, Organizations and Society* 19 (1): 45–82.

Russian Federation. 1998. "Letter of Development Policy for the Third Structural Adjustment Loan." Letter issued by the Russian Ministry of Finance, July 17.

Sachs, Jeffrey D., and Andrew Warner. 1995. "Economic Reforms and the Process of Global Integration." *Brookings Papers on Economic Activity* 1: 1–95.

UNCTAD, "About International Standards of Accounting and Reporting (ISAR)," http://www.unctad.org/Templates/Page.asp?intItemID=2905&lang=1, accessed August 4, 2006.

Voronov, Viktor V., Fattakh V. Zainetdinov, Iurii I. Ivanov, Nikolai P. Kondrakov, Stanislav A. Korolev, Andrei V. Krikunov, Boris E. Pen'kov, Andrei V. Petrov, Anatolii N. Romanov, Viacheslav V. Skobara, Nikolai G. Sychev, and Oleg S. Shakhov. 1999. *Entsiklopediia obshchego audita* [Encyclopaedia of General Audit]. Moscow: Delo i Servis.

World Bank. 1996. *World Bank Development Report 1996: From Plan to Market.* Washington, DC: World Bank.

5   China's Response to Globalization

Manufacturing Confucian Values

Thierry Pairault

> *Le retour aux sources est toujours aussi un modernisme.*[1]
>
> (Michel de Certeau)

The dichotomy between "identity" and "globalization" broadens in a different economic and societal context the classic oppositions between "tradition" and "modernity" or "past" and "present." Midway between the hope to retrieve a prestigious but idealized past and the desire to be realist and modern, or even between an ancestral identity and a prospective otherness, there is some space for a prospective identity, for an adherence to different values under the guise of regaining one's tradition. In China, the revival of Confucian values and thoughts is central to this topic.

The concept of Confucianism (which lacks a literal Chinese equivalent) developed out of a Jesuit desire to comprehend an unknown other. Even though its interpretation was self-serving, it generated "a systematic doctrine and a religion while elevating *ru* [scholars[2]] above *fo* [Buddha] and *dao* [way] as the only legitimate indigenous faith, and delivered *ru* from local eminence to international prominence" (Jensen 2003: 139). Today Confucianism and its manifestation circumscribe encounters between the West and China to such an extent that cooperation and communication are made possible. How many books invite Western businesspeople today to realize their management tasks according to Confucius's guidance but, in fact, review precepts learned in business schools?

If we agree that meaning is socially constructed, the difference between past and present in a culture should be as important as that between two dissimilar cultures. Establishing a link to a historical past by identifying an alleged, transhistorical, olden figure of universality may reduce this difference. In this process, Kongzi [Confucius] was assumed not only as the primordial teacher but also as the symbol of Chineseness. Thus, to Chinese modernization theoreticians of the late 19th and early 20th centuries, Chineseness-ship (i.e. membership of the Chinese community, hence of the Chinese "nation") meant subscribing to Chinese cultural principles, whatever your ethnic group might be (e.g., Manchus as long as they had accepted these principles). This culturalist nationalism (Duara 1993: 1–26) was built up in such a manner that it reproduced the 17th-century Jesuit equation of Confucius and Chineseness; thus the prophet from Lu (part of present-day Shandong province) was regarded as the sole one who could inspire a unified drive toward national recovery and modernization. Ironically, this reproduction of a Jesuit fiction undermines the common presumption of the uniqueness and otherness of China and suggests that China and the West are no more than mere tropisms on a cultural continuum (Jensen 2003: 268).

This reinterpretation of the Chinese past, in order to find out the ways and means to adopt Western knowledge and technology and to build China as another superpower, was primarily conducted under the aegis of Kang Youwei and his school. This process was continued by Sun Yat-sen, then by Chang Kai-Chek in Taiwan, Lee Kwan-Yew in Singapore, and other authoritarian leaders; more recently, hierarchs of Communist China began to follow suit. The main feature of their approaches was a self-characterization, manufacturing Confucian values and modeling out the figure of a modernizer-messiah. This "revival," as Singaporean political leaders used to call it, was also a response to Max Weber's thesis that China experienced some specifically Chinese disablement freezing her economic and social modernization. In this chapter, I intend to unravel how the reinvention of Confucianism has been used to overcome Chinese ills and to foster economic development through the construction of a supposed indigenous thought.

SAVING AND MODERNIZING THE NATION

"The conception of Political Economy as a branch of science is extremely modern; but the subject with which its enquiries are conversant has in all ages necessarily constituted one of the chief practical interests of mankind," stated John Stuart Mill (Mill 1848: pr1). China was no exception, as Yan Fu—the great 19th-century translator of European books, notably of Adam Smith's *Wealth of Nations* —uttered in a letter from 1902 to Liang Qichao: "Despite an ancient understanding of its principles, China has never made a science of [political economy]" (Yan 1902).

Liang Qichao (1873–1929) was the first Chinese personality who reread Chinese classics from an economist's point of view. Liang studied under Kang Youwei (1858–1927), the famous Chinese philosopher and reformist who asserted that the true teachings of Confucius had been perverted in the past and needed to be adapted to the new situation. In 1897, Liang wrote a study entitled *Modern Significance of the Chapter of the Records of the Historian About Those Whose Wealth Increased* (*"Shiji, huozhi liezhuan" jinyi*)[3] where he claimed not only that political economy had existed in China for hundreds of years, even before the Qin dynasty (221 BC–206 BC), but that it had been similar to its modern Western counterparts (Zhu 2004: 182). Comparable assertions can be found everywhere in the literature on Confucian economic thought; in fact, a fundamental ambiguity has nurtured the debate: a confusion between "economic policy" that focuses on the actions politicians may have taken in the economic realm, and "political economy" that focuses on the theory of economic policy. No one can challenge that traditional Chinese "practitioners of government" were concerned with economic policies. The questions they raised were the same as those of their European counterparts (Will 1999: 323–389). Furthermore, it is true that the Chinese people has not elaborated any theoretical framework that may be compared to the Western classical economics. Some years later, Liang rejected the delusive excuse of a Chinese precedence. In his *Theory of a New Citizenry* (*Xinmin Shuo*), written in 1902, Liang considered as necessary the destruction (*pohuai*) of the "national quintessence" (*guocui*): "We must sweep away and refute the rotten and effeminate scholarly theories of the last few thousand years" (Liang 1941a: 65, 128).[4] Therefore, his *Short History of Political Economy Theories* (*Shengjixue xueshuo yange xiao shi*) from 1902 was a careful and methodical analysis of economic ideas from Aristotle to Adam Smith (Liang 1941b: 1–61). To compile this essay, he had read three books translated or written in Japanese. The first book was written by an Irish philosopher and poet, John Kells Ingram (1823–1907), who published in 1885 a *History of Political Economy* in the *Encyclopædia Britannica*. A second book was written by Luigi Cossa (1831–1896), an Italian economist, who published in 1876 *Guida allo studio dell' economica politica* (in 1880, Stanley Jevons translated the book in English and wrote a preface). The third book was by Inoue Tatsukurō (1868–1943), a Japanese economist, called *History of Political Economy* (*Keizaigaku shi*) and published in 1896. Liang's *Short History* was written without cultural arrogance in order to serve China's economic and political recovery.

This attitude contrasted sharply with that of another student of Kang Youwei, Chen Huanzhang (1880–1933). Although Chen was far less influential than Liang Qichao, his state of mind was more representative of current and past Chinese attempts to bridge the gap between tradition and modernity. Chen had accomplished a traditional education; he was one of the last *jinshi*—the highest degree in the old Chinese examination system. Then he studied in the United States at Columbia University, where he defended in 1911 a doctoral dissertation with the title *The Economic Principles of Confucius and His School*. Chen sought to reinterpret Chinese classical thinking in light of the political economy taught by modern Western economists and his professors at Columbia. Digging into the writings of ancient Chinese philosophers and statesmen, he exposed ideas he had drawn from Western economists and then produced a Confucian economic thought. The Chinese title, compared to the English one, he gave to his dissertation is rather evocative: *Kongmen licaixue*, which literally meant *Confucian Political Economy*. Obviously, he thought that the economic principles he described in his dissertation were part of a scientific theoretical corpus.

Chen Huanzhang constructed his thesis following Kang Youwei's teachings; he reread and reinterpreted the Chinese classics in order to advocate new politics and to initiate institutional reforms (*tuo gu gaizhi*); then he extolled the virtues of Western knowledge to promote these reforms (*fang yang gaizhi*). In fact, his reasoning consisted in dressing Western learning with the showy rags of Confucianism. Thus, Liang Qichao's brutal rejection was completely reexamined in favor of a more diplomatic and tactful stand. Instead of repudiating Chinese knowledge in order to prefer the Western one, Chen claimed that the former was the substance and the latter just a tool (*zhongxue wei ti, xixue wei yong*). However, practical experience showed that the latter became the substance and the former was just a mere tool (*xixue wei ti, zhongxue wei yong*). Chen could then "enjoy" himself searching throughout Confucian Holy Scriptures any fact or thought that could suggest a link between economic theories of his days and a reconstructed, ex-nihilo manufactured Confucianism.

Kang Youwei had glorified a political utopia, *The Great Harmony* (*Datong*), which, he assumed, would end up with the abolition of private ownership of land. Chen noted that the influential American political economist Henry George (1839–1897), the author of the highly celebrated book *Progress and Poverty: An Inquiry into the Cause of Industrial Depressions and of Increase of Want with Increase of Wealth: A Remedy* (1879), regarded land property as the main cause of poverty. Thus he advocated land nationalization and the replacement of taxes by a single tax on ground rent. However disputable Chen's interpretation might have been (there was no land "confiscation" in Henry George's books), what really mattered was that Chen aimed to provide evidence (Chen 1974: 296, 489, 533). In his view, the concept of the "well-field system" (*jingtian*)[5] showed that the Chinese Confucian philosopher Mencius (371–288 B.C.) was the forerunner of all socialist thoughts. Subsequently, the Chinese fiscal history had to be read as a battle between those who purportedly praised a "single tax" and those who allegedly were opposed to it (Will 1994: 863–902). Thus, Confucianism would teach a kind of state socialism (Chen 1974: 532)! Chen repeated again and again this device in his thesis in order to establish the precedence of Confucianism. The theory of wage determination and subsistence wage—as Richard Cantillon (1680–1734) and then Adam Smith (1723–1790) had observed—was, according to Chen, expounded by Confucian scholars in earlier times (Chen 1974: 480–496). One chapter from the *Classic of History* (*Shu jing*) foreshadowed some principles advocated by Wilhelm Roscher (1817–1894), the founder of the German Historical School of Economics (Chen 1974: 532). Chen Huanzhang had thus accumulated unassailable "evidences" of the modernity of Confucianism—as well as of its "economics"—all along the 736 pages of his thesis. Does this proceeding fool him? The answer is no. Chen—a clever casuist and an (unknowingly) anti-Weberian scholar—argued that "all the good points of Christianity are found in Confucianism"; therefore, China "is not weak because she followed the teachings of Confucius, but precisely because she did not truly follow his teachings" (Chen 1974: 719–720, 727–728).

Chen Huanzhang as well as the great majority of his Chinese and Western contemporaries did not understand that political economy does not give any formula for good government. The British economist Joan Robinson in her preface to her book *The Economics of Imperfect Competition* had clearly stated that her book "is presented to the analytical economist as a box of tools" (Robinson 1933: 1). In other words, she underlined that she did not give any certainty to the "practitioners of government." Using a given tool to deal with a given predicament in order to obtain a predictable outcome, whether it is good or bad, is outside the scope of any economic analysis, but is a political question. For example, when Chen alluded to the fiscal debate, the fiscal tool was not conceived in order to share out wealth (economic policy) but to share out power (politics) between the Emperor and his dependants. The "well-field system" did not fall within the topic of fiscal theory but within that of political practice. Although the Emperor's ministers expressed their concern about fiscal policy, one should not infer that they worked out any Confucian economics. Conversely, one should consider that these ministers defended some fiscal policy (an exclusive land tax) as they subscribed to some Confucian political principles, such as the "well-field system."

Back on the Chinese mainland, Chen Huanzhang began with proselytizing activities. Until his death, he indefatigably promoted Kang Youwei's idea of a religion of Confucius (*Kong jiao*) or Confucianism, though better identified as "Confucianity" in English. Kang, Chen, and others have drawn an enduring parallel with Christianity,[6] modeling the former on the latter but disparaging the latter with the former. As the latter had its Christmas Day, the former received in 1918 its "Kongmas Day" (if I may coin such a phrase), an annual celebration of Confucius's birth on September 28. In 1929, Chen Huanzhang introduced a Confucius Institute in Hong Kong in order to spread Confucianism and to foster peace all around the world. Instructively, the current Chinese government chose this denomination[7] to name its new propaganda apparatus springing up around the world and whose patterns are very reminiscent of the *Goethe Institut*, the *Pushkin Institute*, and the *Alliance Française*—even if this denomination has not personalized this institution (SCMP 2006, November 14). The new Confucius Institutes, like their forerunner, intend to spread "Confucian values" and to "bring peace to the world" (Xinhua 2006).

Sun Yat-sen (1866–1925) did not recommend, as did Liang Qichao, a harsh rejection of Confucianism. Neither did he attempt, as did Kang Youwei and Chen Huanzhang, to work out a lengthy reinterpretation of the classics so that a new China could be built on foundations that would have been strained. In the collection of conferences that formed the principal book of the Father of the Nation (*guo fu*), *The Three Principles of the People*, also known as *Triple Demism* (*San min zhuyi*), his longest reference to Confucian concepts appeared in his discussion of the Principle of Nationalism (*minzu zhuyi*). Here he suggested that if China were to become again a great power, the country should first succeed in preserving her ancient values.

Sun Yat-sen went even further than Chen Huanzhang. Sun not only mixed principles taken from Western economics with concepts chosen from Chinese Classics, but confiscated for the benefit of an alleged Chineseness what the market economy's pivotal institution is: trust. The Bible has regarded economic practices as a paradigmatic locus revealing values such as trust. Adam Smith, in his *Theory of Moral Sentiments* (1759), examined the social process when individuals adopted moral standards that permitted them to judge others' and their own actions. He explained how people could overcome selfish impulses of the commercial realm—how voluntary exchanges relied on reciprocal trust and mutual benefits so that there might be a "happy commerce" (Smith 1759: 39). To foster growth, even G8 members have been fully aware that "trust and confidence are key ingredients of a well-functioning market economy" (G8 2003).

In fact, Sun Yat-Sen, the Father of the [Chinese] Republic, challenged the authority of the Father of Modern Economics. The notions of trust and confidence have definitely been part and parcel of Chinese moral values; traditional Chinese schoolbooks have instilled these virtues into very young children. For instance in Taiwan, a Chinese reader for primary schools recounted little stories showing high esteem for legendary parents, friends, or merchants who brought credit on themselves as they proved to be utterly trustworthy (Guoli bianyiguan 1994: 33–36). In a similar way, a Chinese literature textbook for second-year students of junior high school began with a text from Sun Yat-sen, followed by a thorough exegesis that emphasized the preeminence of Chinese culture in the matter of trust (Guoli bianyiguan 1987: 1–8). Sun's quotation reads as follows (Sun 1924):

> Regarding trust, China has always emphasized trust when dealing with neighbouring countries or with friends. In my view, Chinese behave more trustfully than foreigners. This is obvious in commercial matters. When Chinese do business, they need no written contracts; they only have to reach an oral agreement that is wholeheartedly trusted. Thus, when foreigners trade with Chinese people, no itemized contract is needed . . . . As a result, foreigners who have done business for a long time in China have always spoken with high esteem of Chinese, saying that Chinese keep their words better than foreigners fulfill their contracts.

Assuming that there is no intentional deception in Sun's remark, at least Sun drives readers into a conceptual jumble. Well trained and fluent in English, Sun[8] could not be unaware that the foundations of any contract, promise, pledge, or agreement are not the outcome of some formal procedures—the writing of a document—but the written as well as the oral expression of the partners' will. Furthermore, Sun should have known that the drafting of contracts was common practice in his country, and that disputes caused by the nonfulfillment of these contracts were everyday occurrences. Sun should have been familiar with an old Chinese legal adage stating that "spoken words cannot prove anything" (*kong kou wu ping*), which is similar to the Latin *verba volant, scripta manent*. Moreover, even if the Chinese state had been unwilling to intervene in private transactions and to codify contractual practices, it had been levying a contract tax since the 10th century and had introduced an aggressive administration to enforce its levy (Hansen 1995); the yield of this tax had been so important for the state's budget that this tax was the first to be restored by the Communist regime in 1950. In China, the dead (according to folk beliefs), ghosts in literature (Wenhua 1984: 136), and beggars (Cui 1936: 118–119) used to sign written contracts—even if to do so the latter had to put their forefinger print on a contract.

A system where transactions between agents were conducted on an *intuitu personæ* basis could have fostered a direct and informal manifestation of their mutual trust, but immediacy and informality would become less suitable whenever this system happened to be increasingly intricate and impersonal, so that it needed more formal and more comprehensive agreements. Chinese state-owned enterprises experienced this consequence after the launching of economic reforms. On March 1, 1996, the *People's Daily* published an article entitled "What is a contract?" The author admitted that these legal documents had become necessary. Yet he acknowledged that the drafting of such contracts had allowed all kinds of exactions, whose victims were the newly reformed state-owned enterprises. He explained that the economic reforms involved the gradual vanishing of the planned economic sector, and the fading away of preestablished economic relations between production units that stemmed from the first days of the regime. According to the journalist, in the current socialist market economy—and in particular in business relations with foreigners—modern enterprises had to sign contracts. But he failed to notice that state-owned enterprises were not prepared for the new rules. Instead, the author stressed the role of foreign businessmen.[9] In fact, such clichés and arguments still further nurture the belief in a distinctive Confucian character as it has already spread in Singapore.

A century ago, when East Asia seemed immutably poor, many Western scholars—especially Max Weber—argued that Confucian-based cultures lacked the qualities needed to undergo a successful mutation into wealthy capitalist countries. Two or three decades ago, as Western countries were experiencing a slow economic growth, most Asian hierarchs' attention was focused on an excessive Western stress on individual rights that according to them became the main reason why Western countries were decaying while East Asian countries were blooming (Zakaria 1994: 111). Pundits and politicians turned this explanation on its head, arguing that Confucianism emphasized essential aspects of economic dynamism. The World Bank was no exception when it published in 1993 *The East Asian Miracle* compendium (World Bank 1993). A further example is Singapore's "cultural revival" (*wenhua liguo*), which was implemented by the former prime minister Lee Kuan-Yew (in charge from 1959 to 1990), who shaped it together with the most conservative as well the most Westernized members of the Singaporean Chinese elite, who had always been fostering the English language to the prejudice of the Chinese tongue and other vernaculars. Accordingly, in 1982, it was decided to offer a fellowship to seven American scholars of Chinese origin[10] plus one Taiwanese scholar so that they drafted in English a Confucian catechism that had to teach schoolboys and schoolgirls the virtues of good citizens. Furthermore, Singapore's rulers published a book of selected readings on moral education (e.g., traditional Chinese stories of virtuous men and women) and an English translation of the classical maxims written with three characters (*San zi jing*) (Chen 1991: 11–18; Chen 2004).

Despite the failure to spread Confucian moral values in the educational network (Riegel 2000: 84), Lee Kuan-Yew insisted in his 1994 conversation with Fareed Zakaria (then managing editor of *Foreign Affairs*) on their importance for the economic development of Singapore and other East Asian countries, such as Japan, Korea, and Taiwan (Zakaria 1994: 109–126). Moreover, to emphasize the actual importance of Confucianism, Lee underlined: "If you have a culture that does not place much value in learning and scholarship and hard work and thrift and deferment of present enjoyment for future gain, the going will be much slower" (Zakaria 1994: 116–117), values, which according to him needed a "well-ordered society" and an "ordered state" (Zakaria 1994: 114). The debate on "Confucian values," highlighted as "Asian values," not only featured a growing stress on Confucianism as a central component of cultural identity, but also secured a static ideology that submitted individual prosperity and societal development to the state. Confucian values, ideals, and social norms have been appealing to authoritarian regimes because they have promised a social and political cohesion between state and society that these regimes would otherwise fail to achieve. Thus, Confucianism was successfully domesticated into an acceptable cultural form by Japanese militarists in the 1930s, Korean and Taiwanese dictators in the 1950s, and Chinese and Vietnamese communists in the 1990s.

This "contamination" of Communist China has been suggested by Fan Heping's recent book on the well-known Japanese industrialist Shibusawa Eiichi (1840–1931) (Fan 1995). The "father of Japanese capitalism," as Shibusawa was called, actually wrote a book entitled *The Analects and the Abacus*, imagining that Confucian values would connect Japanese customs to modern economics realities. Shibusawa initiated a personal friendship with Sun Yat-sen, a fact that helped him to establish the China Industrial Corporation (*Zhongguo shiye huishe*) in 1914 and paved the way for Japan's financial expansion in China (Li 2006). Shibusawa and Sun were loyal supporters of (a rethought) Confucianism as an industrial ideology. In short, this was modernization with "Japanese characteristics" or with "Chinese characteristics," to speak as Chinese Communist hierarchs.

CONFUCIUS TO SERVE AND TO SINICIZE SOCIALISM

Since 1982, with the promotion of a "socialism with Chinese characteristics" (*juyou Zhongguo tese de shehuizhuyi*), the Chinese Communist Party (CCP) considered that it had found the "ideal economic structure" to conduct the modernization of China (Wang 2004). Although the CCP formerly did not extol any Confucian value or ideal, it had always referred to some solidarity between state and society. It had been unable to achieve this sort of cohesion that seemingly could not be realized by imitating Western countries. Thus, it expected to be successful with the revival of a purportedly Chinese uniqueness. Currently, this revival uses words and concepts that are admittedly reminiscent of Confucianism. In 1993, the Ministry of Education under the guidance of Vice Prime Minister Li Lanqing charged Professor Wang Dianqing to realize a study on moral education that would underline Chinese traditional virtues (*zhonghua minzu chuantong meide*). Thus, for a decade that had begun in 1994, Professor Wang conducted experiments—mainly in Peking and Shandong—based on a rather contemporary reading of the eight Confucian virtues (*ba de*). In 2003, Professor Wang delivered a report on his experiments on moral education in primary and secondary schools; he could not but assert: "History reels off records proving that the roots of Marxist ideology are already in the genes of Chinese traditional culture" (Wang 2003; Fan 2003: 1). Obviously, arguments have not much changed since Chen Huanzhang!

Today, the CCP faces a problem that was already formulated by Adam Smith: The sole maximization of individual profits can neither promote economic development nor explain how market economy works. The impediments to economic development met by the Chinese leaders' strategy are threefold. First, this strategy has focused "material incentives"; second, it has disregarded the promotion of institutions supporting the transition to a market economy; third, it has underestimated values that favor mutual understanding and standard behavior. The solution of the first and the second impediments is mainly linked to the reform of state governance; the answer to the third is linked to the restoring of the idea of Confucian virtues.

Actually, China experiences an unsatisfactory economic growth and an even poorer socioeconomic development. "The China miracle," "A miracle with Chinese characteristics," "The tremendous success of China's economic reform," and so on have been the leading economic headlines for the last decade.[11] All these superlatives should not hide that China's economic growth is common standard. From 1960 to 1990, that is, for thirty years, Taiwan, South Korea, and Singapore—like Japan before them—all witnessed an average annual growth rate of 8.7 percent—just the average growth rate of China for the last ten years. In 2005, economic activities in Venezuela, Ukraine, and Belarus showed an annual growth rate of 17.3 percent, 12.1 percent, and 11.0 percent, respectively; they underscored China's "meager" 9.5 percent (as high as that of Kazakhstan). The point is that the developed countries have wondered how they could solve their economic problems. They have envied China's growth rate and have considered it as appropriate to cure Western socioeconomic diseases. But Western countries have never asked the question of whether this growth rate is adapted to the necessities of China's socioeconomic development.

In fact, China's growth rate cannot handle simultaneously urban unemployment, rural unemployment, and surplus labor. On average, job demands in urban centers have exceeded twenty million during the last years; they may even reach twenty-five million in 2007. Despite an almost double-digit growth rate in 2004, 2005, and 2006, Chinese urban economic sectors have only created ten to eleven million vacancies annually; accordingly, ten to fifteen million people in urban centers are left without a job each year (SCMP December 28, 2005, and December 24, 2006). Furthermore, as the economist Yu Yongding underlined in 2002,[12] if China is to solve her unemployment predicament, she must not only create each year twenty million new urban jobs, but she must also generate another twenty million new jobs for rural people. In short, to compete with unemployment and to convert her economic system from a rural into an industrial economy, China is compelled to engender at least forty million new jobs each year for 30 years. In other words, to achieve such an economic modernization, the new jobs to be generated in China each year are, for example, fifteen times the number of the French unemployed (2006). However, as the socioeconomic background is far less favorable in China than in the developed countries, it precludes China from providing extensive social care to her unemployed.[13]

Putting China's economic growth rate into perspective is not enough to display its ambiguity. To cast some light on its significance, I utilize the Harrod–Domar model, which permits the predictive use of a mere counting equation. It delineates a functional economic relationship where the growth rate of the gross domestic product (g) depends on the national saving ratio (s) and inversely on the national incremental capital-output ratio or ICOR (k), so that it is written as $g = s/k$. What does this equation tell us? The ICOR measures the efficiency of the use of capital: the higher the ICOR, the lower the productivity of capital. In China, it is generally assumed that the best ICOR is about two and the worst is about three (it could even be higher, as obsolecent equipment is rather widespread). The average Chinese propensity to save fluctuates from 30 to 45 percent annually—it even peaked at 49 percent in 2005. What do these figures mean?

- Provided that the capital-output ratio is not higher than three and supposing that all available savings are invested, the Harrod–Domar model teaches us that the annual Chinese growth rate should at least be equal to 15 percent and might even reach 20 percent. Yet these figures are much higher than those recorded by the statistical department of the government.

- Assuming that the annual growth rate equals 9 percent (somewhat less than the actual rate but higher than the trend from 1995 to 2004) and provided that the capital-output ratio is not higher than three, the requisite saving ratio should not exceed 27 percent (i.e., 9 multiplied by 3 makes 27); once again, the virtual and the statistical reality are contending.
- We thus have to conclude that the Chinese economic system endures serious capital outflows (out of the formal sector as well as out of China) that may look even more important if foreign direct investments (i.e., capital inflows that amount to some $55 billion) are taken into consideration.

In spite of her economic growth—it does not matter whether disclosed or concealed—the way China shares the wealth that is produced is rather unequal: There is a stark contrast between the urban centers and the countryside, the coastal regions and the interior, men and women, among social and ethnic groups, and so on. The Gini coefficient is used to measure income disparity: The higher this coefficient is (from 0.0 to 1.0), the lower is the share of national income captured by the poorest. In China, this coefficient was at its lowest level (0.10) in the aftermath of the Maoist period, showing equality in poverty; it reached 0.26, then 0.41, in 1984 and 2001, respectively; in 2004, it peaked at 0.53. Since 2001, it has always exceeded the threshold of 0.40 that is considered as the limit when social unrest is likely to appear (Ru 2005: 376). Before the launching of economic reforms, Chinese urban centers did not experience any form of poverty except that commonly shared. Nowadays, the "iron rice-bowl" (*tie wanfan*) is broken: A lifetime employment is no longer guaranteed to anybody; on the contrary, everybody may have to face unemployment. In addition, a retired worker may no longer receive any pension from his or her work unit. A worker may be lucky enough to find a job but his or her income may be insufficient to make a living. Statistical departments continue to discover new forms of urban poverty, but the delays from discovery to registration are so high that official figures list almost 50 percent of people who get some relief from any social welfare provision among "other recipients" (Ru 2005: 165–167).

The present conjunction of circumstances prompts some Chinese economists, such as Zhang Houyi,[14] to state that China unfortunately *latinoamericanizes* (*nanmeizhouhua*) herself. This very pessimistic assessment is still corroborated by the United Nations Development Program (UNDP). According to the UNDP's *Human Development Report 2006*, the richest 10 percent of Chinese people spend an amount of money that is twenty times higher than that of the poorest 10 percent; the former share 33.1 percent of the national income and the latter share a mere 1.8 percent (UNPD 2006: 336). The situation in China not only mirrors a clear-cut difference between the poorest people and well-heeled parvenus, but above all shows a widening wealth gap between city dwellers, who are on average richer (42 percent of China's population), and country dwellers, who are on average poorer (58 percent of China's population).[15] The income earned by the former grew on average 8 to 9 percent annually from 1978 to 2004, while that of the latter only rose by 4 to 5 percent each year (Xinhua 2005a). In addition, per capita annual social welfare expenditures on average amount to 1,765 *yuan* (180 euros) in urban centers, while they reach a ceiling of 14 *yuan* (1.5 euros) in the countryside (Ru 2005: 377). The *China Human Development Report 2005* illustrated significant differences in human development between urban and rural areas. This report calculated a separate human development index (HDI) for urban and rural areas. Urban areas displayed an HDI of 0.816 while rural areas reached only 0.685 (UNDP 2005: 8). Accordingly, Chinese cities rank somewhere between Cuba (52nd among 177) and Mexico (53rd), while the Chinese countryside is placed between the Mongolian People's Republic (133rd) and Bolivia (134th). China as a whole joins Paraguay, Surinam, Saint Vincent, and the Grenadines at the 88th position (UNDP 2005: 219 ssq.).

"Empirically, for a given growth rate, higher relative inequality generally implies a slower rate of reduction in absolute income poverty. . . . The growth elasticity of poverty reduction—the percentage decline in poverty for each percentage point in the growth rate—tends to decline with income inequality (and with the ratio of the poverty line to the mean)," wrote the World Bank in its *World Development Report 2006* (World Bank 2006: 10). Does this mean that China has been sentenced to a never-ending poverty and will never be able to establish any state of welfare?

The concept of "petty welfare" (*xiaokang*) had become for many years the slogan of keynote speeches delivered by Chinese hierarchs. This notion first appeared in the old Chinese Classics. The *Book of Odes* (*Shi Jing*) linked it to a situation where people longed for peace and yearned for moderate wealth in the aftermath of the civil war (Couvreur 1896: 368). The same vision was taken over in the *Book of Rites* (*Li Ji*). Yet its "petty welfare" was then confronted to a prospective "great harmony" (*datong*) (Couvreur 1913: 498, 500). This second concept had delineated a kind of Golden Age when peace was long-lasting and wealth so plentiful that it met people's needs. Kang Youwei revisited this "great harmony" much later in his *opus magnum* precisely entitled *Datong* (cf. earlier discussion). Nevertheless, Sun Yat-Sen has been considered as the first thinker to have thrown a bridge from "petty welfare" to "great harmony" in a modernizing perspective. In fact, a careful reading of the compendium of the Father of the Republic (*guo fu*), *The Three Principles of the People* (*San min zhuyi*), will permit one to come across the phrase *datong* (i.e. "great harmony"), for example, in the title of one of Sun's lectures. On the contrary, the phrase *xiaokang* (*i.e.* "petty welfare") is missing.[16] Indeed, the formalization of Sun's vision is due to Chiang Kai-Chek (Jiang Jieshi), who not only theorized the transition from one kind of society to another, but who experimented with this theory rather successfully in Taiwan.[17] Such a legacy might be rather wearisome to the communist hierarchs, as the generalissimo's visions were somewhat premonitory of theirs.

To uphold his own conception of great harmony, Mao Zedong put China to fire and sword (Great Leap Forward, Cultural Revolution, etc.). In the aftermath of Mao's death, Deng Xiaoping started to utilize the notion of "petty welfare" in order to improve the standard of living of the population. The faintness of this initial endeavor was obvious from the circumstances of its first public formulation. When Deng Xiaoping met with Japan's Prime Minister Ōhira Masayoshi on December 6, 1979, he stated that China's goal was not to modernize and to develop herself as Japan had done, but to become a modest "haven of petty welfare" (*xiaokang zhi jia*). This anecdote was widely reported, for example, in the *Renmin ribao* (*The People's Daily*), on February 26, 2003 (p. 12). This idea was integrated into a new conception of China's socioeconomic development that should be a stage-by-stage process. Deng Xiaoping disclosed the three stages China had to go through (*san bu zou*) when he met with Spain's Vice-Prime Minister Alfonso Guerra González on April 30, 1987. First, China's GDP per capita should reach US $500 before the end of the 1980s. Second, China's GDP per capita should double and reach US $1,000 by the end of the twentieth century. Third, China's GDP per capita should reach US $4,000 during the next thirty to fifty years (Deng 1993: 226).

At the end of 2000, the Chinese government considered that China had crossed the "threshold of petty welfare" (*xiaokang shuiping*). As far as economic development and intellectual life were concerned, China was successful. Regarding material life, demographic issues, and environmental matters, some endeavor was still needed (the rate of achievement of each goal was 96 percent, 90 percent, and 92 percent, respectively). Moreover, the overall rate of achievement of city dwellers was far more successful than the rate of people living in the countryside (96 percent and 93 percent, respectively). Some goals suffered important setbacks. First, the infant mortality rate remained rather high (about 3 percent) and its related goal was only achieved up to 60 percent. Further, female excess mortality and protein diet were far below their target (86 percent for each) (Tongji ju 2004a, 2004b). In addition to these dissatisfactions, the deterioration of social inequalities required policy adjustments.

Two years later, Jiang Zemin, in the report he delivered at the 16th Party Congress on November 8, 2002, took advantage of the notion of "petty welfare" and launched a policy aiming at "building a petty welfare state for all" (*quanmian jianshe xiaokang shehui*). This new policy initiated a major change "from an average state of petty welfare to a petty welfare state for all" (*cong zongti xiaokang dao quanmian xiaokang*). Its goal was no longer to reach a level (*shuiping*) of petty welfare but to build a society (*shehui*) with petty welfare; this meant a shift from economic growth to socioeconomic development (Jiang 2002: 3rd part). In 2005, Wen Jiabao, when he presented the Eleventh Five-Year Plan (2006–2010), explained this policy change (2006–2010) (Xinhua 2005b).

The very title of the Eleventh Plan, *guihua*, not *jihua*, obviously expressed this new course. First of all, it showed a clear-cut break with the socialist past and its soviet-like economic planning that the former designation *jihua* denoted. Second, this new plan has set a new target: As much as the former designation reminded the computation of figures (*ji*), the latter evokes the drafting of norms (*gui*). Quite illustrative of the new deal is the following quotation from the well-known economist Wu Jinglian.[18] At the Forum for Building a State of Petty Welfare held in Peking on December 8–9, 2005 (RMRB 2005a), Wu made it clear that the "building of petty welfare for all" (*quanmian xiaokang jianshe*) is closely correlated with the "pattern of growth" (*zengzhang fangshi*), and therefore the current pattern has to endure drastic changes (*zhuanbian*) if China is to achieve her goals (RMRB 2005b, 2005c):

> Why were the rulers of our country unable to change the patterns of growth in spite of their renewed statements during the last few years? Why, on the contrary, did they still increase its pace and were attached to the old patterns of growth combined with the traditional socialist industrialization mode? . . . In the past, when we discussed our development goals, we only emphasized the quantitative growth of our GDP and disregarded other goals. Today, we must advance our understanding of development. This does not mean that quantitative growth is of no importance; actually, the building of a state of petty welfare depends on quantitative growth. The main issue is not whether we have to sustain a high rate of growth but which pattern of growth has to be fixed and subsequently, if such high rates of growth are sustainable.

The obvious need for a shift from mere economic growth to socioeconomic development has been backed up by the gradual emergence of a new political philosophy that should tackle demands of distributive justice and should ensure social peace. Despite being quite conservative on political questions, Hu Jintao—the current secretary general of the Chinese Communist Party—could not but initiate this change. On February 19, 2005, Hu spoke to top provincial leaders during a seminar where he claimed to be aware that overcoming contradictions (*maodun*) that stemmed from economic growth would require the building of a harmonious society (*jiangou hexie shehui*). Indeed, Hu Jintao's speech was not disclosed before June 26, 2005 (RMRB 2005d). Hu stated that he had been appropriating utopian socialism and that he had traced a descent for his proposal back to Charles Fourier's *Harmonie universelle* published in 1803 in the *Bulletin de Lyon*.[19] Hu's harmony results from actions taken according to the Law, from being urbane with others, and from living in a "civilized" (*wenming*) society. This is the foundation of the following slogan: "Build a harmonious society and praise social civility" (*jiangou hexie shehui cujin shehui wenming*). Obviously, a sort of rejuvenated Confucianism influences Hu's so-called Fourierism.

Yet it is necessary to try a tack other than any Western conception, as China, are we said, is searching for a state of harmony (literally "harmonious society," *hexie shehui*), whereas the West is looking for social peace (literally "social harmony," *shehui hexie*). To make it even clearer, the creator of this casuistic distinction, Li Chen (in charge of the Urban Culture Research Centre of Shanghai's Huaxia Social Development Research Institute), claims that Western sociological theories mainly emphasize "social competition, social networks, state regulation, and social order" and thus sharply contrast with the Chinese concept of harmony (*hexie*) (CCTV 2005). With China's uniqueness being asserted once again, the search for origins restarts. In her recent book, Professor Qin Ling (in charge of the Philosophical Research Department of the Party School of Tianjin's Chinese Communist Party) strived to show how deeply anchored in Confucianism this pursuit of harmony is. Each occurrence of the phrase in Confucius's *Analects* is quoted and receives a lengthy explanation. Yet most of the quotations are rather insignificant with the exception of the following one (Qi 2006: 12; Couvreur 1895: 74–75): "Rites' observance is crucial to harmony. [Hence] searching harmony for harmony's sake, i.e. disregarding the rites, should not be done."

Today, these "rites" are unmistakably formulated by the Chinese Communist Party. Praising harmony is thus to place Confucius in the service of Chinese hierarchs. Qin Ling has been obviously commissioned with this task: In the last part of her book, she has shown that the thoughts of Mao Zedong, Deng Xiaoping, Jiang Zemin, and Hu Jintao have been keeping up with Confucius's conception of harmony. Xinhua's caricaturist eventually ventured to call the Sage from Qufu "Money-spinning Confucius" (*Kongzi cheng yaoqianshu*) (Xinhua 2005c).

This does not mean that Chinese people have gone Confucian once again. The *2005 Bluebook on Education* reported on a recent survey of public attitudes toward, and understanding of the teaching of Chinese classics (*guoxue*) (Yang 2005: 429–432). It is worth noting that 77 percent of the people polled did not have the faintest idea of what the study of the Chinese classics was. Asked what might represent *guoxue* if it was to be understood as the study of the Chinese traditional culture, 56 percent answered they did not know, while 44 percent believed it was the study of the Confucian canon. Asked whether *guoxue* embodied any threat to China's modernization, 60 percent judged it as rather or very risky. Formerly, Confucian values had taught ways of life, such as family ethics. Today, filial piety, for example, has been so loosely endorsed and so rarely practiced that the Chinese Central Television (CCTV) was charged to broadcast spots and programs that had to urge grownup children of elderly people to care for their parents. Indeed, this further use of Confucian values hides the government's inability to guarantee the payment of adequate retirement pensions.

The promotion of Confucian values has given other advantages to the government. The affirmation of harmony is meant to mirror the party rulers' concern for all social groups. According to official figures, in 2005, illegal acts by displaced villagers, unpaid migrant laborers, and laid-off workers resulted in 87,000 serious "disturbances of public order" (SCMP January 20, 2006). Threatened by this important social discontent, the leadership has been eager to consolidate its power, to claim its legitimacy, and to designate a scapegoat. On September 19, 2004, Hu Jintao gave a speech (Kaifang 2004):

> For some time, hostile forces abroad and their media have wantonly attacked our leaders and the political system. Subsequently, our domestic media upholding the flag of political reform have spread Western bourgeois parliamentary democracy, human rights, freedom of the press, etc. To the U.S.-led international monopoly capital, the collapse of the [former] Soviet Union and the Soviet Communist Party was an ideological venture from the very beginning. Their decay does not prove the failure of socialism and Marxism . . . [but] results from Gorbatchev's assault, that favored their "Westernization" and "bourgeois liberalization."

Hu Jintao seems here to embrace New Left intellectuals' advocacy of a Chinese substitute for a neo-liberal market economy that caused the breakdown of welfare systems, a broadening income gap between the wealthiest and the poorest, and a worsening environmental predicament not only in China but also in the United States and other developed countries.[20] Insofar as political necessity does not know any law, Confucius became Marx's best ally. One could finally ask whether China's prospective identity is symbolized by Marx wearing the rags of Confucius.

Insofar as the Confucian revivals are continued by a discourse on Asian values, they seem to give up themselves. If the heterogeneous group of countries that build Asia were to subscribe to a common way of thinking, every faith (including the Christian ones), every political philosophy (including the Marxist one) should convey the same teachings even if they come in a variety of forms—as Nobel Prize Amartya Sen suggested (Sen 1999: 304–306). The wealth gap between the West and the rest of the world is far too huge to be explained by culture alone (cf. de Soto 2005: 13). Such statements inescapably question any form of syncretism as well as the likelihood of Asian values, and lead us to accept universal human values as a fact. Confucian "fundamentalism" that would claim to fight against Weber's thesis would in fact encourage Herman Kahn's fancy prophecies, advocating that Confucian values were the modern-day Protestant ethics (Kahn 1979). "Confucian capitalism," "Asian miracle" (World Bank *dixit*), "Asian values," and other Kahnian myths, no matter if in the West or in Asia, distort the understanding of economic development, regarding it as the triumph of political regimes whose political measures are expected to be fully justified as they are allegedly rooted in cultural continuity and historical depth.

NOTES

1. "Returning to one's roots is also a sort of modernity" (my translation).
2. *Literari* in the Jesuit idiom. There is no convenient translation of the ambiguous Chinese term *ru*; its usual interpretation is rooted in a chapter from the Chinese Herodotus (Sima Qian) accounts, which narrate the life of eminent scholars: *Rulin liezhuan* [Tales from the forest of *ru*]; cf. Jensen (2003: 159–215). The title of this chapter is indeed indebted to Lionel Jensen's book title.
3. Such a cryptic title—at least for the nonsinologist—refers to a chapter made up of a series of biographies of wealthy men written by the great historian Sima Qian.
4. To present a good translation, I have taken up Mark Elvin's wording (Elvin 1986: 124).
5. The "well-field system" was an idealized system of land tenure; the distribution of the land was done according to a scheme reminiscent of the Chinese character for *well*, which looks like the # symbol.
6. The French language does not need such a neologism, for it has *confucianisme* and *christianisme* (cf. Jensen 2003: 186–187).
7. The Chinese wording is not exactly the same; Chen's institute should literally be read as "Institute of Confucianism" [*Kongjiao xueyuan*] and not "Confucius Institute" [*Kongzi xueyuan*].
8. He learned English when he was still a teenager, and then achieved his education in Hong Kong, where later he graduated as a medical doctor (western medicine).
9. In mandarin, "foreign businessmen" and "injuries" are homophonous (*wai shang*).
10. American people of Chinese extraction, as Du Weiming (Tu Wei-Ming) and Yu Yingshi (Yü Ying-Shih).
11. The three quotations are from the titles and the back cover of two mainstream books on China's economic situation: Lin (2003) and Wu (2004).
12. Lectures given at the École des Hautes Études en Sciences Sociales (Paris) in 2002.
13. Gross domestic product per capita measured on a purchasing power parity basis is about US $4,580 in China, amounting to merely 17 percent of France's US $26,920.
14. An interview with Zhang Houyi (November 17, 2005). Zhang Houyi is an emeritus senior research fellow at the Academy of Social Sciences of China; he is the editor of the annual bluebook of private enterprises.
15. To explain the calculation: The number of regularly registered city dwellers (i.e., having a traditional *hukou*) is added to the number of those having a long-term residence permit; all other people are counted as country dwellers (Ru 2005: 197).
16. I have searched a digitalized Chinese version of Sun's work to test for the presence or absence of the two phrases. The digitalized text is available at http://freeman2.com/roc00001.htm. The fourth lecture is entitled *Minzu zhuyi shi shijie datong de jichu* [Nationalism as the basis of a global harmony].

17. Chiang Kai-Chek wrote *Two Additional Chapters on Education and Lei-sure Attached to the Principle of Livehood* [*Minsheng zhuyi yule liang pian bushu*]]; cf. http://freeman2.com/roc00002.ht.

18. Wu holds multiple positions, the most preeminent of which are senior research fellow at the Developmental Research Centre of the State Council of the PRC and member of the Standing Committee of the Chinese People's Political Consultative Conference. He also teaches Economics at the Academy of Social Sciences of China and at China Europe International Business School in Shanghai.

19. This Chinese translation is mistaken. The expression should be translated by "global harmony" (*quan shijie hexie*, literally: "harmony on the whole world"), while Fourier meant the harmony between human beings.

20. Unlike most China's dissidents and human rights activists, New Left intellec-tuals are confident that the CCP can solve China's problems.

REFERENCES

Certeau, Michel. 1975. *L'écriture de l'histoire*. Paris: Gallimard.

Chen, Dongxia. 2004. *Xinjiapo yu Hanguo rujia lunli daode jiaoyu de bujiao ji qishi* [Comparison of and Lessons from Singaporean and South Korean Teach-ings of Confucian Ethics]. http://www.nciae.edu.cn/wlfw/wlzy/ffw/shownews. asp?id=209, accessed January 4, 2007.

Chen, Huanzhang [Chen Huan-Chang]. 1974. *The Economic Principles of Con-fucius and His School*. New York: Gordon Press (originally published by Long-mans, New York, 1911, in the *Columbia University Studies in Political Science* series).

Chen, Qingsong. 1991. "Pingxi xinjiapo 'rujia lunli' kecheng" [Assessing the Singa-porean 'Confucian ethics' Primer], Guoli bianyiguan tongxun, 14; see also http://www.nciae.edu.cn/wlfw/wlzy/ ffw/shownews.asp?id=209, accessed November 29, 2006.

China Central Television. 2005. "Xifang shehui lilun zhong de 'hexie shehui' shi zenyang?" [What about the Western theory of "social harmony"?] http://www .cctv.com/news/china/20050908/100043.shtml, accessed December 14, 2006.

Couvreur, Séraphin. 1949. *Entretiens de Confucius—Les quatre livres*. Paris: Catha-sia (reprint of the edition from 1895).

Couvreur, Séraphin. 1967. *Cheu King, textes chinois avec une double traduction en français et en latin, une introduction et un vocabulaire*. Taizhong: Kuangchi Press (originally published by Imprimerie de la mission catholique, Ho Kien Fou, 1896).

Couvreur, Séraphin. 1950. *Mémoires sur les bienséances et les cérémonies*. Paris: Cathasia (reprint of the edition from 1913).

Cui, Xiaoli. 1936. "Zhejiang Yinxian nongcun zhong 'hui' de zuzhi" [Tontines orga-nization in Yinxian villages, Zhejiang province]. *Dongfang zazhi* [Dong Fang Magazine] 33 (6): 118–120.

Deng, Xiaoping. 1993. *Deng Xiaoping wenxuan* [Selected Works of Deng Xiaop-ing]. Beijing: Renmin chubanshe, vol. 3.

Duara, Prasenjit. 1993. "De-Constructing the Chinese Nation." *Australian Journal of Chinese Affairs* 30: 1–26.

Elvin, Mark. 1986. "The Double Disavowal." Pp. 112–140 in *China and Europe in the Twentieth Century*, ed. Shaw Yu-Ming. Taipei: Institiue of International Relations.

Fan, Heping. 1995. *Ruxue yu riben moshi* [Confucian Studies and the Japanese Model]. Taibei: Wunan tushuchuban gongsi.

Fan, Xufeng. 2003. "Zhonghua chuantong meide geyan" [Aphorisms relating to Ancient Chinese Virtues]. *Zhongguo jiaoyu bao* [Education Daily], February 19, p. 1, http://www.jyb.com.cn/gb/2003/02/19/zy/jryw/1.htm, accessed January 4, 2007.

G8. 2003. Declaration at the Time of the 2003 G8 Summit. http://www.g8.fr/evian/english/navigation/2003_g8_summit/summit_documents/fostering_growth_and_promoting_a_responsible_market_economy__a_g8_declaration.html, accessed November 24, 2006.

Guoli bianyiguan [Institute for Compilation and Translation]. 1987. "Huifu zhongguo guyou daode" [Recovering old Chinese Values]. Pp. 1–8 in *Guomin zhongxue guowen—di san ce* [Chinese Literature Textbook—vol. 3]. Taibei: Guoli bianyiguan.

Guoli bianyiguan [Institute for Compilation and Translation]. 1994. "Gudai xinyong de gushi" [Some old Stories about Trust]. Pp. 33–36 in *Guomin xiaoxue guoyu keben—liunianji* (Chinese Reader for Primary Schools—6th Year). Taibei: Guoli bianyiguan.

Hansen, Valerie. 1995. *Negotiating Daily Life in Traditional China. How Ordinary People Used Contracts 600–1400*. New Haven, CT: Yale University Press.

Kaitang zazhi (Open Magazine). 2004. "Hu Jintao si zhong quan hui jianghua baoguang yanli daji ziyouhua jue bu shou ruan" [In his speech to the fourth plenary session, Hu Jintao called for a fierce crackdown on liberalism]. http://www.open.com.hk/2003_12news1.htm, accessed January 2, 2007 (published in Hong Kong in December 2004).

Kahn, Herman. 1979. *World Economic Development. 1979 and Beyond*. Boulder, CO: Westview Press.

Jensen, Lionel. 2003. *Manufacturing Confucianism. Chinese Traditions and Universal Civilization*. Durham, NC: Duke University Press.

Jiang, Zemin. 2002. *Jiang Zemin zai Zhongguo gongchandang di shiliu ci guojia daibiao dahui shang de baogao* [Jiang Zemin's Report at 16th Party Congress]. http://www.china.org.cn/chinese/2002/Nov/233867.htm, accessed January 4, 2007.

Li, Tingjiang. 2006. *Dazheng chuqi de Seze Rongyi yu Zhongguo* [Shibusawa Ei'ichi and China in Early Taishō Period]. Available from the web site of the Shibusawa Ei'ichi Memorial Foundation, http://www.sal.tohoku.ac.jp/~kirihara/public_html/cgi-bin/shibusawa/Li_c.pdf, accessed December 3, 2006.

Liang, Qichao. 1941a. *Yinbingshi heji (zhuanji zhi si)* [Pieces Compiled in a Studio Where I Drink Chilled Water—Collection of Dedicated Writings 4]. Shanghai: Zhonghua Shuju, vol. 3.

Liang, Qichao. 1941b. *Yinbingshi heji (wenji zhi shi'er)* [Pieces Compiled in a Studio Where I Drink Chilled Water—Collection of Literary Writings 12]. Shanghai: Zhonghua shuju, vol. 5.

Lin, Yifu, Justin, Fang Cai and Zhou Li. 2003. *The China Miracle. Development Strategy and Economic Reform*. Hong Kong: Chinese University Press.

Mill, John Stuart. 1848. *Principles of Political Economy With Some of Their Applications to Social Philosophy*. London: Longmans, Green. http://www.econlib.org/library/Mill/mlP.html, accessed November 16, 2006.

Qi, Ling. 2006. *Hexie shehui sixiang de youlai* [Origins of the Idea of "Harmonious Society"]. Tianjin: Tianjin renmin chubanshe.

Renmin ribao [People's Daily]. 2005a. "Xiaokang zhibiao mingnian chutai 2020nian renjun GDP da 2500 meiyuan" [Petty welfare indicators to be published next year. In 2020 the per capita GDP will reach 2,500 U.S. dollars]. http://finance.people.com.cn/GB/1037/3930254.html, accessed January 4, 2007.

Renmin ribao [People's Daily]. 2005b. "Wu Jinglian: zengzhang fangshi zhuanbian yu quanmian xiaokang jianshe" [Wu Jinglian: Reform the mode of growth and

118   *Thierry Pairault*

erect a petty welfare]. http://theory.people.com.cn/GB/49154/49155/3953348. html, accessed January 4, 2007.

Renmin ribao [People's Daily]. 2005c. "Zengzhang fangshi zhuanbian yu quanmian xiaokang jianshe" [Reform the mode of growth and erect a petty welfare] http://real.people.com.cn:8080/ramgen/1/ zht/zt2005120806.rm, accessed January 4, 2007.

Renmin ribao [People's Daily]. 2005d. "Hu Jintao: Tigao goujian shehui zhuyi hexie shehui de nengli" [Hu Jintao: Promote our ability to erect a socialist and harmonious society] http://theory.people.com.cn/GB/49169/ 49171/3500334. html, accessed January 4, 2007.

Riegel, Klaus-Georg. 2000. "Inventing Asian Traditions: The Controversy between Lee Kuan Yew and Kim Dae Jung." *Development and Society* 29 (1): 75–96.

Robinson, Joan. 1933. *The Economics of Imperfect Competition.* London: Macmillan.

Ru, Xin, Lu Xueyi, and Li Peilin, eds. 2005. *2006 nian : Zhongguo shehui xingshi fenxi yu yuce* [Analysis and Forecast on China's Social Developement—2006]. Beijing: Shehui kexue wenxian chubanshe.

Sen, Amartya. 1999. *Un nouveau modèle économique: Développement, justice, liberté.* Paris: Odile Jacob.

Smith, Adam. 1759. *The Theory of Moral Sentiments.* London: A. Millar. http://olldownload.libertyfund.org/Texts/LFBooks/Smith0232/GlasgowEdition/MoralSentiments/PDFs/0141–01_Pt02_Part1.pdf, accessed November 24, 2006.

Soto, Hernando de. 2005. *Le mystère du capital: Pourquoi le capitalisme triomphe en Occident et échoue partout ailleurs?* Paris: Flammarion.

South China Morning Post. 2006. "Putonghua becomes a top export commodity", accessed November 14, 2006. "Unemployment drives job-hunters across the delta", accessed December 28, 2005. "New jobs in cities top 10m for the first time", accessed December 24, 2006. "Incidents of social unrest hit 87,000", accessed January 20, 2006. http://www.scmp.com.

Sun, Wen [Sun Yat-Sen]. 1924. *Minzu zhuyi di liu jiang* [Sixth Conference on Nationalism]. http://www.folkdoc.idv.tw/classic/p02/ba/ba01/b6.htm, accessed January 4, 2007.

Tongji ju [National Bureau of Statistics]. 2004a. Xiaokang shenghuo biaozhun ji 1980–2000 nian wonghe pinjiazhi [Petty welfare standards and their value between 1980 and 2000]. http://www.stats.gov.cn/tjfx/ztfx/zjxk/P020040215082510057 6434. htm, accessed January 4, 2007.

Tongji ju [National Bureau of Statistics]. 2004b. *2000 nian Zhongguo xiaokang jincheng* [Progress toward Petty Welfare achieved in 2000], http://www.stats.gov. cn/tjfx/ztfx/zjxk/P020040215082510058 7562.htm, accessed January 4, 2007.

United Nations Development Programme. 2005. *China Human Development Report—Human Development with Equity.* Beijing: UNDP and CDRF.

United Nations Development Programme. 2006. *Human Development Report 2006—Beyond Scarcity: Power, Poverty and the Global Water Crisis.* New York: UNDP.

Wang, Dianqing. 2003. "*Da zhong xiao xue zhonghua minzu youxiu chuantong daode jiaoyu shiyan yanjiu*" yanjiu baogao [Evaluation of 'Some Experiments about Teaching the exceptional Chinese Traditional Virtues in Primary, Secondary Schools and Universities']. http://www.meide.org/3/9/1353.html, accessed January 4, 2007.

Wang, Yu. 2004. "Our Way: Building Socialism with Chinese Characteristics." *Political Affairs* January (online edition http://www.politicalaffairs.net/article/articleview/36/1/1), accessed January 4, 2007.

Wenhua tushu gongsi [Cultural Library ltd], ed. 1984. San xi Bai Mudan" [Thrice-fondled Bai Mudan]. Pp. 134–136 in *Zhongguo minjian tongsu xïaoshuo* [Chinese folk tales]. Taibei, Wenhua tushu gongsi.

Will, Pierre-Étienne. 1994. "Développement quantitatif et développement qualitatif en Chine à la fin de l'époque impériale." *Annales HSS* 4 (49): 863–902.

Will, Pierre-Étienne. 1999. "Discussions about the Market-Place and the Market Principle in Eighteenth-Century Guangdong." Pp. 323–389 in *Zhongguo haiyang fazhan shi lunwenji (di qi ji)* [Memoirs on the History of China's Maritime Expansion (vol. 7)].Taibei: Academia Sinica.

World Bank. 1993. *The East Asian Miracle: Economic Growth and Public Policy.* New York: Oxford University Press.

World Bank. 2006. *World Development Report, 2006.* http://siteresources.worldbank.org/INTWDR2006/Resources/ WDR_on_Equity_FinalOutline_July_public.pdf, accessed January 4, 2007.

Wu, Yanrui. 2004. *China's Economic Growth. A Miracle With Chinese Characteristics.* London: Routledge/Curzon.

Xinhua News Agency. 2005a. "Guojia tongjiju diaocha xianshi chengzhen jumin shouru chaju da 10.7bei" [A NBS survey showed that the gap between urban residents income reached almost elevenfold]. http://news.xinhuanet.com/fortune/2005–06/18/content_3103316.htm, accessed January 2, 2006

Xinhua News Agency. 2005b. "Zhonggong zhongyang guanyu zhiding 'shiyiwu' guihua de jianyi" [CPC Central Committee on the drafting of the "11th Five-Year" plan]. http://news.xinhuanet.com/politics/2005–10/18/content_3640318.htm, accessed January 2, 2007.

Xinhua News Agency. 2005c. "Kongzi chengle yaoqianshu" [Money-spinning Confucius]. http://news.xinhuanet.com/school/2005–10/03/content_3556609.htm, accessed January 2, 2007

Xinhua News Agency. 2006. "Kongzi xueyuan heyi kaibian quanqiu?" [Why are Confucius Institutes blooming everywhere?]. http://www.he.xinhuanet.com/yuedu/2006–04/21/content_6810777.htm, accessed January 2, 2007.

Yan, Fu. 1902. *Yu Liang Qichao shu san feng* [Correspondance between Yan Fu and Liang Qichao]. http://rwxy.tsinghua.edu.cn/rwfg/ydsm/ydsm-qw/00102/003.htm, accessed January 4, 2007.

Yang, Dongping, ed. 2005. *2005 nian: Zhongguo jiaoyu fazhan baogao* [The Development Report of China's Education—2005]. Beijing: Shehui kexue wenxian chubanshe.

Zakaria, Fareed. 1994. "Culture Is Destiny. A Conversation With Lee Kuan Yew." *Foreign Affairs* 73 (2): 109–126.

Zhu, Junrui. 2004. *Liang Qichao jingji sixiang yanjiu* [Study on Liang Qichao's Economic Thought]. Beijing: Zhongguo shehui kexue chubanshe.

6 The Export of Cultural Commodities as Impression Management

The Case of Thailand

Frederick F. Wherry

The global interplay of culture (Pieterse 1994: 117–118) and the opportunities for impression management it affords (Wherry 2006, 2008) have increased in number and intensity as a result of globalization. In 2003, the world export of furniture crafted by artisans totaled 16.6 billion, ceramics 1.4 billion, candles and tapers 1.4 billion, and artificial flowers 1.3 billion in current US dollars (World Trade Organization and UNCTAD 2004). Moreover, in 1998 international tourism accounted for 29.3 billion current US dollars in Southeast Asia alone (World Tourism Organization 2003). In the global market for cultural commodities and tourism, cultural objects, the artisans crafting them, and the consumers curious about "exotic" and "authentic" items have become the supporters, dramaturgical props, actors, and audiences engaged in presenting a particular face to the world and in applauding the presentation. How do individual artisans, private export organizations, and government export agencies manage the image presented to the importing world and what are the constraints on its management?

The question of impression management lies at the heart of the global market for cultural goods and services. Erving Goffman offered the concept of impression management to explain how individuals accomplish meaningful encounters. Most importantly, the performers depend on the willingness of the audience to protect the performance—to ignore inconsistencies or small gaffs, to give the performers the benefit of the doubt. The performers exercise tact in response to the tact the audience exercises, making the performance a dynamic management of symbols and meanings. The accomplishment of meaningful encounters through impression management becomes especially important and more complex in a global environment where "migrants and media, tourists and scientists are looking permanently for innovations in other cultures and are interested in 'exotic' and 'authentic' cultures" (Schuerkens 2003: 219). How do cultural producers present themselves as exotic and/or authentic when exporting their handicrafts, their artworks, "their music, their literature, their spirituality, or healing methods to countries of the northern hemisphere" (Schuerkens 2003: 219)? To what extent do local actors influence the understandings that tourists and handicraft importers have about the authenticity of local productions?

And why are some presentations of authenticity more likely to be performed and in turn believed?

As a strategy undertaken by individuals, impression management seemingly occurs outside of, while being wholly dependent on, the social context of the individual's performance (Goffman 1959, 1961). As the individual attempts to maintain face—to construct for her or his audience a positive evaluation of her or his performance—the individual finds her/himself selecting a role. The role repertoire itself is embedded in a social history that gives the role its salience for the actor and the audience. To the extent that national institutions have played a role in constructing the role repertoire, one can say that national institutions have engaged in impression management in general and in role repertoire construction in particular. As the curators of the museum of national history and art assemble exhibits of the different phases of the nation's history and as similar exhibits tour the World's Fairs, the nation-state actively promotes a particular image of its essentialist self. The images become branded by the national tourism agency, which selects particular images of what it means to be a member of a national territory and what resources that territory has to offer outsiders. Not all government institutions actively engage in impression management, and within those institutions that do, identifiable presentation teams take the show on the road. In other words, a homologous presentation of self happens at a national and at an individual level. Of course, there is a great deal of variation in who participates in impression management, in how much they deviate from the standard "line" of who-we-are-as-a-people, and in the types of changes made to the presentation off the cuff. These derivations call into question how the researcher should treat "negative" evidence; are all indications that impression management does not matter for the trade of cultural commodities simply exceptions to the rule? Do all entrepreneurs agree on how they should perform? These questions emphasize that impression management is a process in which local improvisations influence and are influenced by nonlocal expectations. The explanatory value of this process for pathways to success and for the apparent inequalities in cultural commodity markets depends on careful empirical investigation.

In the market for handicrafts, impression management is likely to be an explicit strategy for increasing the economic value of cultural goods and services. To demonstrate how impression management works in the handicraft sector at the level of the national state and of individual entrepreneurs, this chapter explores the case of Thailand. Thailand exported US$ 377 million in furniture made by artisans in 2003. Two other countries whose hand-crafted furniture can frequently be found as ethnic furniture and in handicraft stores, Brazil and Mexico, had export totals of US$ 235 million US$ 198 million, respectively. In the export of ceramics, Thailand ranked fourth in the world; in the export of artificial flowers, Thailand ranked third. In short, Thailand qualifies as a major player in the handicrafts market, making the sector an excellent site for observing "global intercultural interplay" (Pieterse 1994).

This chapter takes Goffman's framework out of its original context of person-to-person encounters and deploys it at the level of the nation-state and national membership symbols as well as the level of artisans and buyers interacting at the local level. The micro-to-macro transition requires a number of caveats. First, one has to identify specific government agencies and their agents (people) in order to see how impression management is carried out at the level of the nation-state. At the same time, one has to identify specific artisans and importers to see how protective strategies are deployed (or not) at the first point of sale. The impression management framework helps us understand what images the nation-state and the artisans are trying to portray, and our observation of their interactions with buyers helps us understand the micro-interactions in which these impressions get worked out (or not). Viviana Zelizer (1999: 212) writes: "Seen from the top, economic transactions connect with broad national symbolic meanings and institutions. Seen from the bottom, economic transactions are highly differentiated, personalized, and local, meaningful to particular relations."

This chapter begins with a modified explication of impression management in cultural commodity markets. Then using historical and qualitative materials, the chapter presents how Thai government officials have engaged in impression management to establish a reputation within the community of nations and to compete more effectively in global markets. Leaving the macro level, the chapter dwells at the micro level to explain how impression management works on the ground. In the conclusion, I underline the implications for engaging in culture work to promote cultural industries in a global cultural market structured as a caste system.

TRADING IMPRESSIONS

Rather than ask what cultural resources the country holds and what special talents its citizens possess as an indication of comparative advantage, I ask what impression the country's leaders wish to make and what perceptions foreigners already have about the country's cultural and human capital. By consuming a country's exported goods and by consuming the country's cultural heritage as tourists, outsiders provide the audience with whom the polity does what Goffman calls face-work. The state creates and maintains face—a positive evaluation of itself during its encounters with others. To maintain face, the government facilitates (or restricts) the export of cultural commodities and encourages (or discourages) the consumption of cultural goods and services by international travelers as well as its own citizens.

Nation-states learned early on that you are what you make, and being known as a "banana" republic is not a badge of honor. To create and maintain face, some governments have been careful to avoid the export of stigma symbols only. By this, I mean the export of agriculture or minerals that mark the country as a place where things are found, not created: a place unaware of the "enlightenment" or if aware, perhaps resigned to the impossibility of its attainment. Stocks of cultural symbols or practices that mark one's country as somehow too ghettoed or too ethnic are not resources that the national government will "see" as marketable, especially if the government is bent on becoming assimilated or acculturated into the global community of nations. For countries such as Thailand that can be praised for their unique cultural traditions and for their capacity to fit in with the rest of the global community, cultural commodities emerge as viable dramaturgical props in the enactment of impression management.

Rather than start with what economists tell us about markets, I start with what sociologists say about encounters and interactions. I use Goffman's work as my starting point for examining the history of the handicraft market in Thailand. Goffman used the metaphor of the actors on the stage and their interactions with the audience to demonstrate how individuals engage in impression management. First of all, it helps that the actors are not in search of a script. Each knows his or her role in the play and no one betrays the rest of the cast by deliberately enacting a foreign script. The cast and its director discipline the actors to make sure that they stick to the script. And the team is circumspect in preparing for their performance, so that they minimize the elements that might derail a believable performance. As long as the audience thinks that the actors are acting in good faith, the audience forgives minor errors by pretending that such mistakes did not occur or by following improvised lines meant to bring the play back on line. The actors respond to the tact of the audience by themselves exercising tact. It is this process of acting in good faith and engaging with the reactions of one's audience that helps us better understand the dynamics of cultural markets.

Nelson H. H. Graburn recognizes that some national governments consciously engage in impression management to promote handicrafts and other cultural productions that portray a favorable image of Mexico to the international community. In *Ethnic and Tourist Arts: Cultural Expressions from the Fourth World* (1976), Graburn recognizes the noneconomic motivations of the state for promoting cultural commodities:

> The government concerns include... promoting a favorable image of regional Mexico... Mexico has long differentiated itself from European Spain and from other Latin American countries; it has glorified the arts of the conquered civilizations... [and] supports many exhibitions, collections, and museums." (Graburn 1976: 117–118)

When the Mexican government proudly supports expressions of *indigenismo*, "that which is Indian and not European" (Graburn 1976: 115), the Mexican government has undertaken boundary work to distinguish its national self from the (Spanish/European) invaders, even as the government also promotes a hybrid image of its national culture. The government uses production and export incentives to generate more of the good images—specifically, those images that mark Mexico's "natural" difference from Europe, and Mexico's pride in that difference.

Beyond the belief and pride in national identity, political and economic struggles may also influence the impressions the national government attempts to manage. Take the example of the role that shea butter has played in the nation-building project of the Ghanaian state. According to anthropologist Brenda Chalfin (2004), shea butter, an indigenous commodity, became popularized through *The Body Shop* and *L'Occitane's* advertisements of Ghanaian and other West-African women gathering shea nuts, pulverizing them, and putting the lotion to traditional uses, just as women have done for many generations. In Ghana, this indigenous commodity reflects, in part, President J. J. Rawlings's attempt to incorporate the regional identity of the north (where shea nuts are gathered) into the national identity of the Ghanaian nation. At the same time, the Ghanaian state is responding to pressures from economic interests within and outside of the nation-state as well as to the conditions of structural adjustment imposed by the International Monetary Fund and the World Bank. As a result, consumers around the world consume an image of African women, close to the earth, that seems to be wedded to a timeless African tradition. This image generates economic value for the product and a positive evaluation of local African (female) traditions.

That the government and its polity's orientations toward the economy are socially conditioned is well known. In *Economy and Society* (1978), Max Weber identifies transcendental beliefs (based in cultural traditions or religious belief) and social conventions (collective practices and rituals) as two orienting factors for economic life. Institutionally oriented studies in sociology have demonstrated how collective understandings shape the institutions that, in turn, influence economic outcomes (Biggart and Orrú 1997; Biggart and Guillen 1999; Dobbin 1994; Powell and DiMaggio 1991). Collective understandings about the national identity and the way that exports represent that identity inform the country's cultural tool kit—"symbols, stories, rituals, and world-views, which people may use in varying configurations to solve different kinds of problems" (Swidler 1986: 273). The tool kit shapes the strategies that actors are likely to pursue as well as the manner of pursuit. In Goffmanian simile, the tool kit is the script, its plot and its ethos, informing the actor of her or his role and shaping how the actors may maneuver around each other.

Indeed, historical events and the understandings that result from them influence "the types, availability, and legitimacy of actors [roles and symbols]" (Biggart and Guillen 1999: 728) salient for promoting cultural commodities. The shared understandings about one's membership in a group characterized by distinct practices, traditions, and outlooks affect how one interprets the meanings (sign-vehicles) carried along in economic transactions, such as what it means to export cultural commodities depicting courtly traditions rather than (or in conjunction with) indigenous commodities evoking images of the savannah or the "wild jungle." Cultural orientations reflect the response of the nation-state to the society of world opinion, the response of world society to the nation's performance, and the adjustments made by the nation-state in response to how the performance is being taken (Goffman 1959).

IMPLICATIONS FOR STUDYING SOCIAL CHANGE

My analysis brings culture and symbolic interaction back into the sociology of development in a way that enables us to better understand the processes of social change. The structural models offered by the dependency and world systems theorists as well as the social systems theories of the neo-functionalists have failed to capture the processes whereby collectivities and the individuals within them construct definitions of the global market situation and how these very definitions effect change. To keep myself out of the tautology of industrious, culturally rich countries doing industrious, culturally rich things, I focus on specific interactions in which old definitions of the situation are recognized, ignored, contested, and/or transformed. I stress that social interactions in particular contexts might have led to different outcomes—that the social system influences and routes, but does not pursue a teleological outcome. The framework I offer and the research strategy I pursue offer an empirical approach for understanding the complex problems of development, globalization, and social transformations.

How the nation-state defines its situation in the world community affects the likelihood that its government agencies will promote and that its entrepreneurs will pursue opportunities in the global handicraft market. In other words, it is not enough to possess stocks of symbolic capital to convert this symbolic capital into economic capital (through export promotion); the nation-state and its entrepreneurs inherit a collective understanding (orientation) of the uses (appropriation) to which different types of symbolic capital ought to be put. It is not only that former agricultural workers are being pushed out of farm, factory, and protected government employment while being pulled into handicraft production and tourist services, but it is also that both the workers and the industrialists "see" (sometimes subconsciously) the production of some types of cultural commodities as a means to protect cultural traditions and to validate a favorable cultural identity for the nation-state. There is a deep structure of inequality in the social status of different nation-states. These relative status positions come from the interstate comparison of prestige and stigma symbols accumulated during periods of war, economic struggle, and political power struggles. This enduring set of status perceptions orients the course of the country's economic development, sometimes diverting economic development energies away from those stocks of symbolic capital easily appropriated but socially stigmatized.

For example, countries willing to import the world's trash might choose not to do so because they do not want the associated stigma of the dumpster; likewise, a country fighting outsiders' perceptions that the country is backward might want to curtail the images that the country exports confirming such negative perceptions. On the other side, prestige symbols assist the country in portraying a positive image of itself. It stands to reason that some national governments will be motivated to support the production and export of material culture that both promotes economic development and presents a favorable image of the nation-state and its polity.

Economic development remains at the forefront of policy debates on export promotion, yet nation-states are responding to and developing a collective identity as well as a national economy. As Robert K. Merton (1957) reminds us, governments engaged in export promotion may be engaged in impression management either intentionally or unintentionally. It may be that policy makers promote non-cultural sectors of the economy as their initial goal but later promote cultural commodities as an emergent goal, as new opportunities and threats present themselves. Alternatively, policymakers may promote non-cultural sectors of the economy, which spill over into the cultural commodity sector, making inputs for production and infrastructure for distribution more accessible for handicraft artisans.

In middle- and low-income countries, the nation-state's and the citizens' orientation toward cultural traditions and cultural commodities privileges some groups or some courses of action over others. Such logics of action encourage divisive social discourse that often translates into sanctioned social polarities: indigenous communities known for their nobility versus those known for "savagery"; similarities versus differences from highly industrialized countries; traditional forms versus innovative designs; regionally specific traditions versus country-wide traditions. The groups and strategies sanctioned by the nation-state's cultural orientation create as much comparative advantage in the handicraft sector as do capital, labor, and knowledge.

Three ideal-typical cultural orientations toward cultural commodities manifest themselves in the strategies that states pursue to promote cultural or other commodities. The way in which nation-states orient themselves toward exporting commodities resembles the way immigrants to the United States orient themselves in order to facilitate their assimilation into the United States (Portes and Rumbaut 1996). First, the already *acculturated* nation-state takes pride in its movement from and preservation of tradition. The country's premodern traditions act as symbols of national identity, unique to the nation. When the nation-state develops a modern bureaucracy, it may keep or revive its traditions as a source of pride rather than see them as the residue from a past to be forgotten. The nation-state actively certifies its cultural traditions through its museums, its schools, and its tourism promotion agency. With a feeling of national pride, the government may invite outsiders to be in awe of sights never before seen. These certifying agents of culture help generate the foreign demand for handicrafts and signal to domestic producers that handicraft production is a modern, legitimate, and significant economic undertaking. The Thai case described in this chapter exemplifies this case (Bayly 1986).

Second, *the assimilated orientation* leads states to mimic the cultural institutions found in core countries (Meyer and Hannan 1979). Exotic traditions are deemphasized as the state highlights its movement from its traditional roots into a modern, enlightened society. The museums, schools, and tourism organizations do not highlight indigenous groups or local traditions that appear to be backward or in some other way embarrassing. Because these cases are not "success stories," the experiences of indigenous cultural industries in states that view themselves as free of indigenous "backwardness" remain largely underresearched. An example would be the indigenous pottery artisans representing the Chorotega culture but operating in Costa Rica, a nation that has *defined out*—rendered invisible—those indigenous elements in the global imagination of outsiders (Wherry 2006).

Third, what I call the reactive state highlights its differences from the model of modernity. Sometimes in response to colonization and/or to historical conflicts with the core countries, the reactive state may accentuate the cultural differences that free it from the rules by which other states are bound. In this case, the state's art galleries, schools, and tourism organizations do not mimic those of the high-income core countries. Instead, the culture-certifying institutions emphasize the incompatible cultural differences, the unique cultural symbols, and the endangered status of those symbols. Such states block the commercial circulation of culturally significant goods.

These acculturated, assimilated, and reactive orientations are ideal types that do not appear as pure forms in any nation-state. An ideal type approximates the most salient characteristics of an observable phenomenon in order to serve as a heuristic device. This typology proves its usefulness to the extent that it enables the analyst to discern why a particular state chooses some of its cultural resources for export promotion to the exclusion of other cultural resources that could also be exported.

METHODS AND DATA

Some of the data for this study come from the national census bureau, but a few key statistics are provided by other published studies. The qualitative data were compiled in a field survey of artisans in Thailand. I conducted the semistructured interviews in Thai with the assistance of four Thai research assistants. I also realized a number of interviews with some other artisans not using the interview schedule as well as with Thai exporters, community leaders, and other key informants. Snowball sampling would have exacerbated selection bias because I would have been led to prefer some networks of artisans to others. By randomly selecting artisans and other informants, I avoided any one informant's circle of reference. The multiple-entry-point strategy offered me a diverse set of views on how the handicraft communities have emerged and where the community's workshops can be found. Thus, I attenuated selection bias in my choice of key informants.

In Thailand, the major source of my archival data is Chiang Mai University library's Lanna Cultural Collection in the university's main library. These archival sources offered limited information on my study communities, and the newspaper clippings contained therein were not collected systematically. Because the information contained in the archive was not better for other villages whose organization it described, I have no reason to believe that the scope of the information about the villages in the archives reflects the quality or authenticity of those villages. It most likely reflects resource constraints. I consulted existing studies on the topic, especially a recent economic analysis of a Tawai village (Luechai and Siroros 2002) and an anthropological analysis of the San Pa Tong district (Jamaree 1996).

PRESENTATION TEAMS AT THE WORLD'S FAIRS

From historical accounts comes evidence that presentation teams, financed and assembled by national governments, acted strategically to promote particular images of their cultural identity. One sees impression management underway at the World's Fairs, where the community of nations gathered together observed one another's performances and carried away written accounts of who had advanced, who stagnated, who approached "civilization," who "savagery."

Thai historian Thongchai emphasizes that the Thais entered the World's Fair in order to perform a symbolic battle and that they understood that the event offered a tournament in which the *savage, barbaric, civilized,* and *enlightened* represented the four stages of cultural development. As much as possible, Thailand wanted outsiders to consider their kingdom as "civilized," but to accomplish this goal, the Thais had to distinguish themselves from the "barbaric" and the "savage." They had to both tantalize outsiders with Thailand's exotica and also gain recognition for Thailand's scientific progress and its similarities to the "civilized" and the "enlightened" world—the top two categories of the civilization scale. In other words, the Thais have preserved their culture by adapting it to the globalizing pressures coming from the West and by performing in a language and in a style that the West understands.

To walk this fine line between the exotic and the scientifically advanced, Thailand chose to ignore the financial constraints that at times might have prevented the country from participating in the World's Fair. The Kingdom of Siam did not shy away from sending "a village, people, and a dancing troupe" whenever the funds could be spared:

> In most cases, Siam displayed crafts, arts, and natural products from all over the country. . . . On the other hand, Siam usually took the opportunity to show its technological progress in such areas as postal and telegraphic services, railways, or the first modern map made in Siam. (Thongchai 2000: 541)

Although the fair offered the colonizing powers justification for subjugating "savage" peoples, the Thai proudly participated because they had never been colonized, but they had achieved economic and social development on their own terms, marking them as a "civilized" (though not enlightened) country.

To guard their status as a "civilized" country, the Thai delegation practiced dramaturgical circumspection in the location of its exhibit relative to other types of nation-states at the World's Fair. Usually, Thailand found itself among the independent countries of the Far East. Sometimes, Thailand found itself "among the exotic, the half-civilized, or the inferior civilizations, such as among Haiti and the Caribbean islands at the Chicago Fair" (Thongchai 2000: 541). Only when the Paris Fair organizers assigned Thailand a place among the colonies in 1900 did the Thai delegation insist on being moved, and moved to a place among the non-colonized nations. That Thailand was *never* colonized, there could be no confusion.

Participation in international exhibitions produced objective knowledge about national cultures and about progress. Such knowledge enabled the colonizers to rule without too much outright opposition. In the colonizer's representation of the world was a "realness" that verified the position of the subordinate relative to the superordinate. In his discussion of how Egypt was represented at the World Fairs, Timothy Mitchell writes:

> "England is at present the greatest Oriental Empire which the world has ever known," proclaimed the president of the 1892 Orientalist Congress... "She knows not only how to conquer, but how to rule." The endless spectacles of the world-as-exhibition were... by their technique of rendering imperial truth and cultural difference in "objective" form, the means of its production. (Mitchell 1989: 222)

The representations of the World Fairs also served an important political function in the heart of colonial countries. In her discussion of India, the East India Company, and the British Empire, Carol Breckenridge highlights the timing of the first World Fair in 1851; it brought the East to the attention of the British public and generated support for and fascination with the costly expansion of the British empire. Over time, the World's Fairs set the stage for the commodification of the exotic in the global marketplace (Karp and Lavine 1991).

PRESENTATION TEAMS AT TODAY'S
PRIVATE-SECTOR FAIRS

From the state-sponsored World's Fairs, the representations have moved to the international craft, gift, and furniture fairs. The fairs serve as a place for the handicraft entrepreneurs to be reminded of their position within the hierarchy of value and to challenge that position. Mark Narongsak, the Vice-President of the Northern Organization of Handicraft Manufacturers and Exporters (NOHMEX), reports:

> [At] the Bangkok International Gifts (BIG) . . . two years ago we [the members of NOHMEX] tried to make a common area where we mixed together ceramics, furniture, lamps, and other handicrafts instead of each person having a separate booth. We made a nice, integrated display.... Lots of buyers came to our stand because it had everything there together. Then last year, our booth was very big. Now [our elders have] come to join us and we have about 180 factories or small entrepreneurs who have just started to come and join us [in the association]. [2]

The Thai delegates have used the international fairs as an opportunity to see how other entrepreneurs present their products and discuss matters of comparative advantage. At the beginning of 2005, Pansak Vinyaratn, the Prime Minister's chief policy advisor, suggested:

> Producers and retailers [should] add "Thainess" to the designs of their products to attract both domestic and international consumers, and differentiate the products from imported ones.... [T]he charms of Thai culture could create a kind of "mysterious allure" to attract consumers.... Things will continue to sell as long as the "seductive force" of a product or service is not yet clearly identified. (Sujintana 2005)

With the government's financial backing and the Queen's encouragement, creative destruction has reactivated cultural understandings and steered the national economy along a culturally oriented course.

As a recent study from the Sasin School of Business has shown, culture pays in quality where labor loses to neighboring competitors (Suvit, Krittinee, Ake, and Naphisara 2003). Currently, the Thai government is trying to understand how to "brand" Thailand (itself a process of impression management) so that the country's image enables Thai products to compete in quality rather than in price. Low-cost competition from China and other countries in the region has made Thai products and services less desirable for price-oriented consumers. In order to promote economic development, the Thai government has focused on creating synergy with the existing images that global consumers already have about Thailand as a place, about the people that inhabit the place, and about the products produced there. The Thai government has acknowledged what a number of studies have shown: The particular country that produces goods and services influences how consumers evaluate its output, all other things being equal (e.g., Bilkey and Nes 1982).

DRAMATURGICAL DISCIPLINE BY THE NATIONAL GOVERNMENT

The Thai state began to discipline the micro-interactions of its citizens in the 1950s to create an impression of Thai culture for outsiders that would combine the uniqueness of the Thai with the conformity of the nation to world (highly industrialized, Western) standards. The common opinion was that there should be no confusion between the modernizing, market-loving Thais and their backward, communist-sympathizing neighbors. The military-led government secured Thailand this distinction by imposing mandates on how Thais should behave and what they should wear, especially in the presence of foreigners. By the time of Prime Minister Sarit's rule, the state outlawed pedicabs because they represented a premodern era. Furthermore, the army-sponsored radio stations instructed the Thai citizens daily in the virtues of cleanliness and orderliness. Men were to kiss their wives goodbye in the morning, a custom borrowed from the West. In the same sense, people were to greet one another with "Hello" instead of "Where are you going?" Visitors to government buildings were to wear Western-style clothing rather than the now-outlawed traditional dress. In short, Sarit visibly revived the push from the old era, *samai gon*, to the new one, *samai mai* (Wyatt 2003).

Although the Thai state began moving away from the "primitive" and exotica in its modernizing push, those cultural elements continued to exist in the country, waiting merely to be activated. More importantly, the Thai monarchy actively promoted courtly craft traditions and local craft practices as legitimate and respectable ways of affirming Thai identity (Van Esterik 2000). Mauricio Peleggi (2002) has documented the history of cultural heritage promotion in Thailand and how the remembrance for things past has translated into a thriving sector of the Thai economy. In his analysis, Peleggi notes that Thailand's history as never colonized and the country's esteem for its monarchy gave the Thais cultural continuity with Thailand's past. As a result, the national preoccupation with culture led the state to establish its legitimacy through its capacity to provide social protections and to generate prestige symbols through rapid economic development.

As international tourism brought rapid economic development to communities across Thailand, a varied set of community rituals—activities "structured to evoke and communicate meanings" (Wuthnow 1996: 99)—have generated and maintained a favorable impression of the nation's culture. Community rituals provide opportunities for the mutual monitoring of behavior and the collective shaming of those who dare ruin the group's image. For example, the state visits have been captured in photographs that hang prominently on the walls of artisans who have been certified as the purveyors of traditional culture. Queen Sirikit has awarded certificates to master craftspeople, who humbly receive and proudly display these marks of distinction. At the provincial level, the Chiang Mai Provincial Authority has worked with local artisans to develop the Chiang Mai Brand—marking products as traditionally processed and its producers as purveyors of local knowledge. Photographs of Prime Minister Thaksin adorn the walls of those artisans whose products carry the region's label. Talented artisans find their works displayed at regional meetings of the Association of Southeast Asia Nations (ASEAN) and at various United Nations functions. One handicraft entrepreneur remarked that being invited to exhibit one's work for ASEAN is an honor, though it makes no money. "Everyone knows" if one has been invited to participate in these events, and it serves as a reminder that loyalty to traditional images does pay.

THE LOCAL STAGE FOR CASTING CASTE AND PROTECTING PERFORMANCES

What do the importers do to facilitate the performance of identity on the part of the Thai handicraft entrepreneurs and the Thai government? How do the importers affirm the legitimacy of Thai claims that some economic exchanges are not legitimate on cultural grounds? One example of this is the export of religious objects from Thailand. Rather than accuse the Thai exporter of highlighting the story in order to make more money, the buyer grants the exporter the benefit of the doubt. Of course, religious symbols are off limits and the seller probably has a sincere belief in the sacredness of the object being sold. The object receives more economic value because of this sincere belief. By deferring to the seller, the buyer protects the performers in the enactment of their meaningful culture from a sovereign, never colonized country that should be preserved and respected.

The sellers of cultural commodities portray authenticity as the cachet that their products bring to the market. One of the worst things that can happen is for buyers to believe that handicraft artisans are faking the authenticity of their goods and personal intentions—doing and saying whatever may turn a profit. In fact, a number of informants and feature stories in the newspapers indicate that some entrepreneurs moved into handicraft production or sales in response to the uncertainties in the mainstream economy: An architect now designs Thai-style furniture for export; a mid-level manager of a private firm now exports ceramics; a farmer now sells his handbags in Paris, Milan, and Tokyo (Crispin 2003). As one set of opportunities disappears, the industrious respond with creativity. This response is conditioned on the willingness of the global market to pretend not to know that some of the celebrated cultural entrepreneurs are not themselves artisans and have started to learn about their local traditions and culture in an effort to participate in response to Thailand's financial crisis. Likewise, the entrepreneurs exercise tact in portraying themselves and the artisans producing for the market as individuals getting back to their roots.

EXERCISING TACT, REGARDING TACT

Take the example of the Thai spirit house. The spirit house does not require an original to verify its authenticity because the proof of the object's authenticity lies within its use-value and within the ceremonial enactments that enable its utility. In the sacred domain, the spirit house shelters ghosts and spirits displaced from the land by the arrival of humans who chop down the trees that host the spirits. As a person will clear land to build a house, the person will remove a multitude of homes for the spirits. In return for the displacement, the human occupants of the land should build a miniature house, the size of a Western birdcage, ranging from about one by one and a half feet to a much larger structure that can be three feet in height or more. The size of the spirit house depends on the ages and the types of trees removed. As the age of the displaced tree increases, so too does the attention given to the spirit house honoring the tree's removal. It is believed that older trees host more impressive spirits.

Each day, a representative of the household shall pay homage to the displaced spirits in return for the peace and tranquility that come with having one's guardian spirits appeased. At both homes and business establishments, the human occupants of the land set out offerings to the spirits and whisper prayers while holding lit joss sticks. The offering consists of fermented rice wrapped in a banana leaf, a garland of flowers, lit candles, and red joss sticks. The supplicant recognizes the power of the spirits to grant peace and tranquility (Anuman Rajadhon 1988). In the supplicant's personal life, the prayer recognizes that life is uncertain and that accidents happen. In the supplicant's professional life, the prayer suggests that market forces create instability and endanger survival. With so much change produced by life's natural cycle and by the global market's incursion into all corners of the world, the supplicant seeks protection wherever it may be found. Those selling the spirit houses in the West extract this sacred narrative of peace, protection, and spiritual balance and transfer it from its sacred context to a profane market context. Instead of advertising the merits of spirituality, some Western marketers have used the form of the spirit house as an attention grabber for ornate birdcages.

Consider the Thai response to this violation of the sacred; then observe the tact exercised by the foreign buyer in response to the tact deployed by the Thai respondent. In the market transaction for spirit houses, the Thai producers and sellers have had to think about the distinction between the sacred and the profane. One informant constantly used the English phrase "the real one" (*khong ching*) to discern the spirit house from the birdcage as he discussed the dilemma that he faced. According to the informant, everyone in Thailand knows about the sacred meaning of the spirit house. Its Thai name translates as "the house in which the spirits are invited." To permit the spirits to feel welcomed in the house, the human occupant of the land invites the Buddhist monks to the property to hold a special ceremony welcoming the spirits to their new home. As the spirit house ages, the human occupant becomes concerned about the spirits' new home: The spirits do not exit the dilapidated house without a proper ceremony that invites them into their new home. The old spirit houses, in fact, have to rest beneath the old *Bo* tree, which holds sacred significance as the place where the Buddha was enlightened. For this reason, one will see lots of old, broken spirit houses discarded beneath these gnarled trees.

If the Western buyer claimed that he had customers willing to pay up to US $1,000 for very old teak spirit houses, the informant agreed to furnish these items under a set of specific conditions. If the buyer wanted an antique spirit house for artistic purposes, the Thai seller would provide it, but it would take some time to have the monks come and decommission it properly. However, if the buyer only wanted a birdcage that resembled a spirit house, the Thai seller would instruct the artisans to build a new spirit house and to set the object out of doors during the rainy season to make it look old. For inauthentic uses of the sacred item, the Thai would use inauthentic processes. The informant stressed: "We can't treat a real spirit house as if it's just any old kind of thing." Explaining what the object *is not* makes more salient what the object *is*. This explanation also requires the pricing negotiation to start afresh. The buyer can purchase a sacred object, but the buyer has to understand that the object is sacred and has to pay an appropriate sum to honor the item's special powers (e.g., Goffman 1961: 73).

This cultural intertwining led to several differentiations in order to protect the performance of authenticity and to generate satisfaction for the buyer who observed the rather astute performance. The buyer has thus participated in the creation of new product categories without defining what those categories must be. Such interactions do not rob more powerful economic actors of their influence on what is produced, but the interactions do constrain the buyers who themselves want to enjoy the show and who themselves are managing an impression that other buyers and the selling interlocutors might have about the buyer. Sensitive to innovation and quick to recognize how local innovations may benefit the buyer in the final place of sale, the buyer is happy to be carried away to a certain extent by the drama of presentation and counterpresentation.

CONCLUSION

The qualitative research methods used in this research demonstrate that the economic strategies of some nation-states and their entrepreneurs will depend largely on what the goods and services say about strongly held beliefs on cultural identity. If the cultural heritage being represented saves face or is likely to spark a positive evaluation of the country by socially significant outsiders, it is more likely that the national government will attempt to assemble material resources and that local entrepreneurs will capitalize on the global market demand for cultural goods and services, especially if the government and its entrepreneurs are looking for their inclusion in the global community. Therefore, the material conditions of government and private sector actors are not the only constraints or the only motivations for economic action. Indeed, artisans participate in international exhibitions even when they lose money doing so, and governments have sent entire presentation teams to the World's Fairs even when doing so constituted a financial sacrifice. I argue that the willingness to sacrifice for the production and distribution of certain types of cultural commodities and the willingness of others to assist explicitly or implicitly (dramaturgical protection) depend on how the country's cultural heritage has been defined in the minds of outsiders and insiders in global and local market spaces.

To conclude, countries require assistance in managing impressions (definitions of the situation) perhaps as much as they need support for managing their institutions and their macro-economy. The ideal types presented in this article enable comparisons by country according to their integration in the global community rather than by their physical location or their structural position in the global economy. In other words, these definitions of particular economic situations may explain intraregional variation in country performance in cultural markets. Are countries with similar geography and roughly similar economic, political, and social positions in the world system enjoying different levels of market demand for their cultural goods and services because of the way that they and others have jointly defined the country's cultural situation? The answer to this question depends on empirical investigations yet to be launched on a larger scale. The theoretical approach developed here offers some guidance for such investigations. A modified version of Goffman's impression management helps us thus to study the possible processes and outcomes of social change.

ACKNOWLEDGMENTS

The author gratefully acknowledges support from the American Sociological Association's Travel Award Grant (SES-0548370), supported by the National Science Foundation.

NOTES

1. Author interview with Mark Narongsak on December 14, 2001.

REFERENCES

Anuman Rajadhon, Phya. 1988. *Essays on Thai Folklore*. Bangkok: Thai Inter-Religious Commission for Development and Santhirakoses Nagapradipa Foundation.

Bayly, C. A. 1986. "The Origins of Swadeshi (Home Industry): Cloth and Indian Society, 1700–1930." Pp. 285–321 in *The Social Life of Things: Commodities in Cultural Perspective*, ed. Arjun Appadurai. New York: Cambridge University Press.

Biggart, Nicole W., and Mark Orrú. 1997. "Societal Strategic Advantage: Institutional Structure and Path Dependence in the Automotive and Electronics Industries of East Asia." Pp. 201–239 in *State, Market, and Organizational Form*, ed. Ayse Bugra and Bhelul Usdiken. Berlin: Walter de Gruyter.

Biggart, Nicole Woolsey, and Mauro F. Guillen. 1999. "Developing Difference: Social Organization and the Rise of the Auto Industries of South Korea, Taiwan, Spain, and Argentina." *American Sociological Review* 64 (5): 722–747.

Bilkey, Warren J., and Erik Nes. 1982. "Country-of-Origin Effects on Product Evaluations." *Journal of International Business Studies* 13 (1): 89–99.

Chalfin, Brenda. 2004. *Shea Butter Republic: State Power, Global Markets, and the Making of an Indigenous Commodity*. New York, Oxford: Routledge.

Crispin, Shawn W. 2003. "Weaving Entrepreneurs." *Far Eastern Economic Review* 166 (14): 32–34.

Dobbin, Frank. 1994. *Forging Industrial Policy: The United States, Britain, and France in the Railway Age*. New York: Cambridge University Press.

Goffman, Erving. 1959. *The Presentation of Self in Everyday Life*. Garden City, NY: Doubleday.

Goffman, Erving. 1961. *Encounters: Two Studies in the Sociology of Interaction*. Indianapolis, IN: Bobbs-Merrill.

Graburn, Nelson H. H. 1976. *Ethnic and Tourist Arts: Cultural Expressions from the Fourth World*. Berkeley: University of California Press.

Jamaree, Pitackwong. 1996. "Disorganized Development: Changing Forms of Work and Livelihood in Rural Northern Thailand." PhD thesis, School of Oriental and African Studies, University of London, London, UK.

Karp, Ivan, and Steven Lavine. 1991. *Exhibiting Cultures: The Poetics and Politics of Museum Display*. Washington, DC: Smithsonian Institution Press.

Luechai, Chulasai, and Nataworn Siroros. 2002. "Networks and Clusters Development in Northern Thailand." Chiang Mai, Thailand: SMEs Institute of Chiang Mai University Working Paper.

Merton, Robert King. 1957. *Social Theory and Social Structure*. Glencoe, IL: Free Press.

Meyer, John W., and Michael T. Hannan. 1979. *National Development and the World System: Educational, Economic, and Political Change, 1950–1970*. Chicago: University of Chicago Press.

Mitchell, Timothy. 1989. "The World as Exhibition." *Comparative Studies in Society and History* 31 (2): 217–236.

Nederveen Pieterse, Jan. 1994. "Globalization as Hybridization." *International Sociology* 9 (2): 161–184.

Peleggi, Maurizio. 2002. *The Politics of Ruins and the Business of Nostalgia*. Bangkok: White Lotus Press.

Portes, Alejandro, and Ruben G. Rumbaut. 1996. *Immigrant America: A Portrait*. Berkeley: University of California Press.

Powell, Walter W., and Paul DiMaggio. 1991. *The New Institutionalism in Organizational Analysis*. Chicago: University of Chicago Press.

Schuerkens, Ulrike. 2003. "The Sociological and Anthropological Study of Globalization and Localization." *Current Sociology* 51 (1/2, 3/4): 209–222.

Sujintana, Hemtasilpa. 2004. "Retailing: Consuming with a Difference." *Bangkok Post Year-End Economic Review 2004*, http://www.bangkokpost.com/ecoreviewye2004/retailing.html, accessed February 10, 2005.

Suvit, Maesincee, Nuttavuthisit Krittinee, Ayawongs Ake, and Phasukavanich Naphisara. 2003. "Branding Thailand: Building a Favorable Country Image for Thai Products and Services." *Sasin Journal of Management* 9 (1): 21–26.

Swidler, Ann. 1986. "Culture in Action: Symbols and Strategies." *American Sociological Review* 51 (2): 273–286.

Thongchai, Winichakul. 2000. "The Quest for 'Siwilai': A Geographical Discourse of Civilization Thinking in the Late Nineteenth and Early Twentieth-Century Siam." *Journal of Asian Studies* 59 (3): 528-49.

Van Esterik, Penny. 2000. *Materializing Thailand*. Oxford: Berg.

Weber, Max, Guenther Roth, and Claus Wittich. 1978. *Economy and Society: An Outline of Interpretive Sociology*. Berkeley: University of California Press.

Wherry, Frederick F. 2006. "The Nation-State, Identity Management, and Indigenous Crafts: Constructing Markets and Opportunities in Northwest Costa Rica." *Ethnic and Racial Studies* 29 (1): 124–152.

Wherry, Frederick F. 2008. *Global Markets and Local Crafts: Thailand and Costa Rica Compared*. Baltimore: Johns Hopkins University Press.

Wuthnow, Robert. 1996. *Poor Richard's Principle: Recovering the American Dream Through the Moral Dimension of Work, Business, and Money*. Princeton, NJ: Princeton University Press.

Wyatt, David K. 2003. *Thailand: A Short History*. New Haven, CT: Yale University Press.

Zelizer, Viviana A. 1999. "Multiple Markets: Multiple Cultures." Pp. 193–212 in *Diversity and Its Discontents: Cultural Conflict and Common Ground in Contemporary American Society*, ed. Neil J. Smelser and Jeffrey Alexander. Princeton, NJ: Princeton University Press.

7 Informal and Formal Economy in Caracas

Street Vending and Globalization

Mathilde Gauvain

Whoever has walked in the streets of Latin American or African cities has been able to remark the numerous street vendors that can be found in the centers of the towns. These vendors are the most obvious among the workers of the informal sector, but they are not the only ones: Employees and owners of microenterprises, women working at home, agricultural workers, and servants belong to this economic sector that occupies more than half of the active population that we define in this chapter as the workforce that contributes to national production, that is to say, laborers (employed or unemployed) in the formal or informal sector. The statistical institutes in northern countries do not include "illegal" or "extralegal" labor in their active population, but the Statistical Institute of Venezuela does so, as do most of the other institutes in southern countries.

Contrary to what the experts of the International Labor Organization (ILO) have expected, informal work has dramatically increased during the past 20 years in the developing world, and in particular in Latin America and the Caribbean. As a matter of fact, even if street vending or craft industries have some traditional roots, we can draw a parallel between the development of the informal economy and the advent of the neo-liberal credo in southern countries. In fact, the informal sector has two origins. On the one hand, it is linked to a precapitalist organization based on social and familial links aiming at providing an income for the household, and not accumulating capital. On the other hand, it is a sector characterized by the absence of "typical" forms of employment, for example, well-paid and stable jobs.

Nevertheless, this situation deeply differs from one country to another. For example, Mexico has a long experience of what is called *ambulantes* (itinerant sellers): Street vending has existed since the 1950s, corresponding to the reign of the powerful PRI (*Partido Revolucionario Institucional*) that created syndicates of street vendors and passed agreements with them to keep the control on these informal workers (Cross 1997). In Venezuela, the situation is far different, to the extent that street vending was much less developed until the 1980s. There were street markets considered as a survival of the old colonial tradition of the central place that is similar to Caracas's old *Casco historico*[1] and some other cities such as Maracaibo.

The traditional central place of Latin American cities—built according to the architectural principle of the *cuadricula*—predominates in Latin American cities: a central square, two main axes (north/south and west/east), and roads drawn parallel and perpendicular to each other. This place has been used as a street market since the 18th century. Street vending has been mostly concentrated in poor districts and in the *Casco historico*. The historic center built by the Spaniards was almost entirely destroyed in Caracas, but the area around the traditional central place, including the political center and the ancient economic center (*El Silencio*), was assimilated to the *Casco historico*.

Globalization has a large influence on the increase of the informal sector, mainly because of processes of privatization and the decreasing production costs, initiated by an increasing national and international competition that led to an important unemployment for nonskilled or low-skilled people and to precariousness, and this has encouraged the development of the informal economy. Globalization has contributed to transform parts of informal workers into "entrepreneurs," but we should not forget that their choices and actions are often structured by a "sense of necessity" (cf. Bourdieu, 1979). According to Pierre Bourdieu, every member of a social class learns during his socialization process a particular *habitus*, put up by social practices that determine social representations and actions. In fact, the working class does not try to imitate the upper classes because these people are strongly limited in their economic capacities. The working class is weighed down by heavy economic constraints that lead its members to conform their desires to basic necessities.

In order to understand the links between globalization and informal economy, we concentrate our analysis on street vending in Caracas. This chapter is based on an ethnographic observation of the *buhoneros* (street vendors) at different places in the municipality of Libertador in Caracas, in the district of Sabana Grande, a huge pedestrian boulevard in the middle of the city; in the terminal of Nuevo Circo; in the popular district of Catia; in the West side of the town; in the historic center El Silencio; and on semidirected discussions with street vendors. In this chapter, we first discuss the definition of informal economy with a special focus on street vending in Caracas. Then we present the main theoretical frameworks that explain informal economy. Finally, we present current debates on globalization and informal economy in order to tackle the results of the emergence of global markets on the transformation of informal economy and the organization of informal workers.

INFORMAL ECONOMY IN CARACAS

As in every country of Latin America, the informal economy in Venezuela includes an important part of the active population.[2] In 2001, 80 percent of the jobs created in Latin America belonged to the informal economy (World Labour Confederation 2002). In Venezuela, the word *buhoneros* is used for street vendors. If most of the workers of the informal economy use this expression to describe themselves and their activities, some of them find it pejorative and prefer to name themselves "informal workers." In the streets of Caracas, street vendors earn their living by selling many different goods: clothes, pirated CDs and DVDs, products of hardware trade, food (*arepas, cachapas, perros calientes*), cigarettes, books, juridical publications, and services: phone rental, manicure, piercing, and so on.

The informal sector started influencing the individuals' mental representations with the expansion of street vending after the crisis of the 1980s due to the devaluation of the bolivar in 1982 (the value of the national currency was based on the U.S. dollar up to this time), the countershock in the petroleum market in 1987, and budget measures taken by the different governments according to the Structural Adjustment Plans of the International Monetary Fund (IMF). Street vending is the most obvious part of what is called the "urban informal sector" (Chávez O'Brien 1993; Lacabana 1993), because it takes place in the public space and not in some hidden workshops that the inhabitants of the "formal city" never see. Street vending concerns almost 30 percent of the informal workers (Zanoni Lopez 2005). To some extent, people identify the informal economy in urban areas with street vending.

Even if about 50 percent of the active population works in the informal sector in 2007, street vending is just one of its expressions. There are numerous criteria to distinguish and to define the informal sector: The term occurred for the first time in economics in the "Kenya" report of an International Labor Organization (ILO) mission in 1972 (ILO 1972) to characterize small and labor-intensive production structures that were kept out of official statistics. Aiming at simplifying the work of national statistical institutions, the 1993 definition of the informal sector by the Fifteenth International Conference of Labor Statisticians (ICLS) only included one category of informal workers: the employees of informal enterprises. The National Institute of Statistics (Instituto Nacional de Estadisticas) of Venezuela has defined the informal sector as including any worker or entrepreneur in enterprises of less than five employees, except independent professionals who possess a diploma, such as physicians, lawyers, and so on. This definition of the informal sector is quite common among institutions working on statistics and corresponds to the criteria of the ILO. According to the ILO, the definition of the informal sector includes independent workers (except professionals and technicians), unpaid family members, employees, employers of enterprises with less than five laborers, and domestic laborers. Before 1999, the ILO also included microenterprises with less than 10 laborers, but this changed in order to statistically restrain the informal sector. Another reason was the increase of the tertiary sector in developing countries that contributed to create small-sized service enterprises that fulfilled the formal obligation to register as a firm. With this methodological modification, in 1999 the informal sector represented 46.4 percent of the nonagricultural employment, and concerned about 50 percent of women (Tokman 2001).

Before discussing the current framework of informal work as a socio-economic practice and the influence of globalization on informal work and trade, we present our research field (cf. Carr and Alter Chen 2001). In Caracas, the capital of Venezuela, street vending is mainly concentrated in the *municipio* (municipality) of Libertador, the most important of the five municipalities that form the city of Caracas (Libertador, Chacao, Baruta, El Hatillo, and Sucre). Libertador (named after Simon Bolivar's nickname) coincides with the *ciudad* (city) of Caracas. It is situated at the west side of the metropolitan area of Caracas. It is the most populated and the poorest municipality, and it includes the historic town center, whose origins go back to the Hispanic colonization (*el Casco historico*). We notice again that street vendors (*buhoneros*) prefer to occupy town centers in Latin American cities, a fact that brings up in the whole area the same discourse on the occupation of urban public spaces by vendors who use it in a commercial intention when they set up their *puestos* (stands) on sidewalks, *plazas* (places), or even roadways.

The character of these positions depends on the attitude of political actors toward the sellers. Thus, finding sedentary street vendors or itinerant ones in Latin American towns is a good clue for the importance of state tolerance. In Caracas, the *puestos* are most often made of a horizontal plank put on trestles or boxes, on which you can find products. Furthermore, a sunshade protects the vendor and his or her goods. This construction shows that informal street vending is well tolerated. Instead, there are places where sellers have no other option than to put a blanket on the ground that can be folded up as soon as the police arrive.

According to the national census of 2001 and the census of the Alcaldia Mayor (main council) of Caracas in 2002–2003, Caracas had 48,675 people working in the streets, 38,458 of them working in the municipality *Libertador*, of a total of 4,000,000 inhabitants. The real number of people working in the streets of Caracas had increased during the previous 5 years, due to the tolerance of the *Chávez* government toward the urban informal economy. Today, we can consider that almost 1.5 million people dedicate themselves to informal trade. Among them, there are 450,000 street sellers, half of them concentrated in Caracas (CEDICE, 2006). There are almost 20,000 *puestos* of street vending in *Libertador*, even if several people may work on the same *puesto*.

Only a very small fraction of the street vendors with whom we have talked live in the formal city. Some of them have chosen to work as a *buhonero*, but often this is a conditioned choice. Very few have decided to set up a business in the streets because it allows them to earn money and to make tax-free benefits. The owner of the *puesto*, who is quite often a family member most often employs street vendors. One of them, José,[3] is 25 years old. He started his career in street vending by working for his cousin, who has a *puesto* in *Sabana Grande*, one of the biggest boulevards of the city, a former upper-class *paseo* that is now occupied by almost 1,000 stands and that has become one of the centers of illegal and extralegal business. As José knew the coordinator of the punto where he was employed (the boulevard of *Sabana Grande* has been divided into five parts, called *puntos*, whose different parts have been arranged by a coordinator who has rented the different areas), he could obtain a space to set up a stand. He considers himself an entrepreneur. But his case is quite rare, because he has managed to organize an association of street vendors in his district, and as he has been one of those who have lived in the formal city, outside of the slums, called *barrios* in Caracas.

Contrary to men, women admit that they prefer to leave the street. Yet when street vendors are asked whether they would like to set up their business in a commercial center, men and women disagree. Men consider that leaving the street would mean making less money whereas women prefer better working conditions, as sun, rain, and pollution are hard to withstand every day. Moreover, women often work with their children: sleeping babies and young children staying the entire day with them at the stand.

The sharing of the public spaces of street vendors is quite difficult to understand, as it is a kind of illegal network between political leaders, the police, and the municipality. In order to encourage the street vendors to modify this sharing, the local government has given them financial help when they create cooperatives. Our interviewee Miny works in the historical center, in a small street between the *Plaza Bolivar*—the name of the Venezuelan *Plaza Mayor*—and the *Plaza de la Revolucion*, selling t-shirts and caps with the image of Hugo Chávez, and movies on the Bolivarian revolution. In this area, street vendors sell these kinds of products, leftist books, and reviews, as they consider themselves "Chavist." They created a cooperative in 2003. The municipality gave them red stands in order to control street vending in the area. Contrary to this permission, informal activities are totally prohibited on the *Plaza Bolivar*. This example permits us to grasp the quite ambiguous attitude of the local government toward informal economy.

The relative increase of the informal sector can be proven by the fact that since 1999, workers in the informal sector have represented more than 50 percent of the active population (Instituto Nacional de Estadisticas). The active population was calculated by the INE as the part of the population over 15 years that had a job or was employed in the week of the survey.[4]

According to the CEDICE investigation of 2004,[5] women represented almost 62 percent of the street vendors. The gender question is quite important in issues concerning informality. In the informal sector, women are concentrated in the two subsectors of home-based workers and street vendors, sectors where data are rare. This fact can be explained by methodological problems to collect data on home-based workers who remain largely invisible. On the other hand, the topic of street vending is most often tackled from an urban development point of view that concentrates on the number of street shops. Neither the number of laborers nor the working conditions of street vendors are tackled. Furthermore, there is an obvious gender discrimination as it is much easier to accept that a woman works in the informal sector, for example, the "secondary" labor market, by reference to the distinction between the primary labor market formed of jobs that are well paid, stable, and with good working conditions and opportunities for promotion, and the secondary labor market with less well paid and precarious jobs (Piore and Doringer 1971). Often a female income is considered as a "second" and/or additional income in the household.

Nevertheless, huge differences exist within the informal sector. On the one hand, there are women preparing food in a *rancho* (slum) kitchen and going to the streets to sell the food to *buhoneros*; on the other hand, there are enterprises that import illegal products made in Central America or in Asia. The informal sector cannot be considered just as a survival sector for poor people, even if it is an aspect of the inherited *habitus* of poor laborers. The informal sector must also be conceived of its collateral damages to a liberal practice that encourages "free trade." Moreover, weak states do not have the means to make people obey to national laws and rules, a situation that is still reinforced by corruption.

Differences existing within the informal sector are also based on gender. In January 2005 47.8 percent of the active (except the unemployed) male population and 46.5 percent of the active female population worked in the informal sector (INE 2004). But 8.3 percent of men working in the informal sector are employers, versus only 3.6 percent of women. Seven percent of women working in the informal sector are family helpers, but only 2.4 percent of men (INE 2004). These data show that global gender discriminations are also valid in the informal sector. Women are visible here because most of the informal workers' associations, defending their rights, are associations entirely composed of women.

In Caracas, the municipal government tried to apply methods used in Lima and Mexico that consisted in relocating the street vendors to some popular covered markets. This relocation was rather successful in Lima: The municipality tried to get the historical center recognized as "patrimony of humanity" by UNESCO, a standing that was eventually decided in 1991. The same holds true for the historical center of Mexico, which was added to the UNESCO list in 1987.[6] After this recognition, the municipality of Lima created the *campos feriales,* a kind of popular malls, in order to successfully relocate street vendors, because these markets were built close to the center. This strategy was not really successful in Mexico because of the important number of street vendors, their long-established formal associations, and syndicates linked to political parties, inherited from the PRI policy (Cross 1998). In Caracas, this strategy never worked because of the ambiguous attitude of the government that wanted to protect these voters, refusing to take severe measures against street vending.

In 1999, the government of Venezuela introduced an important constitutional reform that instituted the Bolivarian Republic, named after Simón Bolivar, the *libertador* who led the independence war of Gran Colombia in 1811. The Chávez administration has also supported a new outline of theoretical references and political measures that set up the *proceso bolivariano* (Bolivarian process), considered as an institutional, political, economic, social, and cultural "revolution." This "revolution" has been instituted by the head of government, but the change consists of giving people more power with new decision structures, organized at the level of the community, in order to avoid traditional bureaucratic structures considered as corrupt and inefficient. The idea of a new "socialism" developed by President Chávez has led to a political polarization between government supporters and members of the opposition. This polarization has still been enlarged by the socioeconomic gap between the lower classes and the upper middle class. The government's policy toward street vending has been influenced by the fact that this policy is supported by the lower classes, which the street vendors belong to. The attitude of the government toward the informal economy is rather vague because of the fact that the government has tried different measures with contradictory discourses in order to keep the votes of both the street vendors (who most often want to stay in the streets, or who at least want to be relocated to interesting places), and the inhabitants and the formal vendors, who have claimed a "clearing of the streets."

To conclude on this topic, we can underline that the strategies adopted by different governments in order to solve the issue of the informal commerce have corresponded to a spatial point of view and not to an economic point of view. As in the past, it has been found difficult to "formalize" the informal economy, so that municipal public powers and urbanism instead of economics were charged with the finding of a solution. This represents an important shift in the theoretical framework of the informal sector and will allow us to avoid the theoretical confrontation between informality and globalization, which is set up by the problematic of women's informal work.

THEORETICAL FRAMEWORKS OF INFORMALITY

Bruno Lautier, who has seen two different ages of informality, has summed up the history of the notion "informal economy" and "informal sector" and its access to global visibility. The first period covers the years from 1971 (date of the first occurrence of the notion, used by Keith Hart [Hart 1971], who underlined the necessity to obtain a second household income because of inflation) to 1987, when politics "discovered" informality and tried to conceive policies of formalization that aimed at integrating microenterprises into a legal framework. From 1987 to 2004, a "second age of informal economy" started, characterized by social riots as an answer to budget restrictions, implemented by the International Monetary Fund (IMF). One of the most exemplary riots occurred in Caracas on February 27, 1989, known as the "*Caracazo*," due to the increased prices of public transport.

This second approach appeared because of a lack of harsh policies against informality. The informal economy could then be considered as a palliative sector in the face of the inefficiencies of the market and newly created inequalities. According to this idea, the theoretical framework of informality should be linked to sociological studies on marginality, as well as to geographical studies on the fragmentation of the town. In fact, there has been a strong link between informality and poverty, as the informal sector normally grew during an economic crisis. This statistical fact let scholars think that people who are first affected by an economic crisis find a job in informality in order to survive. Yet these people are often the least skilled, the most precarious, the poor; these disadvantages continue to persist in the informal sector.

In the informal economy, even if average incomes are lower than in the formal sector, people work hard: for example, the working hours of street vendors in Caracas are twice as long as those of formal workers, that is to say, 80 hours per week, and 78 percent of them work seven days per week (CEDICE, 2005).

During the 1980s, several policies of "formalization" of the informal sector were tried, in particular in Colombia. But there are practical problems, such as how to know the enterprises that need help and the reinforcement of enterprises already set up. Here, we can find the fundamental question of the purpose of an informal micro-enterprise: to accumulate capital (as in the case of the standard entrepreneur of economic theory) or to sustain the reproduction of the family household. This important challenge to classic economic theory contradicts the analysis of Hernando de Soto, who thought that the street vendor is a rational economic actor who prefers the informal sector to the formal one because of the high costs of entering a formal business (e.g., administrative costs and taxes).

The other fundamental issue has to do with the classical definition of a plant as an actor of the free market. If the policies of "formalization" succeed, the micro-enterprises shall increase their productivity because of free credits given to them. In this case, they will become more competitive in the local market than non-assisted formal enterprises.

To sum up the different theoretical viewpoints on the links between the formal and the informal economy: There are three main schools of thought, depending on different theoretical approaches and leading to different political solutions. The dualists consider that the informal sector is separated from the formal one, and that there is almost no link between the two sectors. The informal sector is just a way to provide an income to the poor, while economic circumstances around their inclusion into the formal job market do not exist. In this approach, excluded and marginalized people create informality in order to survive in an economic crisis (ILO 1972). In the structural approach, the informal economy is subordinated to the formal one, according to a scheme of "dominate/dominated" (Castells, Portes, and Benton 1989). The aim of subordinating those who work in the informal economy is to reduce the labor costs in a competitive market. Finally, the legalists consider informal work as a rational answer to the high costs of formalized establishments, such as high labor costs (de Soto 1986).

GLOBALIZATION AND INFORMALITY

Globalization is, on the one hand, a movement that has facilitated global connections in the fields of finance, communication, exchange, and trade, and, on the other hand, a kind of utopia that has theorized about the importance of integrating world markets in order to increase the growth of the global economy. Already in the early 1980s, the World Bank defined development as successful participation in world markets. Globalization was considered as the answer to problems of "underdevelopment" and became an ideology that linked free trade to democracy, including the idea that free trade was going to offer people opportunities of getting a job and an income.

The informal economy already existed before the globalization of the last 25 years. But as we have explained, Bruno Lautier in his scholarly work on the historical construction of the meaning of the term *informal* has considered informality as the solution to face poverty, an infinite way of getting an income, and as such a field of development policy.

Nowadays, development is based on the importance of markets, and not as much on agriculture and industrialization, contrary to the situation in the past. The informal economy with its many small enterprises perfectly coincides with this new vision of an individual economic initiative linked to the market.

Nevertheless, analyzing the individual reasons for entering the informal sector, we can assert that people choose their activity because of the fact that they cannot find a formal job. There are different careers (cf. Becker et al. 1961). The interviews I had with some of the vendors in Caracas have shown that there are three ways of entering the job. First, there are people who start quite young in order to help a family member who has a stand. These people become employees by learning the job, and once the other street vendors know them well, and they can afford it, they often get their own stand. Second, there are students who enter the job in order to pay for their studies. But sometimes the work takes so much time that they quit their studies and dedicate themselves to street vending. Third, there are people who have been dismissed from a formal job and who do not manage to find another one. The street is for them a survival strategy. In contrast, people who belong to the first category consider the informal sector as a culture, a part of class *habitus*. Most often, their family members and neighbors (community members) work in the informal sector, as many owners of a stand employ family members to help them.

Contrary to what some ILO experts have expected, informal jobs have thus increased over the past two decades. We can wonder why the informal sector has expanded, whereas the barriers between national economies have a tendency to disappear, thus diminishing taxes.

The first reason is that during the period of economic adjustment, the informal sector has expanded, due to cutbacks in public service and redundancies. The workers of public enterprises that were closed, or of public institutions that were downsized, needed to gain money, to make a living for their household, The informal sector was the only solution under these conditions of mass unemployment.

Second, the economic growth of the past two decades was more or less "joblessness" and was based on capital-intensive investment and growth. Joblessness occurs when labor productivity increases more rapidly than economic growth. From the middle of the 1980s, economic growth in Venezuela was really slow, while formal enterprises introduced new technologies in order to increase labor productivity. Globalization has affected both developing and advanced countries, and has led to a greater competition at the international as well as at the national level. On the other hand, some of the developing countries have pursued economic growth based on high-technology sectors that have privileged highly skilled jobs. Those who did not possess the skills necessary to enter the developing economy were forced to find other jobs, with other barriers than a diploma, such as belonging to a social and territorial network.

Third, according to Rodrick's analysis (Rodrick 1997), globalization encourages competition. Competition privileges capital because large companies can move capital across borders. Instead, labor that does not have the same ability to move and to migrate is disadvantaged. To increase their global competitiveness, more and more investors have moved to countries that have been characterized by low labor costs, or employers have shifted to informal employment arrangements. National competitiveness is especially important in tasks that require low skills, and therefore globalization diminishes wages and increases precariousness. Low-skill workers in developing countries would then have to choose between a formal job with a low salary and an informal job. The difference between the two choices has been reduced due to competition, a fact that partly explains the increase of the informal sector over the last years. Jobs were already characterized by precariousness and low wages had become widespread in this global shifting toward flexibility and nonregulation (Rodrick, 1997).

In Caracas, the development of global markets has influenced the informal economy insofar as it created a shift in the geographical origin of the products sold in the streets. An increasing part of these products has originated in Asia, due to a huge network of importation and smuggling. This importation of new products has also triggered new forms of competition among the local producers that have no interest in formalizing their workshop—some *buhoneros* possess their own workshop where they can produce for several street vendors. The quantity of this type of workshop is still unknown. When put in global competition, people prefer the informal way of producing and selling, especially in the present context of a state trying to obtain the payments of the professional taxes, according to an economic rational choice. The *Seniat (Servicio Integrado de Administracion Aduanaria y Tributaria,* the Venezuelan Internal Revenue) started a huge action in 2003 against fiscal evasion, called *Evacion Cero*: The administration initiated important controls in enterprises and shops in order to help people respect fiscal and labor laws. In this context, being in the informal sector has been a way to avoid taxes and labor regulations.

The idea of a segmented informal market developed by I. Gunther and A. Launov (2006) is quite relevant in this context: Based on the 1998 Ivorian household survey, their econometric model shows that a latent heterogeneity exists inside the informal sector. In fact, expected wages are higher in the formal sector, but there is a "significant differential between expected earnings in the "upper" tier and "lower" tier informal sectors" (Gunther and Launov 2006: 17). We can thus consider that there are two distinct informal sectors in developing countries, the first (the "upper" tier informal sector) being superior to the second (the "lower" tier informal sector) in terms of "significantly higher earnings as well as higher returns to education and experience" (Gunther and Launov 2006: 24). The global context of competition may reinforce this segmentation. In Caracas, it is obvious that there are two different types of informal workers, characterized by different incomes and a different *habitus,* with some of them considering themselves as entrepreneurs who refuse to enter the formal sector.

The actual situation may change in the next few years with the widespread creation of cooperatives that the government has triggered off. In fact, the new Ministry for the Popular Economy (MINEP) has encouraged the development of cooperation, through the constitution of enterprises in cooperatives. Some of them have been brought together with other new institutions of the health and education sectors, with assignments set up in the middle of the communities, and with food distribution in the co-op supermarkets. All these attempts are called a "nucleus of endogenous development." These *nucleos* have been at the core of the country's plan of fostering egalitarian economic development. We can imagine that in the future, people who are involuntary workers in the informal sector may try to organize themselves in this kind of structure as this organization is facilitated by the MINEP, which gives scholarships in topics such as cooperatives, production, and accounting. In mid 2006, the National Superintendence of Cooperatives (SUNACOOP) reported that it had registered over 108,000 co-ops representing over 1.5 million members, with an important tendency to increase its membership. These deep changes in the organization of production and selling underline that the informal sector in Venezuela is at the point of changing its face. In Caracas, we have already met street vendors organized in cooperatives, and even if they are still a minority, this trend will continue in the coming years.

ACKNOWLEDGMENTS

My fieldwork took place in Caracas in April/May 2005 and in July 2006. The fieldwork consisted in participant observations and intensive discussions with street vendors. I thank Mireya Silva, responsible for the popular economy in the City Council of Caracas, and José Chauran, the secretary of SINTRAINOR, which is a labor union of street vendors, for helpful discussions and comments. I also express my gratitude to Alain Musset, who supervises my PhD at the École des Hautes Études en Sciences Sociales, Paris.

NOTES

1. The historical center inherited from the Hispanic colonization was built around the traditional *Plaza Mayor*, called *Plaza Bolivar* in the towns of Venezuela.
2. The active population is composed of people available to the labor market, either employed or unemployed.
3. The names of the interviewees have been changed in order to guarantee anonymity.
4. Translation from the INE definition: "Población Económicamente Activa: Está constituida por todas las personas de 15 años y más, con disposición y disponibilidad para trabajar en el periodo de referencia, que es la semana anterior al día de la entrevista" (cf. www.ine.gov.ve).
5. The *Centro de divulgacion del conocimiento economico para la libertad* is a private institution that tried to organize a huge investigation about informal activity and street vending. Its hypothesis is based on de Soto's theoretical framework. The U.S. National Endowment for Democracy has financed this institution.
6. Cf. http://whc.unesco.org/en/list/.

REFERENCES

Alonso, Ivan, Fernando Iwasaki, and Enrique Ghersi. 1989. *El comercio ambulatorio en Lima* [Street Vending in Lima]. Lima: Instituto Libertad y Democracia.

Becker, Howard S., Blanche Geer, Everett C. Hughes, and Anselm L. Strauss. 1961. *Boys in White, Student Culture in Medical School*. Chicago: University of Chicago Press.

Bourdieu, Pierre. 1979. *La distinction. Critique sociale du jugement*. Paris: Minuit Cambridge, MA: Harvard University Press, 1987).

Carr, Marilyn, and Martha Alter Chen. 2001. "Globalization and the Informal Economy: How Global Trade and Investment Impact on the Working Poor." *Working Paper for the Informal Economy* 1. Geneva: ILO.

Castells, Manuel, Alejandro Portes, and Lauren A. Benton, eds. 1989. *The Informal Economy: Studies in Advanced and Less Advanced Developed Countries.* Baltimore, MD: Johns Hopkins University Press.

Chávez O'Brien, Eliana. 1993. "El sector informal urbano. Estrategias de vida e identidad" [The Urban Informal Sector. Life Strategies and Identity]. *Nueva Sociedad* 124: 82–93.

Cross, John. 1997. "Debilitando al clientelismo: La formalizacion del ambulantaje en la ciudad de Mexico" [Weakening Clientelism: The Formation of the Itinerant Dealing in the City of Mexico]. *Revista Mexicana de Sociologia* 59 (4): 93–115.

Cross, John. 1998. *Informal Politics. Street Vendors and the State in Mexico City.* Stanford, CA: Stanford University Press.

De Soto, Hernando. 1986. *El otro Sendero. La revolución informal.* Lima: Instituto Libertad y democracia (2nd ed., 1987, Editorial Oreja Negra: Bogota).

Doeringer Peter B., and Michel J. Piore. 1971. *Internal Labor Markets and Manpower Analysis.* Lexington, MA: D. C. Heath.

Gunther, Isabel, and Andrey Launov. 2006. *Competitive and Segmented Informal Labor Markets.* Discussion Paper 2349. Bonn: Institut zur Zukunft der Arbeit. ftp .iza.org/dp2349.pdf, accessed January 28, 2007.

Hart, Keith. 1973. "Informal Income Opportunities and Urban Employment in Ghana." *Journal of Modern African Studies* 2 (1): 61–89.

ILO. 1972. *Employment, Incomes and Equality. A Strategy for Increasing Productive Employment in Kenya.* Geneva: International Labor Organization.

International Labor Organization. 1993. Fifteenth International Conference of Labor Statisticians (ICLS), "Resolution Concerning the Informal Sector." *Bulletin of Labor Statistics.* Geneva: ILO.

Kruijt, Dirk. 1993."La Sociedad Informal" [The Informal Society]. Pp. 11–39 in *La Economía de los Pobres.* ed. Yassid Barrera, Miguel Castiglia, Kirk Kruijt, Rafael Menjivar and Juan Pablo Perez, San José, Costa Rica: Facultad Latino Americana de Ciencias Sociales.

Lacabana, Miguel. 1993. "La calle como puesto de trabajo: Reflexiones acerca de la relacion Estado-Sector informal urbano" [The Street as a Working Position: Reflections on the Relation State- Urban Informal Sector]. *Cuadernos del CENDES* 10 (22): 195–210.

Lautier, Bruno. 2004. *L'économie informelle dans le tiers monde.* Paris: La Découverte (Coll. "Repères").

Mascarenhas de Jesus, Gilmar. 1995. "The Territoriality of the Street Markets in Rio de Janeiro." *European Geographer Review* 9: 112–118.

Rodrick, Dani. 1997. *Has Globalization Gone Too Far?* Washington, DC: Institute for International Economics.

Tokman, Viktor, ed. 2001. *De la informalidad a la modernidad* [From Informality to Modernity]. Santiago: International Trade Organization.

Torres Jiménez, Ricardo. 1996. "El comercío en la vía publica como forma de sobrevivencia" [The Business on the Public Way as a Means of Survival]. *Sociologica* 11 (32): 159–169.

World Labour Confederation. 2002. *Travailler dans l'informel: Une chance, un risque, un défi.* Annual Report. http://www.cmt-wcl.org/cmt/ewcm.nsf/0/ dab61a7800c35715c1256eb50046ba52/$file/rapp_2002_econom%20inf_ fr.pdf?openelement: accessed May 5, 2006.

Zanoni Lopez, Wladimir. 2005. *Buhoneros en Caracas: Un estudio exploratorio y algunas propuestas de políticas públicas* [Street Vendors in Caracas: an Exploratory Study and some Proposals for Public Policies]. Caracas: CEDICE.

8 Common Roots, Shared Traits, Joint Prospects? On the Articulation of Multiple Modernities in Benin and Haiti

Dirk Kohnert

ON THE CONCEPT OF CULTURES OF INNOVATION

No culture is inherently good or bad, a simple truth that, however, has to be underlined time and again in view of fashionable but doubtful theses on the "clash of cultures," "rogue states," and "axes of evil." Stimulated by Max Weber's enlightening concept of the Protestant ethic as the spirit of European capitalist development, generations of social scientists searched for similar cultural innovations that could promote economic growth in developing countries. However, outdated hypotheses about monocultural readings of a nation's past or about cultural determinism that were considered inspiring truth turned out to be oversimplifications of little prognostic value (cf. Sen 2004). Nevertheless, they remain cherished by many scholars and development experts, not least because they provide ready-made concepts. Though a tendency still prevails to underrate the role of culture in development, there is a consensus in the social sciences that culture matters.[1] The question is rather: What constitutes the decisive element of culture in relation to development, and how does culture matter (cf. DiMaggio 1994; Elwert 1996; Rao and Walton 2004; Sen 2004)?

A holistic understanding of the linkage between culture and development is the underlying rationale of the concept of *cultures of innovation*, developed by UNESCO (2004), d'Orville (2004), and others. Cultures of innovation are relatively stable modes of cognition, behavior and social organization, directed toward "modernization" and "development." They are often based on shared values and fulfill important roles of orientation, motivation, coordination, and legitimization, concerning the actual performance of innovation processes (cf. Heidenreich 2001). The concept provides a methodological framework for the delimitation and analysis of cognitive and action oriented elements and strategies of innovative agency.

Today, as in the past, cultures of innovation have existed not only in industrialized countries, but in nearly every region of the world. However, there is no one-way direction of cultural change. Both the quest for universal growth inducing cultural essentials in developing countries and the transfer of globalized concepts of structural adjustment, as pushed by international donors during the 1980s, failed. Preconceived ideas that might have had success within the European cultural setting did not act up in the face of the sociocultural heritage of African societies; neither did the opposite, the idealization of *Négritude* or other "authentic" traditional African cultures. It is important for our purpose to take into account the diversity of mutually competitive systems within any given culture. It is not true that anything that is modern is at the same time development oriented, as was demonstrated time and again by the critique of monocausal theories of modernization. The study of occult belief systems showed, for example, the different facets of the modernity of African belief in magic and witchcraft (cf. Geschiere 1997; Comaroff and Comaroff 1999). Depending on their local environment and linkages to transnational social spaces, these occult belief systems played an emancipating or delaying role (cf. Kohnert 2003).

On the other hand, even seemingly static cultural factors such as customs, tradition, religion, or ethnicity that are often considered as barriers to economic growth in Africa have been introduced or adapted to changing social requirements. In many cases, they are not backward oriented but, on the contrary, represent multiple modernities of developing areas (cf. Comaroff and Comaroff 2000; Deutsch et al. 2003; Ferguson 2006; Geschiere et al. 2007). Therefore, it would be misleading to put the blame for lacking development in Africa or elsewhere on the cultural heritage, as supposedly incorporated in "traditional African institutions" that are frequently considered in a simplistic manner as customary barriers to democratization or economic growth. The underlying dualistic concept of culture (modern vs. traditional) ignores the reality of a universe of different coexisting and often competing cultures within a society (cf. Sen 2004). A closer look at these so called sociocultural barriers to growth reveals that African cultures are highly differentiated with substantial instances of "high modernity" (cf. Scott 1998). Cultures of innovation depend on space-, time-, and context-specific frameworks. They are a significant part of development-oriented processes of socialization, influenced by globalization and transnational social spaces (cf. Robertson 1995; Sassen 2001; Pries 2001; Schuerkens 2003).

SPECIFIC CULTURES OF INNOVATION WITHIN THE INFORMAL SECTOR

Multiple Cultures of Innovation Versus Globalized Western Concepts of Modernization

The breeding ground for African and Afro-American cultures of innovation is the informal, not the formal sector. In the following, I prefer to consider the informal sector with Elwert, Evers, and Wilkens (1983: 283), Portes, Castells, and Benton (1989: 12), and Feige (1990: 990) as the sector of the economy that is not, or only insufficiently, recorded, controlled, taxed, or otherwise regulated by state activities. Hitherto, academic interest and research focused on innovations in the formal sector, for example, on the state, national political, or economic elites, that is, the driving forces of change and their innovative agency or management qualities, mostly linked with supposedly universal values of democratization and economic growth, with their globally propagated concepts, like good governance, account-ability, structural adjustment, and free markets (cf. Grindle 1996; UNESCO 2004). Unfortunately, the neglect of informal cultures of innovation prompted the disregard of crucial potentials of innovation, particularly in the poorest African countries and in the African Diasporas of the Americas. Redirecting research toward the informal sector is crucial because of the following reasons.

The first reason is the utmost importance of the informal sector for least developed countries (LDCs) in general and for the African poor in particu-lar.[2] To guarantee the survival of the poor who can no longer merely rely on their local cultural heritage (e.g., traditional norms of reciprocity and solidarity are rapidly disintegrating under the pressure of globalization), we have to look for innovative solutions within their social setting that is the informal sector. The quest for these solutions is strongly influenced by cul-tures of innovation.

However, and this is the second reason. explained in detail later, signifi-cant structural differences exist not only between cultures of innovations of the formal and the informal sector, but also within the informal sector. Both differences have serious repercussions with regard to the developmen-tal trajectory.

Third, the fault lines between the formal and the informal become increas-ingly blurred by globalization. This has been demonstrated with respect to different standards applied to cultural innovations between the so-called "useful" and "useless" development regions by Reno (1998) and Ferguson (2006, 380)[3], who took "governance" criteria for strategic investments of oil-multinationals as examples. The enclaves of the "useful" Africa are no longer delimitated neither by national frontiers, nor by the divide between the formal and the informal, but by boundaries of transnational economic and social spaces. The chains of transnational enclaves of the "useful Africa," for example, of oil multinational enterprises in West Africa (often backed by powerful and hidden national interests), seem to function according to rules and ethics beyond the global discourse on governance or international development cooperation. In these regions, the poor are regularly excluded from the "useful Africa," as shown by the example of the Niger Delta. They have to accept the particular character of globalization, that is, globalized exclusion and marginalization. One way to overcome these adverse effects of globalization for the poor is the quest of the stakeholders for indigenous cultures of innovation.[4]

Finally, globalization is accompanied by new forms of (re-)construction of social and cultural identities and by a new dynamic delimitation of ethnicity.

The strategies of exclusion or of political instrumentation of ethnicity and religion deal with instructive examples (cf. Berking 2003; Kohnert 2003). In addition, globalization is geared toward the integration of new elements of a universal culture that are more often than not adapted to local conditions in order to maintain the identity of the group in question (cf. Berking 2003). Globalization is not just a question of growing uniformity, but at the same time of diversification, the creation of new cross-cultural social spaces of meaning and livelihoods. This kind of "glocalization" (cf. Robertson 1995; Altvater 2003; Schuerkens 2003) is typical for the configuration of innovative groups in the informal sector in Africa and the African Diasporas in the Americas.

Differences Between Formal and Informal Cultures of Innovation

In spite of the strong articulation of modes of production of the formal and informal sector (cf. Elwert, Evers, and Wilkens 1983), there are decisive differences between the cultures of innovation of both sectors. These differences concern both their social and economic structure and the political evaluation of their impact. Generations of innovative Hausa, Fulbe, Igbo, and Yoruba entrepreneurs in West Africa, for example, have contributed to the economic integration of the region through parallel cross-border trade between Nigeria and its neighbors. They established a sustainable culture of transnational trade networks (cf. Meillassoux 1971; Igué and Soule 1992). Even though pursuing similar goals as the regional organization ECOWAS (Economic Community of West African States), they were accused by the latter of undermining national economies because of their illegal activities. Consequently, they were harassed by the state (cf. Meagher 1995, 1997, 2003). With regard to structural differences, one has to note that informal cultures of innovation are mainly based on local oral traditions and empirical indigenous knowledge, whereas their formal equivalents rely heavily on written sources, science, and knowledge on a global level. As a rule, the former is better adapted to its respective natural, economic, social, and political environment with a strong propensity for flexible responses to external shocks (cf. Richards 2006). Even though their relevance is mostly restricted to the micro or meso level, they bear significant potentials for innovations in the poorer groups even on a national level and beyond (cf. Richards 1985; Hountondji 1997; Diawara 2003).

Indigenous cultures of innovation are especially relevant for least developed countries (LDCs), but also for the marginalized population of African descent in emerging industrialized countries like Brazil, notably because of their limited access to resources. Only empirical studies can show to what extent there are still niches for the development of indigenous cultures of innovation of the poor under conditions of "glocalization" (cf. Briggs and Sharp 2004). The outcome depends on the relation of different cultures of innovation to transnational social spaces.

Toward a Comprehensive Approach in the Analysis of Cultures of Innovation

Recognizing the cultures of innovation of the informal sector as distinct from formal sector ones does not suffice. Besides the intersector divergences of formal and informal cultures of innovation, there are strong indicators of intrasector differences. Moreover, one cannot deny the existence of common intersections of informal cultures of innovation. However, recent studies demonstrate that it is crucial to take into account not just the impact of the heterogeneity of the informal sector in general, such as its stratification according to different socioeconomic strata, as recognized by the International Labor Organization (ILO 2002) and the World Bank (2006: 187), but also a structured variety of informal cultures of innovation. The latter may be differentiated according to spaces (geographic as well as social) and cultural settings (e.g., class, gender, ethnicity, religion, etc.).

Therefore, I propose a more comprehensive approach to the analysis of cultures of innovation that takes into account not just inter-sector, but also possible intrasector cleavages and potentials. I focus on the impact of differentiation (class and gender) and its articulation to different regional and transnational contexts.

The articulation of multiple cultures of innovation, of its linkages, and of mutual reinforcement or obstruction is especially interesting with regard to the comparison of cultures in Africa and of the African Diasporas, notably in the Caribbean. What matters in this respect is not just the common sociocultural heritage, but even more its actual embeddedness in common transnational social spaces, as indicated by the ongoing discussion on the concept of the African Diaspora (cf. Cobley 1999; Byfield 2000; Manning 2003; Zeleza 2005). The perspective to rewrite global history "from below," taking African migration over the centuries as an still unfinished process (in the Habermasian sense of an "unfinished project") could contribute to overcome the prevailing Eurocentric interpretation of "modernity" and the linkage between culture and development (cf. Patterson and Kelley 2000; Manning 2003; Zeleza 2005). The deplored weakness of current Diaspora studies (that is, its essentialist character and its lack of systematic cross-reference between actual life-worlds of the homeland and the Diasporas) lets us look for empirically proven links between both, in order to contribute to the advancement of African Diaspora studies (cf. Manning 2003: 506). Hitherto, empirical studies on the current social relations of African communities in Africa and beyond have concentrated on economic aspects (e.g., remittances, capital flow). Cultural linkages have been disregarded or referred to with anecdotic evidence, although their impact is as important as economic factors. The importance of Aimé Cesaire's *Négritude* philosophy (later on adopted by Léopold Sédar Senghor), the U.S.-American Black Power movement on African liberation movements, the self-reflection of Africans (cf. Gilroy 1993), or the current discourse on African Renaissance by politicians of the post-apartheid government in Pretoria bears testimony for the cultural factors.

Multiple Fault Lines: On the Threefold Differentiation of Cultures of Innovation

The boundaries of cultures of innovation do not necessarily run along the formal and informal divide. Their articulation is characterized by a differentiation on three major structural levels:

- Between the formal and the informal sector (*intersector differentiation*),
- Between different social strata of the informal sector (*intrasector differentiation*),
- Between local and global or transnational social spaces (*transnational differentiation*).

Depending on the particular impact of these multiple fault lines, cultures of innovation can supplement and reinforce (synergy effect), or obstruct and even oppose each other, leading in extreme cases to violent confrontations, resembling local "cultural revolutions or "clash of cultures" (including important changes in gender roles). As a rule, at least one of the opposing groups represents itself as an innovative–emancipative force. Its forging and consolidation as culture of innovation can contribute to enhance the chances of goal implementation. The members of these social groups contribute, with their actions that are influenced by particular innovative cultures, to the multiple modernities that are characteristic for the development process of LDCs. Examples are the "cults of counter-violence" (Wilson 1992) that originated in the informal sector during the liberation movements of different African countries. Corresponding *popular modes of political action*, trying to reinterpret traditional communal ideals, and to implement them countrywide, are typical for the transition processes of many African states (cf. Geschiere 1997: 99–100).

Within the informal sector, differentiation may run along class, ethnic, religious, or gender lines. Actors of the different groups may have access to resources, but have divergent possibilities. Thus productivity, income, and political interest depend on class and gender. The same holds for the cultures characterized by the informal sector. An example for the latter is the *njang-njang* movement of Guinea-Bissau in the 1980s, where women defended their newly secured cultural rights that they had obtained because of their active participation in the war of liberation (cf. Jong 1987). After independence (1974), traditional and modern political authorities alike did not want to honor the newly acquired gender equality. This was one of the reasons why some enlightened Balante women created and sustained a gender-oriented religious liberation movement, the *njang-njang*. First limited to their own ethnic group, it later spread nationwide, including witchcraft accusations against dominant rulers on all levels of society (cf. Kohnert 1988). Because of the fact that these intrasector fault lines often have a decisive impact on the implementation of the aims of cultures of innovation, they deserve special attention. I demonstrate this phenomenon by taking the example of interclass differentiation at the grass-roots level between the poor, the middle class, and the upper class.

There is a threefold socioeconomic differentiation of the informal sector that extends to corresponding cultures of innovation.

a. The poor: Cultures of innovation of the poor have as a primordial orientation the assurance of their survival as human beings. But in addition they are often directed toward emancipation from oppression and empowerment; therefore, these cultures empower the group (cf. Altvater 2003: 14–18). The poor are marginalized because of their feeble resources, including a limited individual development potential (lack of education, poor health conditions, etc.). Their survival as human beings depends on the informal sector, as their access to the formal sector is severely restricted (schooling, labor and capital market, housing, health sector, judiciary, etc.). The effects of the neo-liberal adjustment programs have rather spurred the marginalization of the poor in the past decades. Typical actors are migrant workers, the families of small farmers, petty traders, child laborers, and child soldiers. Their culture of innovation is restricted to indigenous innovations. They are vulnerable to external shocks (e.g., disasters, epidemics, economic or political crisis) and liable to harmful external interventions (e.g., warlords, drug and child trafficking). Women, children, and the elderly are disproportionately represented in this group.

b. The middle class: In general, their resources allow the reproduction of the members of this class. They are deeply engrained in the formal and the informal sectors. However, this class can be divided in two subgroups. The lower middle class encompasses those whose resources are endangered and who are threatened by social decline. They take part in the activities of the informal sector mainly to secure a supplementary income. Their innovation culture is characterized by the aim to preserve their acquired economic and social status. Typical actors are wage earners and employees in the formal sector, some greater peasants, and small traders. On the contrary, the upper middle class (senior officers, academics, small and middle entrepreneurs, etc.)

is oriented toward risk prevention and income diversification. Their involvement in the informal sector is meant to consolidate their position in the formal sector, for example, a good career in the civil service. Their innovative culture is directed toward social advancement.

c. Upper class: The rich and powerful: Their livelihood is secured in the formal sector, among others by their affluent resources, and is sustained by social and political networks they are embedded in. They use the informal sector strategically for profit maximizing and risk diversification, for example, by large-scale parallel transborder trade (smuggling and reexport of used cars, drugs, weapons, or humans, etc.), and warlordism. This is predominantly a male domain and the corresponding innovative culture aims at power consolidation. Local rulers frequently use their innovative cultures for the pursuit of vested interests and the suppression of the poor and marginalized, which leads then to the cultural foundations of "markets of violence," anchored at the crossroad of the formal and informal, local, regional, and transnational social spaces (cf. Elwert et al. 1999; Collier and Hoeffler 2004).

Gender specific lines of differentiation of innovative cultures run across these socioeconomic fault lines. Female-related cultures typically aim at assuring the reproduction of the family or the emancipation from male dominance (cf. the example of *njang-njang* in Guinea-Bissau, mentioned earlier). Hence, gender-oriented development is not just a normative end in itself, but can be deemed to have positive repercussions on the economic and political development, too. Further examples are given by Chamlee (1993), who shows that women in the Ghanaian informal sector created an innovative culture of trust-based business relations, and Burger et al. (1996) demonstrated that the culture of social learning was gender specific among coffee growers in Kenya, who predominantly adopted innovations from innovators of the same gender.

African cultures of innovation in Benin and Haiti are well suited for an in-depth study of these articulations, not just because of their common sociocultural heritage but because of the continuing cultural exchange that is not restricted to bilateral contacts and concerns, as well as the exchange of cultures of innovation between Africa and the global African Diaspora. In times of globalization, the figuration of embeddedness of conflicting groups and cultures is influenced in a growing manner by transnational social spaces, a fact that holds true in particular for the articulation of African cultures and societies with those of the African Diaspora. Again, the impact of these multilocal and transnational social spaces is ambiguous; it can be conflict reducing or conflict enhancing.

CASE STUDIES: *VODUN*-BASED CULTURES OF
INNOVATION AND EMPOWERMENT IN BENIN
AND HAITI IN TIMES OF GLOBALIZATION

A significant number of cultural innovations have been inspired by religion.
Well-known examples are the impact of the protestant ethics on the growth of
European capitalism mentioned before, or the popular movement for democratization and human rights, driven by the liberation theology in the Americas
since the 1970s (cf. Smith 1991). In the following, I elaborate on comparative
studies of the less-known example of popular movements for democratization
in Benin and Haiti. They share the strong influence of cultures of innovation
inspired by an enlightened *vodun* (including its Afro-American equivalent),[5]
combined with different denominations of Christian orientation, on the democratic transition and the empowerment of the poor.

The following comparative case studies are intended to generate hypotheses within the framework of the already described theory building. They
underline that any monocausal explanation of cultural change that focuses
solely on religion or another single variable is doomed to fail. The outcome
of cultures of innovation is a process that depends to a large extent on the
link of competing cultures. Only a prudent analysis that takes due care of the
articulation of different strands of cultural innovations and their linkage to
social stratification, transnational social spaces, and globalization makes for
their explicatory and prognostic power.

Benin: Multiple Local Cultures of Innovation

Benin, formerly known as Dahomey, is located at the West African Bight of
Benin, sandwiched between the neighboring giant Nigeria and Togo. It has a
reputation as both the *quartier latin* of francophone Africa and the cradle of
vodun. The Benin democratic renewal (*renouveau démocratique*) that started
in 1989 and put an end to nearly two decades of autocratic socialist rule was
welcomed as a model of democratization in sub-Saharan Africa. Not least
in light of its possible spread, Benin provides an illustrative example of the
impact of innovative cultures on democratization, rooted in and insepara-
bly linked to transnational social spaces, as explained next. Contrary to a
widespread belief, the second wind of change in Benin was less determined
by the effects of the fall of the Berlin Wall, but was prepared and triggered
off by popular indigenous opposition movements. As shown here, they were
inspired by development-oriented ethics of Christian institutions that closely
interacted with agents of change encouraged by a modern *vodun*.

The Ambiguous Role of African Religion And Traditional Leaders

The democratization process in Benin had been initiated and promoted
by the "return of the religious" (Mayrargue 2002). A modern *vodun*,[6]

Pentecostals, and the Catholic Church were united in their opposition to the "socialist project" of the Kérékou era (1972–1989), a project that had become incredible (cf. Tall 1995a, 1995b). While creating different, often conflicting cultures of innovation in the 1980s, these people upheld a common aim, paving the way for the fall of the autocratic Kérékou regime (cf. Banégas 1995a, 1995b). Although the Marxist policy of the Kérékou regime in the 1970s and early 1980s regarded African religions and their representatives as a "relict of feudalism" and was highly suspicious of the role of the Catholic Church, both played important roles as mediator and broker of the *renouveau démocratique*. This resulted in a change of roles in its leading ranks, notably of Mgr. de Souza, archbishop of Cotonou, who became the president of the National Conference and of the interim government. But the failure of the "socialist project" also resulted in a new legitimization of an enlightened *vodun*, of charismatic churches (like the *Chrétiens célestes*), and of new antiwitchcraft movements (cf. Tall 2003: 77, 87). Occult belief systems, notably the belief in magic and witchcraft, incorporated in both the *vodun* and the Pentecostals, played an ambiguous role in Benin's development process (cf. Tall 1995a). Depending on local historical preconditions and the actual social setting in different provinces, not all "traditional authorities" (like village heads and *vodun* priests) were necessarily "progressive." Some of them acted as intermediaries and facilitators of indigenous innovative capacity that promoted development, others operated as stumbling blocks of cultural change (Elwert-Kretschmer 1995; Tall 2003). Thus, on the eve of the electoral campaign for the presidential election in 1991, the contender of Kérékou, and subsequent winner of the election, Nicéphore Soglo was empoisoned but could restore health. The crime was attributed to political adversaries of Soglo, who were accused of employing witchcraft.[7] Later on the incumbent head of state was cured with the help of *vodun* priests of his hometown Abomey. As a result, the Soglo government officially recognized *vodun* in 1996 as one of the important religions of Benin, beside Islam and Christianity.

*Competing Cultures of Opposition Movements
Imposed the Democratic Renewal*

Indigenous opposition movements in Benin can broadly be classified as belonging to two categories: popular movements of resistance "from below" and elitist opposition movements. The former comprised organizations from different denominations, notably trade unions and peasant groups that were opposed to the payment of the per capita tax, and obstructed or circumvented public regional development programs (CARDERs, *Centre d'Action Régionale pour le Développement Rural*), and promoted a general climate of passive resistance and civic disobedience (cf. Kohnert and Preuss 1992). The outlawed communist party (*Parti communiste du Dahomey*, PCD, founded in 1977) that established its headquarters in two rural districts

(Djakotomé in the Mono province and Boukoumbé in Atakora), struggled from 1988 to unite these sociocultural forces in a common opposition and played an outstanding role in the organization of mass protests in December 1989 (cf. Banégas 1995a: 29).

The opposition of the elite, spearheaded by the students' and teachers' unions, was embedded in the informal network of the *quartier latin* of francophone Africa.[8] They had a decisive impact on the democratization process, and on the organization of the sovereign National Conference (1990) in Cotonou. The latter initiated a peaceful alternation of political power structures in Benin at the national level (cf. Nwajiaku 1994; Adamon 1995; Heilbrunn 1995). This *renouveau démocratique,* mainly organized by an educated elite that embraced different ethnic, regional, professional, and religious groups of the civil society, was admired and imitated as an excellent example by other African countries. Though even marginalized groups, such as peasants, and local development associations received a chance to participate (cf. Banégas 1995a; Séhouéto 1994), the grass-roots opposition movements, who had paved the way to this first successful civil coup d'état in Africa, were later disregarded and deprived of the fruits of their resistance.

Indigenous Civic Subcultures in West Africa as Pioneers of Transition

In addition, interactive civic (sub)cultures in different West African countries contributed to indigenous cultural innovations "from below." They were active, for example, in local political theater groups of students, griots (praise singers), and nongovernmental organizations (NGOs) that prepared the political terrain for the process of democratic renewal in Benin, Togo, and the Ivory Coast (cf. Séhouéto 1994; Monga 1995). At the same time, dynamic Fulbe intellectuals acted at the meso and micro level as political and cultural brokers of indigenous cultural change in northern Benin. They promoted a new, more development-oriented ethnic identity, based on the mediation of the aims of the modern nation state and traditional elements of Fulbe culture (cf. Bierschenk 1995).

Bottom-Up Processes of Indigenous Cultural Change and a Transition Dominated By Aid, Local Development Brokers, and Venality

As a result, the transition process in Benin had been promoted not so much by a transfer of Western culture, knowledge, technology, or finance, but by a bottom-up process of indigenous cultural change. Later on, it became formalized and dominated by a top-down propagation of concepts of Western political culture, focusing on institutional change and "good governance," as promoted by official development assistance. Local brokers of development aid accelerated this change in cultural policy, which was not adapted to sustainable development (cf. Bierschenk et al. 1993).

A Globalized Culture of Human Rights Standards Strengthened the Constitutional Court in Cotonou as an Effective Third Tier of Government

However, the imposition of Western standards of democratization had also notable positive effects. Driven by a strong impetus of liberation from the autocratic rule of the past and by globalized standards of Human Rights (backed by the international donor community), the Constitutional Court under the guidance of its first president, Elisabeth Poignon, established a new culture of independent judiciary as an effective counterbalance of power at the national level (cf. Rotman 2004). Unfortunately, this promising development did not trickle down as expected to the lower levels of the Benin judicial system. The latter remained highly corrupt and exposed to the politics of the "African command state" (cf. Kohnert 1997; Elwert 2001). Subsequently, the "politics of the belly" once more gained predominance, even in the decisions of the Benin High Courts, during the roll-back strategy under the second and third Kérékou regime (1996–2006).

The Promising Development of A Free Media As Fourth Tier of Control of the State in the Early 1990s, Weakened By Globalized Standards of Media Markets, Poor Training, and Venality

In the early stages of transition, the free press in Benin, driven by highly motivated local agents of cultural change, acted more as an effective control of government and state administration than public legislative institutions. However, the commercialization and decline of professional ethics of journalism, caused by the daily strife for survival in a highly competitive but limited market, affected the role of the media as fourth tier of state control (cf. Adjovi 2002). Nowadays many tabloids tend to be riddled with venality and tainted by globalized Western standards of the rainbow press (cf. Frère 1995). Well-adapted mushrooming communal and private local radio stations, based on a close intermarriage of international technology transfer, local culture and politics, and commercial radio management, were also helpful in promoting a modern innovative radio culture at the grass-root level since 1997 (cf. Frère 1995; Grätz 1997). This phenomenon stood in strong contrast to the chronically ill-adapted top-down public rural radio extension programs of the former socialist Kérékou regime.

The Newly Established Laissez-Faire Culture, Cultivated as Antithesis to the Centralized Economy of the Socialist State, Had Ambiguous Effects

The ongoing top-down program of liberalization and privatization of state-owned companies (such as the oil company *Société Nationale de*

Commercialisation des Produits Pétroliers, SONACOP) had ambiguous effects. While it was meant to guarantee effective management, in some cases, it rather tended to create a symbiosis and a concentration of economic and political power during the implementation process. Powerful entrepreneurs, enriched by political patronage, transformed themselves into new political leaders and hidden financiers of the government. One flagrant example was the case of multimillionaire Séfou Fagbohoun and his influential political party *Mouvement Africain pour la Démocratie et le Progrès* (MADEP; cf. Adjovi 2002: 8) that won nine seats in the National Assembly in 2003. The general secretary of MADEP, Mrs. Antoine Idji Kolawolé, former foreign Minister, was elected president of the Benin National Assembly on 24 April 2003. In order to cope with the aftermath of political corruption during the Kérékou regime, Fagbohoun was imprisoned and accused of corruption under the new government of Yayi Boni in June 2006 in the course of judicial investigations of the SONACOP scandal.

The Top-Down Approaches of Decentralization Promoted *"Politics of the Belly" Rather Than Actual Empowerment*

Decentralization policy, as promoted by massive development aid since the early 1990s, was readopted and transformed by local political actors according to their own logic and interests. This did not necessarily lead to an increase in local participation, democracy, or legal practices (in the western sense) at the local level (cf. Grätz 1996; Alber 1997; Alber and Sommer 1999; Bierschenk 1999, 2003).

A Long-Established Informal Culture of a Transit Economy, *Consolidated by Globalization and Innovative Entrepreneurs, Promoted More Effectively Economic Growth Than Aid*

Democratization without economic growth is hardly sustainable. In this respect, Benin profited from a long established culture of parallel transborder trade (*Entrepôt Trade*; cf. Igué and Soule 1992), going back to pre-colonial sociocultural West African trade networks of Hausa and Yoruba traders. An innovative shadow economy, pushed by lucrative transnational parallel markets (transit economy toward landlocked neighboring Sahara countries and Nigeria) that flourished in the aftermath of the Nigerian oil boom and the "second wind of change," probably contributed more to Benin's economic growth than the massive influx of development aid (cf. Igué and Soule 1992; Beuving 2004). In this respect, the "politics of the belly," combined with the fragile state monopoly of violence and taxation of the new liberal-democratic state that have often been considered as a barrier to economic growth, created, quite to the contrary, a growth-inducing momentum.

Haiti: Democratic Transition Driven by Subversive Cultures of Innovation and Inspired by Vodun

The specific blend of religious cultures of innovation (*vodun* and Catholicism) that stimulated democratic transition in Benin had an impact in Haiti as well, although in a different manner. Nevertheless, the stakeholders as well as outside observers stressed the common African roots of their venture with lasting repercussions. Haiti is the only country worldwide where African slaves, guided by *vodun* as a liberation theology, defeated their colonial masters, establishing their own free state already in the 19th century. Since the 1980s, subversive cultures of innovation, inspired by *vodun* and Christian liberation theology, again drove democratic transition.

The Haitian Vodun Acted as a Modern Driving Force for Democratic Transition, Along With Transnational Networks of Liberation Theology, Against the Firm Resistance of the Religious and Political Establishment

Since the slave rebellion of 1791–1794 and the subsequent liberation of Haiti, the Haitian variety of *vodun* (*vaudoun* or *vodou* in French spelling, dominated by Yoruba elements and those originating in Dahomey, and imported by the slave trade) was the religion of the people, and crucial in forming the Haitian ethos and nationality. About 90 percent of the population adheres to it. In informal politics, *vodun* had always had a great impact, both on the local and on the national level. Various political leaders utilized the cult with ambiguous effects, ranging from the emancipation from slavery (the only slave rebellion worldwide that succeeded in creating a proper nation-state), to the brutal oppression by the *tonton macouts*, who were assisted by corrupted *vodun* priests under the Duvalier dynasty that ended in political turmoil in 1986 (cf. Laguerre 1990; Rotberg 1997: 28–29; Corbet et al. 1999; Michel and Bellegarde-Smith 2007). However, the overwhelming part of the elite, politicians and development experts alike, publicly denounced it as superstition, relict of the past, and impediment to development (cf. Rotberg 1976: 356).

In addition, the Catholic religion, recognized by the concordat of 1860 as the only official religion in Haiti, tried in vain to eliminate *vodun*, even though it maintained a fragile peace with its rival by incorporating elements of its liturgy in its own service since the 1950s (cf. Corbett 1988). Thus, in fact, the church copied a strategy successfully used already some 300 years earlier by adherents of *vodun*. African slaves had camouflaged their continuing worship of *vodun*, outlawed by the church and colonial authorities, by integrating Christian elements in their religion.

To counteract dictatorship and human rights violation by the Duvalier regime and its successors, a grass-roots movement for the empowerment of the poor and marginalized, called *Ti Legliz* (Creole, literally meaning "small church"), came into being in the 1970s. Religion, both Haitian *vodun* and the Haitian variety of the Christian theology of liberation, played a decisive role.[9]

People progressively transformed these ecclesial base organizations into "grass-root communities" with a threefold vocation, religious, social, and political. The movement gained full momentum with the religious-political campaigns of Jean-Bertrand Aristide, a charismatic Catholic priest of an impoverished parish in Port-au-Prince, in the aftermath of the deposition of "Baby Doc" (Duvalier Junior). Subsequently, the movement expanded quickly, through the formation of thousands of *Ti Legliz* and similar *Tet Ansamn* peasant groups, notably in the countryside and among youth and slum dwellers in the cities. They were considered as cradle of the *Organisation populaire Famni Lavalas*, forerunner of the renowned party *Lavalas* or *Famni Lavalas* (Creole, "family avalanche" in English, referring to the biblical flood), a title borrowed from a popular peasant song (cf. Rotberg 1976; Taylor 1992; Corbett et al. 1999) designed to bring Aristide to power. As a result, the power elite considered the movement as a serious menace. The hierarchy of the Catholic Church has upheld its critical attitude up to the present days (cf. Taylor 1991: 817–819). Politically motivated persecution, intimidation, torture, imprisonment, and murder were at the agenda. Even the U.S. government and the Central Intelligence Agency (CIA), which sided with the Haitian political establishment, realized the revolutionary potential of *vodun* as being greater than that of the Haitian Communist Party at that time (cf. Bellegarde-Smith 1999), an assessment that proved to be quite accurate. Notwithstanding the death of thousands of activists and at least nine unsuccessful murder attempts of the movement's leader, 4 years later, in December 1990, J. B. Aristide became the first freely and democratically elected president in the country's history. The population celebrated the event as a "second independence," with reference to the liberation from slavery some 200 years ago. Yet the traditional power elite, the military and economic establishment, reacted with a rollback strategy. Only eight months later, Aristide, the legitimately elected leader, was ousted for the first time by a military coup on September 30, 1991.

Vodun was officially recognized as a state religion besides Catholicism in April 2003 by the second Aristide government (2000–2004) in a desperate act of populist legislation. The state recognized baptisms, marriages, and funerals performed by *vodun* officials by a decree; this fact constituted a significant step in guaranteeing religious freedom and in breaking down the Haitian social class structure. Thus, during political transition, antagonistic cultures of innovation in Haitian's informal sector, each reinterpreting *vodun* according to their own group's interest, portraying themselves as agents of change and "modernizers," were confronted (cf. Averill 1997).

Popular Music, Stimulated by a Modern Interpretation of Vodun, Was Crucial in Establishing a Subversive Freedom Culture That Promoted Democratic Transition

There is an exceptionally strong relationship between popular Haitian music, power, and politics, as shown by Gage Averill (1997). He established four points: First, "Haitian politics and more generally the struggle for power have been introduced into every arena of musical expression. Popular music, as a discursive terrain, is a site where power is enacted, acknowledged, accommodated, signified, contested, and resisted" (cf. Averill 1997: xi–xv). Second, just as in the area of religion, the instrumentalism of music in politics is highly ambiguous. It can and has been used both, as a tool to justify and to camouflage despotic rule, such as the *noirisme* by Duvalier's regime, or as a struggle for empowerment of the oppressed, as illustrated below in the case of the *angaje* (politically engaged) music of pop groups like Boukman Eksperyans. Third, since the 1950s, the message, songs, and rhythms of *vodun* have increasingly been incorporated into popular Haitian music, albeit not in an unchanged "traditional" way, but in an adapted modern way, corresponding to the actual social and political conditions. Finally, the Haitian diasporas, forced into emigration by economic need or by political harassment, have played a crucial role in creating a Haitian freedom culture (*Kilti libète*, in Creole) with its engaging poetry, drama, and music, linking "traditional" peasant cultures with progressive politics. The "unfinished migration" of the slave trade, combined with a continuous migration of Haitians of all classes, due to different, often opposed economic or political reasons, contributed to a dynamic and inspiring culture that had a profound impact on the essentially transnational composition of Haitian identity, including its intimate relationship to the West African *vodun* cosmology (cf. Averill 1997: 161–207).

The pop-group Boukman Eksperyans was an outstanding example for such *angaje* music. It was part of the popular resistance movement *Operasyon Dechoukaj*[10] that contributed to the fall of the Duvalier regime. Like other popular activists of *mizik rasin*, or new roots-music, such as Manno Charlemagne, Boukan Ginen, and the roots band Ram, they combined the liberating aspects of Haitian *vodun*, as represented by the legend about the *vodun* priest Boukman Dutty (see earlier description), and visions of global syncretism of world religions, with demands for the empowerment of the poor, elements of *rara* carnival, Afro-pop, and American rock music (cf. Averill 1997; McAlistar 2002; Ewen 2003: 11–13).

POTENTIAL OF INDIGENOUS CULTURES OF INNOVATION IN TIMES OF *GLOCALIZATION*

Enlarging the choice by promoting stimuli for innovative actors and by improving the competition of cultures and ideas is an important means to promote development. However, we have to consider the serious problem of asymmetric power relations in a globalized world (cf. Sen 2002: 18–19). The *high modernist ideology* (Scott 1998), still propagated by many Western and African experts alike,[11] is not only tainted by the dangers of

Eurocentrism and top-down approaches. It diverts attention also from exploring the potential of indigenous cultural innovations, but it tends to undermine the informal social and economic structures of indigenous cultures, the ground where local innovations may flourish.

In general, cultures of innovation are powerful stimuli for agents of change. However, awareness does not necessarily lead to political action, and not all cultures of innovation in the informal sector have positive effects on the poor. In order to have a sustainable positive impact, they must be embedded in a social structure that favors development. In particular, their articulation with social stratification and gender is crucial for the outcome of the innovation process.

Indigenous cultural innovations are thus better suited to promote sustainable development than externally induced innovations with questionable potentials of adaptation, notably if they are reduced to one-dimensional categorizations and identities.

Transnational social networks play an increasing role in promoting the interactions of cultures and in transmitting cultural innovations into the informal sector where they may be adopted easier than innovations imposed by official assistance or formal institutions. The impact of multilocal social spaces on the interactive process of cultural change and on the diffusion of innovations in the informal sector is not restricted to the educated elite. It concerns different social strata on macro, meso, and micro levels, as shown in our comparative case study.

To put it in a nutshell, the globalized Western culture of innovation, as propagated by major assistance institutions, does not necessarily lead to empowerment or improvement of the stakeholders' well-being. On the contrary, it often blocks viable indigenous innovation cultures. However, the latter are not per se the better alternatives. All depends on their embeddedness in development-oriented social structures.

ACKNOWLEDGMENTS

This chapter is a revised paper presented at the 16th World Congress of the International Sociological Association, Durban, South Africa, July 23 to 29, 2006. An earlier version of the paper was delivered to the INST–International Conference on Innovations and Reproductions in Cultures and Societies (IRICS), Vienna, December 9 to 11, 2005, also available as an extended online version in the series of GIGA Working Papers, number 25, July 2006, at www.giga-hamburg.de/content/publikationen/pdf/wp25_kohnert.pdf. Thanks for valuable suggestions go to the participants of the conferences just mentioned, and to my colleagues at GIGA, notably Gilberto Calcagnotto, Wolfgang Hein, Steffen Trede, and Janina Dill. The responsibility for any mistakes or inaccuracies in the chapter remains of course with the author.

NOTES

1. In the following, I use the term *culture* in the sense of A. Sen (2002), who underlines that culture has to be recognized as "non-homogeneous, non-static, and interactive"; otherwise, cultural prejudice and determinism lead to alienation, political tyranny, and doubtful theories.

2. In the 1990s, the informal sector contributed an average of 41 percent to the GDP in sub-Saharan Africa (Benin: 41 percent; Ghana: 58 percent) and 29 percent in Latin America, according to tentative estimates of the ILO (ILO 2002: 24; Rotman 1990).

3. Machiavellian terms coined by Reno (1998) with allusion to the French Gaullist interpretation of *l'Afrique utile vs. l'Afrique inutile.*

4. I consider cultural innovations as *indigenous* if they are rooted in the culture of the group, for example, in the sense of Paulin Hountondji (1997), Paul Richards (1985, 2006), Diawara (2003), and Briggs and Sharp (2004), who used the term. Yet the acceptance of foreign influence and its integration in the local imaginary constitute indigenous innovations as well, notably if these external factors are adapted to local conditions.

5. The African religion of *vodun* originated in the precolonial kingdom of "Dāxome" (Dahomey, in present Southern Benin Republic, still considered to be the spiritual center of this religion and of its Latin American derivates). West African slaves, primarily descended from the Ewe, Anlo-Ewe, and other West African groups, brought it to the Americas, where it became transformed and adapted to the specific social and political conditions of various countries, like Haiti (*vodou*), Cuba (*Santeria*), and Brazil (*candomblé*).

6. As represented by the syncretistic movement for the inculturation of Christianity and the reinterpretation of the *vodun* (*Mewihwendo*, or *Sillon Noir*, cf. Adoukonou 1989); or by the *Atingali* and *Glo- and Kpe-vodun*, imported from Ghana already in the 1930s (cf. Tall 1995a, 1995b).

7. Cf. the interview with N. Soglo, *L'Intelligent–Jeune Afrique*, No. 2094, February 27, 2001, p. 33.

8. The expression "*quartier latin*" refers to the high percentage of an educated francophone elite in Benin, compared with other French-speaking African countries (cf. Bako Arifari 1995). However, we should bear in mind that the Benin elite, since the advent of colonial rule, maintained close social and political links not only to Paris but also to their peers in Dakar, Abidjan, and Lomé as well. Therefore, the network of the *quartier latin* is inseparable from the transnational social spaces of French speaking West Africa.

9. One indicator for the close relationship between Haitian liberation theology (*teyoloji liberasyon*) and *vodun* was the linkage with the famous "Boukman's Prayer" as the foundation of the *Ti Legliz* philosophy. The prayer, inspired by the wisdom of *vodun*, had been already used as a call for action by Boukman Dutty, a *houngan* or *vodou* priest who launched the Haitian Revolution, on August 14, 1791, at the Bwa Kayiman Vodun ceremony. Some 200 years later, it contributed again to the formation of Haitian liberation theology (cf. web site: www.margueritelaurent.com/campaigns/campaignone/presswork/freeprisoners.html#prayer, accessed June 16, 2006).

10. *Dechoukaj* or uprooting in Creole, and *mawonaj*, which means resistance, originally from slavery and currently from any form of oppression; this latter expression has the same roots as the English word Maroon.

11. Cf. Kohnert (1995) for a critical evaluation.

REFERENCES

Adamon, Afize D. 1995. *Le renouveau démocratique au Bénin: La conférence nationale des forces vives et la période de transition.* Paris: L'Harmattan.

Adjovi, Emmanuel V. 2002. "Liberté de presse et corruption au Bénin—La dérive du journalisme de marché." Working Paper Number 10, Department of Anthropology and African Studies, Mayence University, Germany.

Adoukonou, Barthélemy. 1989. *Vodun—Sacré ou violence? Mewihwendo et la question éthique au cœur du sacré vodun.* Thèse de doctorat d'état, Sociology, University Paris V, Sorbonne, unpublished.

Alber, Erdmute. 1997. "Le pouvoir local face aux mutations au niveau de l'État. Le cas d'un village bariba." *Cahiers d'études africaines* 37 (145): 137–156.

Alber, Erdmute, and Jörn Sommer. 1999. "Grenzen der Implementierung staatlichen Rechts im dörflichen Kontext. Eine Analyse der Rechtswirklichkeit in einem Baatombu-Dorf in Benin." *Afrika Spectrum* 34 (1): 85–111.

Altvater, Elmar. 2003. "Globalisation and the Informalisation of the Urban Space." Working Paper, Caracas: www.polwiss.fu-berlin.de/people/altvater/Altvater-informal.pdf, accessed August 2, 2006.

Averill, Gage. 1997. *A Day for the Hunter, A Day for the Prey: Popular Music and Power in Haiti.* Chicago: Chicago University Press, Studies in Ethnomusicology.

Bako Arifari, Nassirou. 1995. "Démocratie et logiques du terroir au Bénin." *Politique Africaine* 59: 7–24.

Banégas, Richard. 1995a. "Mobilisations sociales et oppositions sous Kérékou." *Politique Africaine* 59: 25–44.

Banégas, Richard. 1995b. "Le processus de transition à la démocratie—Action collective et transition politique en Afrique. La Conférence nationale du Bénin." *Cultures et Conflits* 17: 137–175.

Berking, Helmuth. 2003. "'Ethnicity is Everywhere': On Globalization and the Transformation of Cultural Identity." *Current Sociology* 51 (1/2, 3/4): 248–264.

Beuving, J. Joost. 2004. "Cotonou's Klondike: African Traders and Second-hand Car Markets in Benin." *Journal of Modern African Studies* 42 (4): 511–537.

Bierschenk, Thomas. 1995. "Rituels politiques et construction de l'identité ethnique des Peuls au Bénin." *Cahiers des sciences humaines* 31 (2): 457–484.

Bierschenk, Thomas. 1999. "Herrschaft, Verhandlung und Gewalt in einer afrikanischen Mittelstadt (Parakou, Benin)." *Afrika Spectrum* 34 (3): 321–348.

Bierschenk, Thomas. 2003. "Political Decentralisation. How Great Expectations in Paris, Berlin and Washington are Dashed in Parakou/Benin, or why it is Amazing that Democratic Reforms Work at all." Unpublished paper delivered at the AEGIS-conference on "How people elect their leaders. Parties, party systems and elections in Africa south of the Sahara," Hamburg, March 22–23.

Bierschenk, Thomas, Georg Elwert, and Dirk Kohnert. 1993. "The Long-Term Effects of Development Aid: Empirical Studies in Rural West Africa." *Economics* 47 (1): 83–111.

Briggs, John, and Joanne Sharp. 2004. "Indigenous Knowledges and Development—A Postcolonial Caution." *Third World Quarterly* 25 (4): 661–676.

Burger, K., P. Collier, and J. W. Gunning. 1996. "Social Learning—An Application to Kenyan Agriculture." WPS-93.5, Centre for the Study of African Economies, University of Oxford. www.csae.ox.ac.uk/workingpapers/pdfs/9305text.pdf, accessed August 7, 2006.

Byfield, Judith. 2000. "Introduction—Rethinking the African Diaspora." *African Studies Review* 43 (1): 26–28.

Chabal, Patrick, and Jean Pascal Daloz. 1999. *"Africa Works." Disorder as Political Instrument.* Oxford: James Currey.

Chamlee, Emily. 1993. "Indigenous African Institutions and Economic Development." *Cato Journal* 13 (1): 79–99.

Cobley, Alan. 1999. "Forgotten Connections, Unconsidered Parallels: A New Agenda for Comparative Research in Southern Africa and the Caribbean." *African Studies* 58 (2): 133–155.

Collier, Paul, and Anke Hoeffler. 2004. "Greed and Grievances in Civil War." *Oxford Economic Papers* 56 (4): 563–595.

Comaroff, Jean, and John Comaroff. 2000. "Privatizing the Millennium—New Protestant Ethics and the Spirits of Capitalism in Africa, and Elsewhere." *Afrika Spectrum* 35 (3): 293–312.

Comaroff, John, and Jean Comaroff. 1999. "Occult Economies and the Violence of Abstraction: Notes from the South African Postcolony." *American Ethnologist* 26 (2): 279–303.

Corbett, Bob. 1988. Introduction to Voodoo in Haiti. www.webster.edu/~corbetre/haiti/voodoo/overview.htm, accessed June 22, 2006.

Corbett, Bob, Patrick Bellegarde-Smith, Guy Antoine, Max Blanchet, and Mark Gill. 1999. Democracy and the Ti Legiz Movement. www.webster.edu/~corbetre/haiti/misctopic/ti-legliz/democracy.htm, accessed June 12, 2006.

Deutsch, Jan-Georg, Peter Probst, and Heike Schmidt, eds. 2003. *African Modernities—Entangled Meanings in Current Debate*. Portsmouth, NH: Heinemann.

Diawara, Mamadou, ed. 2003. *L'interface entre les savoirs paysans et le savoir universel*. Bamako: Le Figuier.

DiMaggio, Paul. 1994. "Culture and Economy." Pp. 27–57 in *Handbook of Economic Sociology*, ed. Neil J. Smelser and Richard Swedberg. Princeton, NJ: Princeton University Press.

D'Orville, Jean. 2004. "The Culture of Innovation and the Building of Knowledge Societies." Pp. 21–28 in *Dialogue among Civilizations—A Culture of Innovation and the Building of Knowledge Societies*, International Expert Symposium, Moscow, 9 to 11 November 2003; Conference Reader "Dialogue Among Civilizations" series, directed by Jean d'Orville, ed. Tina Bovermann and F. W. Russell. Bureau of Strategic Planning, Paris: United Nations Educational, Scientific and Cultural Organization (UNESCO).

Elwert, Georg. 1996. "Kulturbegriffe und Entwicklungspolitik. Über 'soziokulturelle Bedingungen der Entwicklung.'" Pp. 51–87 in *Kulturen und Innovationen*, ed. Georg Elwert. Berlin: Duncker & Humblot,

Elwert, Georg. 2001. "The Command State in Africa. State Deficiency, Clientelism and Power-locked Economies." Pp. 419–452 in *Entwicklungspolitische Perspektiven im Kontext wachsender Komplexität*, ed. Steffen Wippel and Inse Cornelssen. Forschungsberichte des BMZ 128. Bonn: Weltforum.

Elwert, Georg, Hans-Dieter Evers, and Werner Wilkens. 1983. "Die Suche nach Sicherheit—Kombinierte Produktionsformen im sogenannten informellen Sektor." *Zeitschrift für Soziologie* 12 (4): 281–296.

Elwert, Georg, Stephan Feuchtwang, and Dieter Neubert eds. 1999. "Dynamics of Violence. Processes of Escalation and De-Escalation in Violent Group Conflicts." Berlin: Duncker und Humblot. *Sociologus*, Special issue 1.

Elwert-Kretschmer, Karola. 1995. "Vodun et contrôle social au village." *Politique africaine* 59: 102–119.

Ewen, Stephen. 2003. *Exogenous Development vs. Endogenous Development in Haiti*. BA thesis, Florida Atlantic University, Jupiter, FL, http://bellsouthpwp.net/e/w/ewenste/stephen_ewen_thesis_2003.pdf, accessed September 14, 2005.

Feige, Edgar L. 1990. "Defining and Estimating Underground and Informal Economies: The New Institutional Economics Approach." *World Development* 18 (7): 989–1002.

Ferguson, James. 2006. *Global Shadows: Africa in the Neo-liberal World Order.* Durham, NC: Duke University Press.

Frère, M. S. 1995. "Pluralisme médiatique au Bénin: L'heure des désillusions?" *Politique Africaine* 57: 142–148.

Geschiere, Peter. 1997. *The Modernity of Witchcraft. Politics and the Occult in Postcolonial Africa.* Charlottesville, VA: University Press of Virginia.

Geschiere, Peter, Birgit Meyer, and Peter Pels, eds. 2007. *Readings in Modernity in Africa.* Oxford: James Currey.

Gilroy, Paul. 1993. The Black Atlantic—Modernity and Double Consciousness. Cambridge, MA: Harvard University Press.

Grätz, Tilo. 1996. "Tote, Helden, Rächer. Moral und lokale Politik in Tanguieta (Benin)." Pp. 150–158 in *Afrika und das Andere. Alterität und Innovation,* ed. Heike Schmidt and Albert Wirz. Münster: Lit.

Grätz, Tilo. 1997. "Lokale Radiostationen in Afrika. Radio Rurale Locale Tanguieta (Benin)." *Nord-Süd aktuell* 11 (4): 699–708.

Grindle, Merilee S., ed. 1996. *Challenging the State: Crisis and Innovation in Latin America and Africa.* Cambridge Studies in Comparative Politics. New York: Cambridge University Press.

Heidenreich, Martin. 2001. *Innovation und Kultur in europäischer Perspektive.* FS "European Integration and Global Society." Paper, Universität Bamberg, www.uni-bamberg.de/sowi/europastudien/innovationskulturen.htm, accessed July 7, 2006.

Heilbrunn, John R. 1995. "Social Origins of National Conferences in Benin and Togo." *Journal of Modern African Studies* 31 (2): 277–299.

Hountondji, Paulin J. 1997. *Endogenous Knowledge: Research Trails.* Dakar: Conseil pour le Développement de la Recherche économique et sociale en Afrique (CODESRIA).

Igué, John O., and Bio G. Soule. 1992. *L'État-entrepôt au Bénin: Commerce informel ou solution à la crise.* Paris: Karthala.

International Labor Organization. 2002. *Women and Men in the Informal Economy—A Statistical Picture.* Geneva: ILO.

Jong, J. T. V. M. de. 1987. "Jangue-jangue—La politique par le bas en Guinée-Bissau." *Politique Africaine* 28: 108–112.

Kohnert, Dirk. 1988. "Socialism Without Liberation—Land Reclamation Projects in Guinea-Bissau." *Sociologia Ruralis* 2/3: 161–175.

Kohnert, Dirk. 1995. "New Markets for Local Experts in Africa?" Pp. 63–74 in *Responsibilities to South Consultants in Developing Countries,* ed. Michael von Hauff and H. Werner. Ludwigsburg/Berlin: Verlag Wissen und Praxis.

Kohnert, Dirk. 1997. "Verfassung und Rechtsstaatlichkeit im Demokratisierungsprozeß Benins 1989–1996." Pp. 169–195 in *Verfassunggebung in der Dritten Welt,* ed. Joachim Betz. Hamburg: Schriften des Deutschen Übersee Instituts, No. 37.

Kohnert, Dirk. 2003. "Witchcraft and Transnational Social Spaces: Witchcraft Violence, Reconciliation and Development in South Africa' s Transition Process." *Journal of Modern African Studies* 41 (2): 217–245.

Kohnert, Dirk, and Hans J. A. Preuss. 1992. "Vom Camarade zum Monsieur: Strukturanpassung und Demokratisierung in Benin." *Peripherie* 46: 47–70.

Laguerre, Michel S. 1990. *Voodoo and Politics in Haiti.* London: Macmillan.

Manning, Patrick. 2003. "Africa and the African Diaspora: New Directions of Study." *Journal of African History* 44: 487–506.

Mayrargue, Cédric. 2002. *Dynamiques religieuses et démocratisation au Bénin—Pentecôtisme et formation d'un espace public.* Thèse de doctorat en science politique, Université Montesquieu, Bordeaux-IV, IEP Bordeaux-CEAN.

McAlistar, Elisabeth. 2002. *Rara! Vodou, Power, and Performance in Haiti and Its Diaspora*. Berkeley: University of California Press.

Meagher, Kate. 1995. "Parallel Trade and Powerless Places: Research Traditions and Local Realities in Rural Northern Nigeria." *Africa Development* 22 (2): 5–19.

Meagher, Kate. 1997. "Informal Integration or Economic Subversion? Parallel Trade in West Africa." Pp. 165–187 in *Regional Integration and Cooperation in West Africa*, ed. Réal Lavergne. Trenton, NJ: IDRC, Africa World Press.

Meagher, Kate. 2003. "A Back Door to Globalisation? Structural Adjustment, Globalisation & Transborder Trade in West Africa." *Review of African Political Economy* 30 (95): 57–75.

Meillassoux, Claude, ed. 1971. *The Development of Indigenous Trade and Markets in West Africa*. London: Oxford University Press.

Michel, Claudine, and Patrick Bellegarde-Smith, eds. 2007. *Vodou in Haitian Life and Culture*. Houndmills, Basingstoke, Hampshire: Palgrave Macmillan.

Monga, Celestin. 1995. "Civil Society and Democratisation in francophone Africa." *Journal of Modern African Studies* 33 (3): 359–379.

Nwajiaku, Kathryn. 1994. "The National Conferences in Benin and Togo revisited." *Journal of Modern African Studies* 32 (3): 429–447.

Patterson, Tiffany Ruby, and Robin D. G. Kelley. 2000. "Unfinished Migrations—Reflections on the African Diaspora and the Making of the Modern World." *African Studies Review* 43 (1): 11–46.

Portes, Alejandro, Manuel Castells, and Lauren Benton, eds. 1989. *The Informal Economy: Studies in Advanced and Less Developed Countries*. Baltimore, MD: Johns Hopkins University Press.

Pries, Ludger, ed. 2001. *New Transnational Social Spaces. International Migration and Transnational Companies in the Early 21st Century*. London: Routledge.

Rao, Vijayendra, and Michael Walton, eds. 2004. *Culture and Public Action*. Stanford, CA: Stanford University Press. and Washington, DC: The World Bank.

Reno, William. 1998. *Warlord Politics and African States*. Boulder, CO: Lynne Rienner.

Richards, Paul. 1985. *Indigenous Agricultural Revolution: Ecology and Food Production in West Africa*. London: Unwin Hyman.

Richards, Paul. 2006. "The History and Future of West African Rice—Food Security and Survival in a West African War Zone." *Afrika Spectrum* 41 (1): 77–93.

Robertson, Roland. 1995. "Glocalization: Time-Space and Homogeneity—Heterogeneity." Pp. 25–44 in *Global Modernities*, ed. Mike Featherstone, Scott Lash, and Roland Robertson. Thousand Oaks, CA, New Delhi, London: Sage.

Rotberg, Robert I. 1976. "Vodun and the Politics of Haiti." Pp. 342–365 in *The African Diaspora*, ed. Martin L. Kilson and Robert I. Rotberg. Cambridge, MA: Harvard University Press.

Rotberg, Robert I., ed. 1997. *Haiti Renewed—Political and Economic Prospects*. Cambridge: Brookings Institution Press, The World Peace Foundation.

Rotman, Anna. 2004. "Benin 's Constitutional Court: An Institutional Model for Guaranteeing Human Rights." *Harvard Human Rights Journal* 17: 281–314.

Rotman, Janet L. 1990. "The Politics of Informal Markets in sub-Saharan Africa." *Journal of Modern African Studies* 28 (4): 671–696.

Sassen, Saskia. 2001. "Cracked Casings: Notes Towards an Analytics for Studying Transnational Processes." Pp. 187–208 in *New Transnational Social Spaces*, ed. Ludger Pries. London: Routledge.

Schuerkens, Ulrike. 2003. "The Sociological and Anthropological Study of Globalization and Localization." *Current Sociology* 51 (3–4, 1/2): 209–222.

Scott, James C. 1998. *Seeing Like a State. How Certain Schemes to Improve the Human Condition Have Failed*. New Haven, CT: Yale University Press.

Sen, Amartya. 2004. "How does Culture Matter?" Pp. 37–58 in *Culture and Public Action*, ed. Vijayendra Rao and Michael Walton. Washington, DC: World Bank, and Stanford, CA: Stanford University Press.

Séhouéto, Lazare. 1994. "Kulturelle Aktivitäten Jugendlicher als Trojanisches Pferd der Modernisierung des Politischen in Westafrika. Zur Vorgeschichte der Demokratisierungsprozesse." Pp. 29–41 in *Afrika hilft sich selbst. Prozesse und Institutionen der Selbstorganisation*, ed. Anna Maria Brandstetter. Münster: Lit/ Vereinigung von Afrikanisten in Deutschland (VAD).

Smith, Christian. 1991. *The Emergence of Liberation Theology: Radical Religion and Social Movement Theory*. Chicago: University of Chicago Press.

Tall, Kadya Emmanuelle. 1995a. "De la démocratie et des cultes voduns au Bénin." *Cahiers d'Études africaines* 36 (1): 195–208.

Tall, Kadya Emmanuelle. 1995b. "Dynamiques des cultes voduns et du Christianisme céleste au Sud-Bénin." *Cahiers des Sciences Humaines* 31 (4): 797–823.

Tall, Kadya Emmanuelle. 2003. "Les nouveaux entrepreneurs en religion: La génération montante des chefs de cultes de possession à Cotonou (Bénin) et Salvador (Brésil)." *Autrepart* 27: 75–90.

Taylor, Patrick. 1992. "Anthropology and Theology in Pursuit of Justice." Callaloo 15 (3, *Haitian Literature and Culture, Part 2*): 811–823.

UNESCO. 2004. *Dialogue among Civilizations—A Culture of Innovation and the Building of Knowledge Societies*. International Expert Symposium, Moscow, 9 to 11 November 2003; Conference Reader "Dialogue Among Civilizations" series, directed by Jean d'Orville, ed. Tina Bovermann and F. W. Russell, Bureau of Strategic Planning. Paris: United Nations Educational, Scientific and Cultural Organization (UNESCO).

Weber, Max. 2002. *The Protestant Ethic and the "Spirit" of Capitalism and Other Writings*. Ed., trans., and with an introduction and notes by Peter Baehr and Gordon C. Wells. London: Penguin Books; first published 1904 in German, "*Die protestantische Ethik und der Geist des Kapitalismus.*"

Wilson, Ken B. 1992. "Cults of Violence and Counter-Violence in Mozambique." *Journal of Southern African Studies* 18 (3): 527–582.

World Bank. 2006. *World Development Report 2006: Equity and Development*. Washington, DC: Oxford University Press.

Zeleza, Paul T. 2005. "Rewriting the African Diaspora—Beyond the Black Atlantic." *African Affairs* 104 (5): 35–68.

9 Rethinking "Free-Trade" Practices in Contemporary Togo
Women Entrepreneurs in the Global Textile Trade

Nina Sylvanus

For the FIFA World Cup 2006 in Germany, Chantal Almeida[1] obtained the exclusive retail rights to distribute the official fabrics of Togo's national football team, *Les Eperviers*. She shared a stand with the public relations agency charged to promote the image of Togo to the world. Hence, public relations and merchandising provided a commercial niche for this Togolese businesswoman, in addition to a larger market share at the *Grand-Marché* of Lomé, where she has been the only wholesaler to sell these fabrics.

In the three decades from the 1960s, 1970s, and 1980s, this type of incentive would have been considered a prestigious enterprise, but only as an extension of her principal activities: the control of the import of European-produced fabric into the African market. Indeed, Mrs. Almeida and, prior to her, her mother operated during a period when a small number of women traders monopolized the distribution of wax prints throughout West Africa and certain parts of Central Africa. Her colleagues were called "Nana-Benzes," a term associating the image and authority of the mother or grandmother—"Nana"[2]—to the symbol of their success—a (Mercedes) Benz. Mrs. Almeida is in fact the descendant of a historical figure of Lomé's textile market. For three generations these female entrepreneurs have established a highly competitive system of economic control over textile distribution networks, crafting Lomé into a regional capital of textile distribution, controlling both prices and the final destinations of these European-produced commodities. Soon, Nana-Benzes' economic power became a symbol of success throughout the African continent, an image notably conveyed through western media.[3] According to Nana-Benzes' descendants, however, it is the process of globalization that has ended their success: Large profits and prosperity would belong to the past. A niche market, such as the *Eperviers* market share, has in fact become a necessity if not a prestigious repositioning for these women entrepreneurs despite the enduring representational ethos that the Nana-Benz symbol conveys throughout the region.

The discourse on the decline of a trading elite, as employed by Nana-Benzes' descendants, contrasts with the perpetuated symbol of their success in a transformed trading environment since the early 1990s. The current fragmentation of the textile market in Togo and its geopolitics are directly linked to the process of decentralization and the shifts in production in the direction of China, that is, the reorganization of the global economy. However, this transformation is not merely a phenomenon of late modernity as authors such as Appadurai (1996) have suggested. The Nana-Benzes who have historically primarily operated in the context of semiprotected markets, that is, colonial and postcolonial European-dominated networks, have actively contributed to the current development. Their trade practices stimulated the emergence of parallel networks of competition that emerged in the early 1970s—networks, animated by women traders excluded from Nana-Benzes' market share, exploring Indian and Pakistani textile manufactures. The reorientation of the bipolar flow of cloth commodities can be considered as the first step of the current process of disintegration and the ultimate decline of the Nana-Benzes in the 2000s. Current trade practices have accelerated these forms of disintegration. A new generation of female traders—*les Nanettes*—is at the heart of these newly emerging trade connections that have in part replaced Nana-Benzes' formerly protected trading spaces. While Mina textile traders have dominated the trade in European textiles in close connection with European firms—based on a particular agreement with the Togolese state that granted them a highly beneficial fiscal regime—the numeric significance of these women traders, however, when compared to other female traders in the market is relatively small. Indeed, they represented only 2 percent of the total female trade population in Lomé's Grand-Marché during the early 1970s (cf. Cordonnier 1987: 109). Today, trade continues ever more and constitutes these women's principal activity in Togo, but the number of high-income entrepreneurs in the textile trade remains small. An important shift in the current reorganization of the textile trade, which is linked to the change from Nana-Benzes to *Nanettes*, resides in the fact that the *Nanettes* represent a heterogeneous group that operates beyond postcolonial connections and "ethnic" origins.

The rise of the *Nanettes* and their entrepreneurial success relates to the making of global trade networks, in particular with Chinese textile manufactures in Shanghai and the Shandong region. Their engagement in these highly beneficial commodity circuits has provided them with a sense of new economic possibilities. But the profits derived from these markets are linked to the notion of risk that implies a model of flexibility. Although Nana-Benzes would only engage in one economic niche, the *Nanettes* alternate between different niches to maintain their entrepreneurial success in a context of economic uncertainty.

A paradox underlies this dynamic. While the *Nanettes* seek to restore the Nana-Benzian model, that is, the control over distribution networks, they in fact reinforce the competitiveness of the market ensuing free-trade mechanisms and the multiplication of economic players and networks. The increased participation of actors in these new trade connections baffles the possibility of monopolistic control. Indeed, Chinese manufacturers prefer to interact with a variety of traders rather than to rely on a restricted number of interlocutors as the Nana-Benzian model suggested. Nevertheless, most *Nanettes* continue to explore new products with the intent to control their distribution for the most expansive time period to accumulate the largest profit.

These transformations take place against the backdrop of political and economic changes in Togo, including structural adjustment programs and CFA devaluation that opened up for free-market policies. Free markets are also fragmented markets. Some scholars including anthropologists have seen the present neo-liberal moment as characterized by the contradictions of "millennial capitalism," a process that according to the Comaroffs (Comaroff and Comaroff 2000) and Ferguson (2006) helps create a sense of "abjection." This chapter attempts to constructively intervene, by demonstrating through an analysis of networks, trading practices, and commodity signification that although recent global transformations of production affect local commercial structures and consumption practices, they do not do away with them. Rather, the arrangements that exist locally contribute actively to shaping how globalization works as part of a process of entanglement. As such I adopt an understanding of globalization that allows for the articulation of the "global" and the "local," against a conceptualization of the global as a pervasive, top-down force, where the local is considered to be a repository of authentic cultural meanings and the site of resistance to global forces. I wish to nuance this simplistic view of global processes by considering that the local comprises the global at various levels, rather than being in opposition to it (Ong and Collier 2005). In line with Friedman, I would argue that the "the global simply reflects the emergent properties of the articulation of numerous local processes" (Friedman 2004: 180).

To frame my analysis of the current reorganization of entrepreneurial practices, based on fourteen months of ethnographic fieldwork in Togo, I assume a perspective that argues against neo-liberal or institutional theories that view economic behavior as structured by mere profit maximization. New patterns of competition are addressed here so as to explore the degree to which and the way in which local structures are constituted in the context of global relations by looking at the transformation of trade practices, both synchronically and diachronically. I propose a systematic analysis of the transformation of this trade system and strategy with the "liberalization" of the market, a phenomenon primarily due to the penetration of Asians. Although the opening of the market to increasing competition, de facto liberalization, has occurred, this however does not refer to an entirely new—neo-liberal—market scheme as such because, in my view, it is not more capitalistic than the previous system. This case study demonstrates that new forms of trade practices in contemporary Togo are not part of a new strategy, but rather they refer to an adaptation to increasing global competition in the local market. By looking at the long-term transformations of the textile market and its principal actors, I suggest that current changes are not merely the result of what globalizers call neo-liberalism but that local socioeconomic practices have equally contributed to allow for the current moment of unprecedented competition. Indeed, Chantal Almeida's mother, who was an influential Nana-Benz, would have never imagined that one day her daughter would have had to share her business with competing *Nanettes*, those newly emerging women entrepreneurs who illegally import counterfeited copies from China and thereby provide Asian textile manufacturers with the blueprints essential for Togo's market domination. However, the monopolistic trade practices in which Mrs. Almeida's mother and fellow Nana-Benzes had engaged for several decades stimulated alternative accesses to rents in a context of economic uncertainty.

To illustrate this argument, I use ethnography to illuminate the local-level nuances that confound globalization theories. Ethnographers of globalization (Marcus 1995; Burawoy et al. 2000; Burawoy 2001; Gille and O'Rian 2002) contend that focusing on a micro-level site promises to ground global processes by connecting macro dynamics to micro processes. I attempt to employ ethnography by drawing on what Burawoy identifies as "global ethnography"—the replacing of "abstract globalization with a grounded globalization that tries to understand not only the experience of globalization but also how that experience is produced in specific localities" (Burawoy 2001: 158). In this chapter, I follow what Marcus calls the "thread of cultural processes" (Marcus 1995: 97) to ground those processes that are often dealt with only in the most general terms, attempting to offer insight into economic and cultural complexities brought on by global dynamics. In the sections that follow, I first sketch out Togo's economic and political context in connection to the role of the textile trade and the importance of the commodity at stake. I then focus on three sections: (1) the historical conditions under which women textile traders took over the textile trade, (2) early forms of market deregulation and extraversion, and (3) changing conditions of competition and new forms of entrepreneurship. My concluding argument addresses the paradoxical relation of monopoly power and free-trade dynamics.

REVISITING TOGO'S POLITICAL AND ECONOMIC CONTEXT

Until the beginning of the 1980s, Togo was called, like Rwanda and Burundi, *"la petite Suisse"*—little Switzerland—because of its apparent stability and prosperity. Togo's authoritarianism was relegated by most Western decision makers to the benefit of the image of a developing country. The characteristics of political and economic governance were not taken into account. The "straddling" (Bayart 1989: 112) between the political and economic field became one of the pillars of the Eyadéma regime.[4] Its apparent stability contrasted with the experiences of its neighbors, Ghana, Benin, and Nigeria.[5]

These perceptions were reconsidered in the 1980s with the weakening of the political and economic pillars of the regime. The agenda of the international financial institutions changed when they adopted the "Washington Consensus," shifting its focus from state development to the liberalization of the market. International aid decreased in connection with structural adjustment policies. In addition, the end of the cold war accentuated the reduction of foreign aid. A discourse promoting "democratization" accompanied these policies. International pressure, political reform movements, and popular protest in the streets of Lomé erupting in violence forced Togo's "tyrannical government" (Ellis 1993: 456) to partially cooperate. Togo's period of transition, which was intended to end with a national conference and free elections, was subject to still more violence, and was followed by a series of strikes that paralyzed Togo's economy, not to mention thousands of Togolese fleeing to the neighboring countries (Heilbrunn 1993; Macé 2004).

From 1991 to 1994, political chaos durably weakened the country's economy: Most Nana-Benzes left their businesses behind and flew to Benin if they did not pay for local militia to protect their merchandise. After Eyadéma's reelection in 1993, which Ellis considered to be the result of a series of maneuvers and intimidations, Eyadéma incited the entrepreneurs to regain the country. Xenophobic slogans were spread through the media in order to reach Togo's diaspora: "Don't leave the economy to foreigners" or "foreigners are taking over the market, come back before it's too late"[6]. In 1994, Nana-Benzes returned to Lomé, characterized by a transformed socioeconomic environment.

Lomé's reputation as the supposedly "safest capital in West Africa[7]" was substantively weakened and its economic role in the region deteriorated. Its Beninese neighbor, however—which had experienced a successful period of transition embodying a "model of democratization" to the international community—benefited from Togo's economic situation. Indeed, Benin partially replaced Togo's role as a regional center of trade, notably for textiles.

As Piot pointed out, "Lomé remains in a kind of limbo" (Piot 1999: 47). High unemployment, a decrease in schooling, and lack of opportunities for graduates have contributed, among other factors, to a situation of social precariousness in a context of severe economic recession. The impoverishment of the population encouraged the growth of parallel economic activities that large parts of the population depend on. However, these "informal" trade structures have been deeply affected by economic uncertainty (Piot 2006: 172) not only because of currency devaluations but also because of the increase in the availability of cheap products imported from East and Southeast Asia, especially China. Value structures and notions of authenticity have been blurred, not only for traders but also for consumers. Indeed, new consumption practices have emerged with the multiplication of these commodities that contributed to the fragmentation of market hierarchies and the status systems. Among these new products, textiles play an important role, and notably those fabrics imitating European-produced wax cloth. This leads us to our next point, essential not only for the understanding of current fragmentations of trade networks, economic practices, and consumption structures in a context of political deterioration, but also for the understanding of the role and the sociocultural significance of textiles in this region. This will permit us to underline the prestige of those who are involved in this trade.

COMMODITY CIRCUITS

Transactions that link Togolese traders to global networks of textile production have a particular character because of their value and their local signification. Cloth used for dress is central because of the power of the dressed body to symbolize notions both of identity and group, that is, both of self and of society (Tranberg Hansen 2000). Wax cloth has that power, and those who are engaged in its distribution even more so.

The specific status of wax prints in connection to local orders of signification and value goes back to an entangled historical process that has linked Europe, Asia, and Africa since the 19th century. Indeed, the creation of interconnections or *"branchements"* (Amselle 2001) has operated since the late 16ᵗʰ century when Indian-produced cottons were first traded by Portuguese merchants to the coasts of Africa and during the 19th century when the French exported "Guinée cloth" from Pondicherry to West Africa[8] (Tirthankar 1996). Among other commodities in circulation on the trade routes of the East India Company were fabrics from Java, so-called *batik*. These batik textiles that traveled from Europe to the Dutch Indies were in fact reproduced in British and Dutch textile manufactures for the Javanese market. A series of political and economic factors contributed to their subsequent introduction into the Gold Coast (cf. Nielsen 1979; Cordonnier 1987; Picton 1995) at the end of the 19th century. European-produced batik for the West African market is called "wax cloth," a designation probably derived from its original mode of production in Java. Wax fabric was particularly appreciated on the Guinea Coast, where it was adapted to local consumption needs and desires and where it was rapidly integrated in local trade structures. Because of its quality and its chromatic possibilities, wax cloth attained the status of a luxury commodity by the early 20th century not only in the Gulf of Guinea but also in the West African hinterland. Until today, wax cloth retains this status of a special commodity in its capacity to "clothe" a person with a specific social identity. Its economic success originated in a unique process of adaptation of a European industry to West African consumer desire and need. Those who have dominated this market since the late 19th century—Dutch and British textile manufacturers—remain associated to the value and representation of the wax fabric today.

Given the historical, social, and cultural importance of these commodities, those who have been engaged in their trade have also benefited from their special status. In Lomé, a small group of women traders—the Nana-Benzes—have carved out a particularly powerful position in controlling large distribution networks of wax cloth throughout the region, carving Lomé into a central position in the West African region.

HISTORICIZING WOMEN ENTREPRENEURS IN TOGO

The powerful position Togo's Nana-Benzes had established was mutually linked to the trade in wax cloth and to the design specificity of the commodity. The early specialization in the trade of wax prints during the colonial period allowed for the creation of a particular economic regime that only a small number of traders participated in. Their marginality as women traders and their belonging to the Mina ethnic minority group was an advantage for their economic activities, because they were not seen as a threat to both the colonial and the postcolonial state. Maneuvering between these distinct political and economic spheres, the Nana-Benzes established a regional trade network, engaging in an early form of economic globalization by establishing transnational trade connections. Although they considerably contributed to Lomé's role as a regional center of trade—a status that was beneficial to large portions of Togo's population—it also led to forms of economic marginalization for those excluded from the lucrative textile trade.

The Nana-Benz era was closely associated to companies such as Unilever, with whom they had negotiated exclusive retail rights. It was indeed beneath the colonial radar that gender-specific labor roles evolved: Men were recruited into the colonial state administration whereas women took over "informal" trading spaces, previously operated by men. Togolese men holding positions within the French colonial administration were often descendants from influential merchant families who had been engaged in the precolonial palm oil trade with Europe. Mina women had participated in precolonial trading activities, but men had then limited their economic autonomy. During the early colonial period, women had benefited from male labor recruitment and had successfully exploited the opportunity to position themselves as the intermediaries between agents and businessmen. Since the early 20th century, Mina women have been in charge of the distribution networks of European manufactured commodities by providing hinterland markets with the means of subsistence goods and Western luxuries, such as textiles (Cordonnier 1987). In order to advertise metropolitan commodities, women had taken over the role of marketing agents themselves and had carefully promoted new consumption desires. European trading companies granted them credits, creating durable, yet ambivalent, economic relationships. Female capital accumulation had thus been reinforced and women's status generally increased (Bay 1982; House-Midamaba and Ekechi 1995). Since the 1930s, the crafting of a female entrepreneurial space had put a small group of textile traders into a hegemonic position by providing women sociopolitical influence and economic power in the West African region. The flexibility of their operational structures—reinforced by their marginality as Mina women—had provided them with the capacity to adapt to a wide range of situations, including colonial trade restrictions. In 1933, for example, Lomé's market women organized a strike against French colonial taxation, putting into question the established social hierarchy and defending their economic interests (Almeida-Ekué 1992).

To maximize financial gains and more profitable control of market space during the colonial period, a group of Mina women had monopolized a lucrative textile trade network throughout the region, linking European centers of textile production to West African Togo. In the 1960s, they positioned themselves at the core of a transnational trading space, effectively reinforcing their economic power. Their power was to be deemed official via the foundation of an influential female business association: the *Association Professionnelle des Revendeuses de Tissu* (APRT)[9] (cf. Cordonnier 1987; Heilbrunn 1996). Although Nana-Benzes were urged to create this structure in order to formalize access to the lucrative textile trade by incorporating more members (so that other women traders could benefit from this trade), Nana-Benzes redeployed this associational instrument to reinforce their authority. Despite the incorporation of approximately 800 textile traders into this business association, only the founding members had direct access to European firms. This interest group of ten women shared not only the access to their suppliers, but they established even more a system of mutual understanding (*modèle d'entente*), an oligopolistic type of organization where each textile wholesaler would monopolize the distribution of approximately fifty design patterns. In this system, each Nana-Benz held a monopoly power generating a guaranteed income with her control over wax-cloth designs that had come to be part of West African dress orders. Depending on the trading licence the state would agree on, the subaltern members of this trade association could access a small portion of Nana-Benzes' market share (an agreement obliged them to sell a small percentage to these traders).

Since each Nana-Benz individually controlled the designs that were exclusively attributed to her, Nana-Benzes' interests did not conflict. Their institutionalized umbrella allowed them to influence and to negotiate trade policies. In exchange for the dispensation from taxation, these women provided the state with their cars, thus providing the artifice of the early postcolonial state. Nana-Benzes would use their "gender" and "ethnic" origins in an adaptable way and for shifting purposes. Their marginality as an ethnic minority group had operated as an advantage beneath the colonial and postcolonial radar because they were not viewed as a threat to the formal economic sector. Trading off institutional propaganda for economic interests was part of their reservoir of knowledge and proved to be an element of historical continuity. Moreover, their economic power became an instrument of social and political emancipation: Several traders chaired the feminist wing of the only authorized political party and others broadly invested in real estate acquisitions.

This institutionalized postcolonial arrangement carved out a flexible position of power vis-à-vis changing postcolonial governments but also vis-à-vis international centres of textile production that Nana-Benzes significantly influenced with their orders. They crafted Lomé into a regional capital of textile distribution, controlling both prices and the final destinations of European imported textiles. Nigerian, Congolese, Ivorian, and other transnational trading networks met at the crossroads of Lomé's textile wholesalers in order to purchase the much-desired fabrics. Depending entirely on Nana-Benzes' willingness to sell their merchandise, they could make the success of regional traders. This influential position granted them a reputation throughout the West African region so that they began to incarnate a model of gendered entrepreneurial success.

Nana-Benzes' economic power continuously progressed. They were exposed to very little competition in light of their internal agreement guaranteeing each Nana-Benz the control of a specific market segment. In consequence, those excluded from the trade in wax cloth explored external economic opportunities. These attempts or parallel modes of investigating in new commercial ventures could be conceptualized, following Bayart (1989, 2000), as "strategies of extraversion."[10] This is part of the logic of what Ekholm-Friedman (1991) has referred to as prestige good systems in the Congo. These systems operate by monopoly over the import of certain goods, in particular foreign goods, that function as means of high-ranked payment, and that provide the basis of hierarchy and of political control.

EXTRAVERSION AND EARLY FORMS OF MARKET DEREGULATION

Regardless of the incorporation of about 800 women traders in the Lomé textile market and its cyclical opportunities, several traders preferred to create their own entrepreneurial networks in the early 1970s. In reaction to the highly protected markets controlled by the Nana-Benzes as direct intermediaries of European firms, these women aimed at breaking this "tradition." These ruptures took different forms. Some women became importers of wax-cloth spin-offs, whereas others would bypass the formal system of wax-cloth distribution. Although the trajectories of several traders, which we discuss next, have not been conceived as a direct form of competition to Nana-Benzes' activities, they have nevertheless paved the way for future market fragmentation and trade liberalization. As such these trajectories of extraversion, using external dynamics to innovate local trade practices, have appeared as a predecessor of current trade liberalizations and opportunities that Togo's *Nanettes* have creatively engaged in over the past fifteen years.

Jacqueline Lassey

During the 1980s, Jacqueline Lassey appeared as a successful women trader who had made a fortune comparable to that of some Nana-Benzes by engaging in a parallel economic venture. Like most textile traders, she was part of the APRT carrying out medium-scale activity in the retail of wax cloth. Restricted by state license and unable to progress toward large-scale activity, she was one of the first Togolese traders to engage in trade with Indian and Pakistani textile manufactures. Since the early 1970s, Indian businessmen had invested in Nigerian textile mills—and notably in "fancy-print" production[11]—but their physical presence had been limited to Nigeria and parts of Ghana. When Mrs. Lassey made her first trip to explore textile units in India and Pakistan she not only brought with her samples of fancy prints available in the *Grand-Marché* in Lomé, but she also brought patterns she had designed with a local craftsman. During this first trip, she visited several textile firms, but she selected only two plants she considered most competent to produce her designs. At the beginning, as she remembers, this was not an easy task, because manufacturers were reluctant to accommodate Jacqueline Lassey's requests.

> The finishing of their fabrics was dumpy; it was glossy and cheap looking. They didn't understand that Africans like the finishing being matt. . . . The fabrics were stiff and they had a taste of salt. I had to teach them everything and together we made samples over and over again until tait bon.

Mrs. Lassey alludes to the difficulties she had encountered during her early experiences with Asian manufacturers. Indeed, Indian and Pakistani manufacturers had to discover that Africans particularly care for quality. It was only after a transitional period of multiple temptations that the fabrics would appear suitable to Jacqueline Lassey, who then agreed to sell them on the market. Although these first attempts were not all successful, she decided to continue this venture.

While traveling to Karachi on a regular basis, where she kept on working with her Pakistani suppliers to improve quality and refine design, she was able to obtain several good selling fabrics and to establish a significant network of clients. Gradually the quantity of her imports increased attaining up to six containers per month. She held the exclusive distribution rights for these commodities just like Nana-Benzes did for wax prints. When she created a fancy print called "Cha-Cha-Cha," the success was without precedent to the point that this fabric achieved the popularity of noble wax prints—reflected in the unusually high prices this fabric could sell for. Mrs.

Lassey's success, stipulated by means of significant capital accumulation, became most apparent when she opened, in addition to her three shops at the *Grand-Marché* in Lomé, seven further wholesale shops throughout Togo. Unlike Nana-Benzes, whose single retail location was situated in the central market, Jacqueline Lassey was able to incarnate an additional benchmark of entrepreneurial success, a model several women traders followed. The success of these entrepreneurs was rooted in the making of external trade relations by means of extraversion that would operate according to the Nana-Benzian monopoly power.

This development contributed to a first phase of the reorientation of the bipolar flow of cloth with the entry of Indian and Pakistani producers in the 1960s reflected in the shift of the formation of a triangular trade constellation. This system directly emerged from local incentives of Togolese traders in their attempt to create a market that would not conflict with Nana-Benzes' interests and allow them to control a share of the African print segment. While traders such as Jacqueline Lassey were not perceived as a threat to Nana-Benzes' economic regime—because they evolved in different social and economic circuits, and because their trade of fancy prints did not directly interfere with the trade of wax prints—they however contributed to the current fragmentation of the textile market by providing a blueprint for neo-liberal market schemes, a topic to be discussed in more length later.

During the 1970s and 1980s, several attempts had been made by individual traders to circumvent Nana-Benzes' monopoly power. In the early 1980s, Ghislaine Ekué set up a parallel market for wax prints, which she imported from Liberia via her husband's business partner's connections. Although these imports could not compete with the large quantities the Nana-Benzes imported from Europe, Ghislaine Ekué, however, periodically deregulated their market.

Although the consequences of these early forms of market deregulation did not significantly affect Nana-Benzes' control over textile distribution, they indirectly contributed to their current transformation by providing a blueprint for future generations. Indeed, the *Nanettes* explored the trade routes women entrepreneurs like Jacqueline Lassey had invested in beforehand to innovate and transform local trade structures that appeared to have collapsed as a result of the economic and political chaos Togo had been drawn into since the early 1990s. This resulted in a declining purchasing power for commodities. In the early 1990s, a variety of traders had diversified their external economic relations by turning themselves, in addition to Pakistani and Indian centers of trade, to alternative locales. The Persian Gulf and China became popular trade destinations, a development that Bayart considers to be the consequence of the "ongoing economic crisis and the devaluation of the CFA franc in 1994, which has reduced the competitiveness of European products on African markets" (Bayart 2000: 238). It is my intent to question the relation between trade liberalization, the decline of former economic players, and the appearance of new actors and commodities in the Togolese market space by looking closely at the trajectories of those women who are said to have "brought globalization to Togo." Indeed, Nana-Benzes hold the *Nanettes* responsible for having brought Chinese low-cost commodities into the market and for subsequently driving Nana-Benzes out of business. Further, the *Nanettes* are stigmatized as operating on the margins of the law. To explain the success of some of these new businesswomen, the Nana-Benzes consider to have emerged *ex nihilo* in the textile trade, rumors in Lomé's central market associate the *Nanettes* with criminal activities such as drug smuggling. These accusations, however, appear as a continuum of former accusations in relation to Nana-Benzes' capital accumulation. Indeed, a series of rumors—partially fueled by the state, which was concerned that Nana-Benzes power might represent an oppositional threat—accused Nana-Benzes of witchcraft practices. Togo's present situation of economic and political limbo, as Piot has pointed out (1999: 10), offers a fertile ground for rumors and accusations. Under these circumstances, it is likely that "informal" or economic activities are enhanced. Indeed, several *Nanettes* have organized the import of Far-Eastern textiles at the margins of official fiscal and taxation legislation, and few of these women are officially registered at Togo's Chamber of commerce. While most of these illegal imports are tolerated, several *Nanettes* have encountered difficulties with the law. Yet the *Nanettes* consider themselves as having brought consumption democratization to Togo: "Finally everybody can dress in wax prints: China wax is beautiful!" states a successful Nanette.

I consider these trajectories, in line with Hart (2002), as "spatially interconnected sets of practices that actively produce and drive the process we call 'globalization'" (p. 14). What do these practices tell us about the transformation of the Togolese trade space and notions of flexibility and competition? Have these transformations emerged merely because of the sociospatial change that has taken place in the context of intensified global integration? Nana-Benzes view their decline as the consequence of free-trade dynamics. But the shift from semiprotected markets in which Nana-Benzes had formerly operated to "free markets" has been strongly linked. There has been an order that has organized the present "disorder" of change, disintegration, and fragmentation (cf. Friedman 1994).

DECLINING HEGEMONIES: CHANGING CONDITIONS OF COMPETITION AND THE EMERGENCE OF NEW FORMS OF ENTREPRENEURSHIP

What was long perceived to be invariable—the Nana-Benzian model of success and its stable economic environment—revealed itself to be cyclical. As I have already stated, when the Nana-Benzes returned to Lomé in 1994 after a period of political turmoil, the regional economic agenda had changed. The port of Cotonou had taken over Lomé's economic activities and Cotonou's

central market—*Dantokpa*—was now the privileged place for textile distribution in the region. Unilever had withdrawn from the textile market it had
organized for almost a century, and Vlisco, the Dutch wax-print producer,
had taken over these African distribution units of Unilever's. Determined
to succeed in this endeavor, Vlisco reoriented the trade policies Unilever
had implemented in Togo—policies that had originated in the colonial and
postcolonial period. This reorganization not only implicated that fabrics
were now to be distributed also in Cotonou and other regional capitals, but
also it foresaw that Nana-Benzes did not have exclusive retail rights over
distribution circuits. The dismantling of their "cartel" was notably accentuated by the integration of younger women, a step that Vlisco considered
fundamental in an attempt to rejuvenate its customers.

Simultaneously to the reorganization of the trade in wax prints, large
amounts of counterfeited copies of these Dutch produced fabrics have
appeared. Although imitations have entered the African market since the
mid-1990s, it is only since the beginning of the 21st century that these copies are produced in China in the same technique as the original Dutch prints.
Not only has this change challenged the latter's authority and has been frag-
menting former hierarchies of value, but it also resulted in the multiplication of networks and heterogeneous actors. The Togolese case provides
thus nuanced inside into how Chinese manufacturers entered the African
market.

Antoinette Mensah

With Lomé's political and economical collapse, several traders explored
new economic opportunities. The case of Antoinette Mensah provides an
emblematic example. In 1995, she traveled for the first time to Bangkok,
along with several fabric samples she wished to reproduce for the Togolese
market. In Bangkok, she encountered a Thai entrepreneur who introduced
her to a colleague in Hong Kong. The latter, head of several textile-manu-
facturing units, was keen to accommodate this African client that he considered potential. Akin to Jacqueline Lassey's experience in Pakistan and
India, Antoinette Mensah stayed in Hong Kong, where she worked with
this Chinese manufacturer for several weeks. Just like Jacqueline Lassey,
she remembered that it had been difficult to "work with them and to make
them understand what exactly these textiles had to look like. . . . There
is more to it than just copying the designs . . . the thickness of the cotton
is important . . . and delicacy, softness, and refinement matter equally!"
After several weeks of hard work, Antoinette Mensah judged the results
to be satisfying enough to try them on the market. To promote these copies, she named them after her daughter, Soso. When "Super-Soso" fabrics
appeared on the market they encountered an immediate success—a success
directly linked to the postdevaluation period of the CFA franc. Indeed, with
purchase power being reduced by 50 percent, this imitation of a high-quality

fabric in subordinate quality revealed itself to be highly successful. Wholesalers from throughout the region came to Lomé to purchase super-soso cloth, which Antoinette Mensah had detained the exclusive retail rights for. Monthly arrivals of four 40-foot containers assured her monopolistic position for over one year until copies of super-soso entered the market. In fact, drawing upon Antoinette Mensah's innovation, a group of Togolese traders had meanwhile successfully reproduced Mrs. Mensah's prints in the vicinity of Bombay. With this process of what economists call "creative destruction," Antoinette Mensah's monopoly came to an end.

Although Mrs. Mensah had successfully exploited this highly beneficial market, she conversely experienced its risky facets. But driven by the fantasy of reestablishing a monopolistic position and becoming a local figure of notability and success, she has been willing to play the game. Many of her colleagues from Lomé's *Grand-Marché* also pursue this risky quest, in part because Antoinette Mensah has come to represent a model of economic accomplishment that has not seemed as unrealistic to achieve as the Nana-Benzian pattern. Indeed, for these new entrepreneurs it has appeared "normal" to engage in flexible trading ventures, that is, to switch from one market segment to another depending on economic opportunities. As such, the intensification of activities of Togolese traders, who are now exploring the Persian Gulf, and especially Dubai,[12] have demonstrated this trend (cf. Marshal 1997). The trivialization of external economic relations based on high mobility instantiates the *Nanettes'* modus operandi in a context of increased competition where individual risk is highly valued. This contrasts with the Nana-Benzian model.

Exemplifying this new model, Antoinette Mensah quickly adapted to the transformation of the market by exploring a new trade avenue: China's Shandong region. When traveling to Hong Kong, one of her contacts incited her to go to Shanghai, where numerous textile manufacturers are located. Although she was skeptical at the beginning, notably of "the Chinese" as she told me, she soon established a commercial relationship with a Shanghai-based company that was interested in reproducing wax prints in "Dutch" quality for the African market. Vaunting her technological inventiveness, Mrs. Mensah took on, once again, an advisory role. In 2001, this new fabric arrived in Lomé where it was marketed as "Mondial wax"—the first Chinese wax prints to enter the market. It became a key product in Togo, Ghana, Benin, and Nigeria, where it was sold for a tenth of the original Dutch fabric cost. Mondial wax allowed Antoinette Mensah to reestablish monopoly power over a niche market.

In contrast to common perceptions that attribute market transformation to the "invasion" of Chinese low-cost commodities, Antoinette Mensah's story reveals that local actors have contributed to this shift. At Lomé's *Grand-Marché*, many voices claim that she "brought Mondial wax to Africa." Indeed, some Nana-Benzes have accused this *Nanette* of having initiated what in 2005 resulted in a significant reorganization of the market with approximately 10 competing Chinese firms. While Antoinette Mensah had been able to access rents, she lost her monopoly power a few months after Mondial wax had entered the market. Her Shanghai-based manufacturer not only expanded his customer network while simultaneously selling containers of the same product at different prices throughout the region (engendering severe competition and the overproduction of fabrics), but also competing Chinese manufacturers entered this market segment. Mrs. Mensah did not foresee this change and seemed overrun in light of the turn of events.

CONCLUSION

The stories of Togo's textile traders reveal that the current fragmentation in the organization of the global textile trade has appeared in articulation with local transformations. As Antoinette Mensah's trajectory suggests, the recurring attempt to restore monopoly power in fact stimulates the diversification of the market. It increases the market's competitiveness and engenders free-trade dynamics while it simultaneously produces the multiplication of networks and actors that results in a decrease of profits.

In fact, numerous *Nanettes* have gone out of business and only a few have been successful. Nevertheless, many of them continue to explore these risky trade avenues with the hope of controlling a market segment for a short time. How can we account for this seemingly paradoxical engagement? And why is it that despite increased competition and limited profits these traders continue to explore these risky markets? Only a perspective from "below" informed by ethnography can explain the cultural complexity of these contradicting processes and contribute to a more refined comprehension of globalization. I have argued that *Nanettes'* economic behavior is rooted in what I call the fantasy of the Nana-Benzian model: the possibility of creating durable access to rents. This fantasy provides a motivation for women traders in Togo today because it offers a possibility in a transformed local trade environment with few opportunities for sustainable accumulation. As such, it is not profit maximization per se that structures *Nanettes'* economic behavior (to continuously explore and engage in new trade networks) as a neo-liberal or institutional approach would suggest, but rather the prospective idea of temporal success that motivates them. It is this culturally and historically rooted desire associated with monopoly power that has been central in the deregulatation of former hierarchies of trade and, in consequence, of its organization.

As I have argued earlier, and as the cases of Jacqueline Lassey and Ghislaine Ekué have illustrated, these changes are embedded in earlier attempts to circumvent Nana-Benzes' restricted markets. This paved the way for parallel networks to emerge, as we have seen in the trajectories of extraversion of the 1970s, particularly in the case of Jacqueline Lassey. In fact, the latter provided a blueprint for traders such as Antoinette Mensah, who adapted it, which in turn provided an opportunity to welcome Far Eastern manufacturers into the West African market. Taking into account these interrelated and dialectical dynamics, I would argue that processes of global economic restructuring need not only be framed by history, but they should take into account that the "local" and the "global" appear as an intertwined articulation. As the Togolese example illustrates, global processes, that is, the recent shift in the organization of the African textile trade, work out as interdynamic articulations where the "local" appears to structure certain aspects of the "global."

The stories of declining Nana-Benzes such as Chantal Almeida and emerging *Nanettes* like Antoinette Mensah illustrate that new forms of trade practices in contemporary Togo are not part of a new strategy or a new, neoliberal market scheme, but rather refer to an adaptation to increasing global competition in the local market. It is this adaptation that has reorganized local forms of trade, which have led to increased flexibility and individualism. As the trajectory of Antoinette Almeida has illustrated, it is the failing attempts to restore monopoly power, inspired by the Nana-Benzian model, that creates increased competition in the local market. The transformation in the organization of the West African textile trade on a global scale with the shift to China appears to be the consequence of these local attempts, remembering the image of the invisible hand of the market.

NOTES

1. The names of families and persons have been altered.
2. The term *Nana* derives from an archaic *éwé* form—Nana meaning mother—that according to Weigel (1987) would have undergone an emphatic reduplication to finally mean grandmother or elder woman, while in Ghana this word is employed as an aristocratic title for men. The term *Nana-Benz* results from the fact that these Nanas preferred to use in the 1960s Mercedes Benz cars to pick up their merchandise.
3. Since the 1970s, there have been numerous articles in European newspapers, journals, and several TV reports on Togo's Nana-Benzes. A recent documentary *Mama Benz and the Taste of Money* (Karin Junger 2001) reflects the continuous interest in the subject of women, power, and entrepreneurship in Africa.
4. Gnassingbé Eyadéma, who participated in the coup against Togo's first president—Sylvanus Olympio—came into power in 1967. He was sustained by the army and created a one-party system.
5. In this regional configuration, there was little competition, so that Lomé became a regional center of trade with its deep harbor, progressively evolving into an "*Etat-entrepôt*" (Igué and Soule 1992) and benefiting from high tax incomes.
6. I found these slogans in interviews I conducted in 2003 with several textile wholesalers who were in Cotonou, Benin, during this period.
7. A notion often used in West Africa.
8. The entangled history of the textile trade illustrates what Bayart points out in his *Africa in the World: A History of Extraversion*, namely, that "it is not

possible to dissociate the history of sub-Saharan Africa over the past century from the effects of the globalization which has been busily weaving its social fabric since the European commercial expansion of the fifteenth century and, more specifically, since the nineteenth century, clearly a crucial period" (Bayart 2000: 235).

9. Professional association of textile retailers.

10. Bayart applies this principle to the degree in which African societies engaged in relations with their external environment, which he defines as "crucial to the constitution of their internal politics" (Bayart 2000: 218). As such, he stresses the importance of external elements as ways of innovating endogenous dynamics. Although Bayart primarily employs this notion within the political sphere/field, I tentatively use it to illustrate how women entrepreneurs in Togo build on external economic environments to innovate and transform local trade practices.

11. Fancy prints entered the West African market in the 1930s. Produced exclusively in Europe for African markets until the late 1950s, fancy prints represented a cheaper alternative to the expensive wax prints while drawing on a distinct iconographic repertoire. Fancy-print production was shifted to Africa during the late 1950s and significantly expanded in the postindependence era.

12. The comparative advantage of Dubai, despite a 2 percent export tax rate, notably resides in its function as a regional hub, where traders can purchase all types of products and notably Far Eastern commodities. Airlines have adapted to this trend by offering interesting fares to West African traders: British Airways has flight arrangements from Accra and Lagos via London to Dubai, and Emirate Airways offers daily direct flights from Lagos to Dubai.

REFERENCES

Almeida-Ekué, Sylvie. 1992. *La Révolte des Loméennes*. Lomé: Les Nouvelles Éditions Africaines du Togo.

Amselle, Jean-Loup. 2001. *Branchements*. Paris: Flammarion.

Appadurai, Arjun. 1996. *Modernity at Large: Cultural Dimensions of Globalization*. Minneapolis: University of Minnesota Press.

Bay, Edna G., ed. 1982. *Women and Work in Africa*. Boulder, CO: Westview Press.

Bayart, Jean-François. 1989. *L'État en Afrique. La politique du ventre*. Paris: Fayard.

Bayart, Jean-François. 2000. "Africa in the World: A History of Extraversion." *African Affairs* 99: 217–267.

Burawoy, Michael. 2000. "Manufacturing the global." *Ethnography* 2: 147–159.

Burawoy, Michael, Joseph A. Blum, Sheba George, Zsuzsa Gille, Teresa Gowan, Lynne Haney, Maren Klawiter, Steve H. Lopez, Seán Ó Riain, and Millie Thayer. 2000. *Global Ethnography: Forces, Connections, and Imaginations in a Postmodern World*. Berkeley: University of California Press.

Comaroff, Jean, and John Comaroff. 2000. "Millennial Capitalism: First Thoughts on a Second Coming." *Public Culture* 12 (2): 291–343.

Cordonnier, Rita. 1987. *Femmes africaines et commerce. Les revendeuses de tissu de la ville de Lomé (Togo)*. Paris: L'Harmattan.

Ekholm-Friedman, Kajsia. 1991. *Catastrophe and Continuity: The Transformation of an African Culture*. London: Harwood Academic Press.

Ellis, Stephen. 1993. "Rumour and Power in Togo." *Africa: Journal of the International African Institute* 63 (4): 462–476.

Ellis, Stephen, and Yves Fauré, eds. 1995. *Entreprises et entrepreneurs africains.* Paris: Karthala.

Ferguson, James. 2006. *Global Shadows: Africa in the Neo-Liberal World Order.* Durham, NC: Duke University Press.

Friedman, Jonathan. 2004. "Globalization." Pp. 179–197 in *A Companion to Anthropology of Politics*, ed. David Nugent and Joan Vincent. Malden, MA: Blackwell.

Gille, Zsuza, and Sean O'Rian. 2002. "Global Ethnography." *Annual Review of Sociology* 28: 271–295.

Hart, Gillian P. 2002. *Disabling Globalization. Places of Power in Post-Apartheid South Africa.* Berkeley: University of California Press.

Heilbrunn, John R. 1993. "Social Origins of National Conferences in Benin and Togo." *Journal of Modern African Studies* 31 (2): 277–299.

House-Midamaba, Bessie, and Felix Ekechi, eds. 1995. *African Market Women and Economic Power. The Role of Women in African Economic Development.* London: Greenwood Press.

Igué, John, and Bio G. Soule. 1992. *L'État-entrepôt au Bénin: Commerce informel ou solution à la crise?* Paris: Karthala.

Macé, Alain. 2004. "Politique et démocratie au Togo 1993–1998: De l'espoir à la désillusion." *Cahiers d'Etudes Africaines* XLIV (4): 841–885.

Marcus, George E. 1995. "Ethnography in/of the World System: The Emergence of Multi-Sited Ethnography." *Annual Review of Anthropology* 24: 95–117.

Marchal, Roland. 1997. "Doubai: le developpement d'une cité-entrepôt dans le Golfe." *Les Etudes du CERI* (28) : 1–36.

Nielsen, Ruth. 1979. "The History and Development of Wax-Printed Textiles Intended for West Africa and Zaire." Pp. 467–498 in *The Fabrics of Culture*, ed. Justine Cordwell and Ronald D. Schwartz. The Hague: Mouton.

Ong, Aihwa, and Stephen J. Collier. 2005. "Global Assemblages, Anthropological Problems." Pp. 3–21 in *Global Assemblages. Technology, Politics and Ethics as Anthropological Problems*, ed. Aihwa Ong and Stephan R. Collier. Malden, MA: Blackwell.

Picton, John. 1995. *The Art of African Textiles. Technology, Tradition and Lurex.* London: Barbican Art Gallery and Lund Humphries Publishers.

Piot, Charles. 1999. *Remotely Global. Village Modernity in West Africa.* Chicago: University of Chicago Press.

Piot, Charles. 2006. "Jeux de frontière: La lotterie des cartes vertes au Togo." *Politique Africaine* 101: 171–181.

Tranberg Hansen, Karen. 2000. *Salaula. The World of Second Hand Clothing and Zambia.* Chicago: University of Chicago Press.

Tirtankar, Roy. 1996. *Cloth and Commerce. Textiles in Colonial India.* Walnut Creek, CA: AltaMira Press.

Weigel, Jean-Yves. 1987. "Nana et pecheurs du port de Lomé." *Politique Africaine* 27: 39–47.

10 Outcomes and Perspectives

Ulrike Schuerkens

TRANSFORMATIONS OF LOCAL SOCIOECONOMIC PRACTICES AND GLOBALIZATION

The focus of this book is on transformations of local socioeconomic practices in most regions of the world. The main contribution of the book is that it explores this concept in a world characterized by globalization. The empirically rich chapters invite us to a discussion of this topic by economic anthropologists and economic sociologists. In this, the book opens up a discussion of a domain hitherto reserved to economics that has been investigated by anthropologists or sociologists for a rather short time period (Van Binsbergen and Geschiere 2005). The strategy of the book is to further the dialogue with economists by proposing an understanding of countries of the North, the South, and the East in which the world is not as commodified as economists often think, but where socioeconomic aspects of life are present in abundance and no longer hidden. Often ancient production systems have been virtually destroyed or revitalized in the process of globalization that has characterized our world (Cook 2006). In this sense, the case studies in this book are not presented as an ethnographic evidence of socioeconomic practices but their value renders possible a rigorous investigation of broad theoretical issues within a specified social context.

The economic markets we can find in most of the studies are considered as social phenomena (Edelman and Haugerud 2006). The understandings of these economic situations permit us to obtain information about the conditions of socioeconomic practices. Capitalism in its neo-liberal global manifestation shapes identities and defines values (Causa and Cohen 2006). Even if scholars have reflected on this phenomenon only recently, people all over the world have found that they are included and/or marginalized in unanticipated ways. Globalization produces desires and expectations but decreases the certainty of work and appears less constrained by the costs of concrete labor (Dunning and Muccielli 2002). The current globalization encourages casualization, outsourcing, and the hiring of cheap workers (women, immigrants). It widens social and economic disparities between rich and poor regions and makes the latter the working regions of the former.

The culture of the neo-liberal economy is the consumption of consumers on a global marketplace. Some of these consumers obtain their identity less by their local cultural history than by consumer items they can buy. Even in countries such as China, contacts with media and advertisements have fueled domestic demands for several decades. New consumption patterns appear beside unprecedented levels of inequality between the Chinese coast and the impoverished countryside. In Thailand, non-traditional commodity production, as F. Wherry has shown in this book, has created opportunities for private domestic and international capital. Growth in nontraditional export sectors has accompanied changes in economic policies of Southern countries. Expanding niche markets, as F. Wherry has demonstrated, are included in private-sector development. They entail a set of global relations, symbols, and labor processes that encompass bankers, local producers, and bureaucracies. Even in Africa, as N. Sylvanus has displayed, the neo-liberal trade philosophy is part of a larger agenda that aims to fundamentally restructure African economies. In China, the pedagogical program of propagation of a rich culture of consumerism inculcates acquisition desires, even if the majority of the goods are not yet distributed in regions where television programs create a yearning for commodities that are elements of a distant culture. The permitting of advertisements in Chinese television programs since the end of the 1970s allowed the culture industry to create huge groups of "consumers-in-training" (Schein 2006: 220) who wish to participate in the global culture of capitalism. This sort of training may be conceived of as a cultural development in which transformations of cultural habits are initiated by leading groups.

In fact, the consumption style that the transnational model has created is only accessible to a small part of the populations in the geographic South, a portion that some scholars estimate to be only 20 or 30 percent of the population (Mattelart et al. 1984). This fact needs an explanation: The hierarchies that have been elaborated are shaped by an ethnic and cultural hierarchical ordering that may be easier to apply in some countries than in others. Cultural differences become thus a key alibi for economic disparity (Miller 2006). In this sense, culture is a barrier to development in the same way it was in the colonial differentiation of racial groups in some countries and between different countries.

Even more importantly, individuals who invest much time and energy in economically productive activities and do not meet their social obligations risk being regarded as deviants who are negatively sanctioned. Social rules that highly value egalitarian socioeconomic practices, as in many African countries, may thus have the tendency to explain failures of entire groups. The neo-liberal credo can enter in opposition to given social practices and may expose adapters to social sanctions such as accusations of theft or witchcraft, a phenomenon that is widespread in African countries south of the Sahara (cf. Geschiere 1997).

Some chapters in this volume stress the extent to which Southern societies have been influenced by the market stereotype. The authors show how actors can move in and out of market circuits. They display changes of socioeconomic practices in societies that have been considered as "anthropological" societies that are dominated by reciprocity and gift giving. The results show that it is more and more difficult to single out "premodern" remnants as obstacles to economic development (Perrons 2004). They put in question Western development experts that keep imposing in Africa or elsewhere in the South forms of community development that these experts would not uphold in their own societies.

The results of the book reveal that the peoples of southern, eastern, and northern regions are not helpless victims of the neo-liberal credo but that they are capable of creatively engaging in a selection of socioeconomic globalized practices. In this way, these populations may continue doing what they have been doing for a long time using only other resources. The different chapters show that there is industrial growth from below: Artisans may adapt special strategies of price settings and payment in a market system of global dimensions. Objects are invested with different emotional appeals, as F. Wherry displays for Thailand. Nevertheless, there are processes of rapid commodification. The results of these studies complement and even occasionally counteract models of economics that are more and more implemented by transnational elites in southern countries. The development discourse that has been a product of the world originating from World War II was strongly changed in the 1980s under Structural Adjustment Programs. The consequences of the neo-liberal credo that followed have created options for anthropological and sociological correctives in the institutional infrastructure of development (World Bank and International Monetary Fund). Poverty eradication, gender mainstreaming, and microfinance are openings that permit us to speak of the beginning of a dialogue of economists, sociologists, and anthropologists. The intention to give the recent Nobel Prize for Peace (2006) to the founder of the Grameen Bank in Bangladesh may be considered to further such a dialogue (Goldberg 2005). This book tries to provide some conceptual and descriptive elements toward this dialogue.

Anthropologists have often tried to project a utopian vision of a non-commodified society on the people they studied. They can be suspected to compensate for the intimacy and meaning they are missing in their home society. This nostalgic anthropological tradition of *authenticity* may be the opposite of the transformations of socioeconomic practices we have studied in this book. But, as our studies show, these particular aspects of the socioeconomic life can no longer be dissimulated. Many experiences and predicaments of today's South and of the world at large can be instructively considered from a socioeconomic perspective. The desire to make natives dependent on the market that was created, for example, during colonialism in large parts of Africa, Asia, and Latin America changed its character in the last decades: In the developing world, as our case studies reveal, people have become consumers in societies more and more characterized by the neo-liberal credo.

THE DIFFERENT CONTRIBUTIONS TO THIS COLLECTION

The first chapter tackles the social responsibility of economic elites in Germany. The author, P. Imbusch, presents the results of a study that has focused on the reactions of economic elites in the global economic competition and their societal responsibility. He tries to find out where these actors stand: Do economic profits lead automatically to positive societal results or should enterprises, as more or less public institutions, accept societal responsibility? In Germany, Imbusch could find over the last decades a shift from the traditional national model of the Rhenanian capitalism to the model of a globalizing neo-liberal capitalism. In most western European states, political elites consider themselves to be actors who should assist the local industry with political measures favoring casualization, deindustrialization, flexibilization, and a decrease of taxes so that enterprises find favorable frameworks supporting their economic activities under conditions of global competition. This shift to an Anglo-Saxon form of capitalism has implied that a majority of Germans, including large parts of the middle classes, had to accept precarious jobs and/or face new sorts of poverty, as well as social exclusion. This model has more and more been criticized in Germany during recent years, according to the results of a content analysis of newspaper articles, and the prestige of economic elites has been characterized to a greater extent by negative elements, such as corruption, self-centered interests, and so on (Imbusch and Rucht 2007a). In public newspapers and the papers of the economic sector, global processes of competition that have led to a deregulation of labor markets have progressively been discussed as stemming from self-evident economic constrains. Yet Imbusch and Rucht have studied the changing ethics of social responsibility under different governments (left- and right-wing) and have found that conservative parties underline that the pursuit of economic interests favors the general benefit of a society, whereas left-wing governments may possibly discuss the potential conflict between an economic performance ideal and social responsibility (2007a). Another interesting point of this study is that large enterprises with more than 100 employees have spent four to five times smaller amounts of money in percentage terms on social activities than smaller enterprises. Economic elites are furthermore interested that the state contributes to the creation of optimal conditions for economic competition and that it avoids intervening in the economy (2007a). This favored option is linked to the acceptance of the neo-liberal credo that considers social responsibility more or less as an option for private people than for enterprises. Nevertheless, social responsibility, according to the author, continues to be linked to public relations departments in enterprises but becomes a strategy used to improve the image of the given enterprise. "Image construction" is thus part of economic strategies under global competition that no longer permit people to value societal responsibility as an obligation, but only as a voluntary act. Therefore, we find currently top managers underlining a combination of conflicting logics: They increase their salary and the gains of stock option holders; they underline corporate social responsibility, and realize huge dismissals by delocalizing or unionizing enterprises.

This chapter gives important details on socioeconomic practices in a Western country. It shows that economic elites consider globalization and worldwide economic competition as a self-evident fact that influences their economic choices. Mass unemployment of large groups is considered as compatible with the quasi-natural economic competition that directs the activities of economic actors. Only in recent years, left-wing intellectuals and the ecclesiastical hierarchy have begun to put in question this understanding. Yet a powerful institutional infrastructure supports this vision so that it is difficult to criticize economic elites. In the last part of this conclusion, we discuss alter-globalization movements, which seem to be currently the only credible actors who, confronted with established economic structures, may influence the future economic life of the populations in the northern hemisphere.

The chapter by N. Bandelj tackles free-market reforms in Central and Eastern Europe. She asks what the adoption of neo-liberal reforms drives and argues that there is some divergence in the process in the region, despite uniform pressures from international financial organizations and the European Union. She demonstrates that the International Monetary Fund (IMF) and the World Trade Organization (WTO) have played a major role in implementing neo-liberal policies. These institutions argued for rapid changes in the region, with a goal of rapidly creating markets and eliminating former "socialist" economic structures. This neo-liberal concept of transformations was based, according to N. Bandelj, on the belief in a natural progression of economic development toward capitalism, whereby benefits of markets and privatization would become obvious soon after the first shocks. A further important factor in the transformation process was the beginning of the integration into the European Union linked to agreements on "trade-related issues, political dialogue, legal harmonization, and other areas of cooperation." (51) During "the EU accession process, Central and East European applicants had to adopt their institutional frameworks to the . . . common European legislation." (51) What is interesting in her chapter is the demonstration that neo-liberal ideas were already worked out during the socialist period. Domestic decision makers had become familiar with Western economic principles and adapted, according to local political and economic situations, policies concerning privatization, foreign direct investment liberalization, tax policy, and so on. N. Bandelj shows that the argument that neo-liberalism has been the result of free-market policies is rather weak and that "differences across countries should be understood as embedded in socialist legacies, and shaped by domestic political forces." (46) But the author also underlines that the support of neo-liberalism by the European Union and powerful international financial organizations had a tendency to trigger adoption and not resistance by the political leaders of these countries. Yet further outcomes and political measures will depend, according to N. Bandelj, on possible development strategies, "balancing simultaneously other domestic political interests and international pressures." (53)

The chapter by A. Mennicken discusses the introduction of international auditing standards in post-Soviet Russia. The author considers that these standards constitute much more than a neutral technical instrument for financial control and that they have been endowed in view of wider demands for international conformity. These standards have been included in the creation of new market-oriented economical structures and the transplantation of Western patterns. A. Mennicken carried out her study in Moscow: for example, in a leading Russian audit firm, and a European Union-funded audit reform project. She writes: "Auditing standards, in particular international standards, were introduced as a means of creating a jurisdiction of professionalism that could help ground, protect, and represent a realm of new capitalist expertise." (82) The acceptance of standards was considered to demonstrate the willingness to reform and to reintegrate into the world of international business. A. Mennicken underlines that the reform of auditing contributed to the development of the market infrastructure and to the establishment of international recognition and legitimacy. In her conclusion, the author argues that the "global determination (of auditing standards) works through as well as against local differences." (94)

Th. Pairault's chapter is interesting insofar as he asks whether Western capitalism has been transforming China into a neo-liberal paradise. He underlines that some of the groups to be left out of economic growth include ethnic minorities, migrant workers, and people in the countryside. (Mohapatra et al. 2006) He shows that state involvement and economic growth are not the antonyms that they appear to have become. In fact, China has grown by ignoring most of the policy prescriptions of the World Bank and the IMF. A large state sector in the economy was maintained. Insofar as the country was opposed to an approach of the international funding institutions that tried to implement one policy for all countries, China could respect local socioeconomic situations by founding its development on cultural roots such as those provided by Confucius. Chinese leaders only adopted the external advice they believed appropriate and continued to refer to a cultural tradition that they could find in Confucius's ideas. The results have been mixed, as T. Pairault demonstrates: Growth rates have been impressive, accompanied by growing social inequality. China has become one of the most important economies during the last decade. Her integration into the world economy is important in domestic public opinion, and the public mood is optimistic that the economy can overcome the challenges of international competition. Provided that political leaders redistribute economic benefits, economic growth may result in beneficial social consequences for this large country. For China, globalization may also mean that transnational elites and political leaders of Western countries may engage with groups and individuals who try to foster rights and interests that avoid the social consequences of an uncontrolled capitalism. China's next challenge is certainly to achieve higher social equity. Some of the ideas on social welfare that Th. Pairault evokes go in this direction. In this sense, development processes in societies like China create alternative forms that combine local socioeconomic practices with international integration. To what extent these forms will be successful is still an incredible process to watch in the coming years.

If we insist on Confucius and his special importance for the economic development of some Asian countries, the German scholar Max Weber had already thought one century ago that the region influenced by this cultural tradition would be particularly apt in comparison to any other part of the non-Western world to adopt a capitalism that had been developed in other parts of the world. In fact, important elements of this tradition are the main interest in education: a readiness to perform according to high standards, and the capacity to work hard (cf. Weber 1991: 200); other aspects are a high appraisal of wealth, self-moderation, acceptance of discipline, diligence, perseverance, and an orientation at the actual life-world. It is obvious that these attributes and attitudes favor economic success and that they resemble personal characteristics of the Protestant ethics that Weber (1984) had considered to be important for the Western capitalist success story. As one scholar has underlined, in South Korea, Taiwan, and Singapore, "[the] whole population was determined to 'live better'" (Bon 1992: 10). In China, the long tradition of the Confucian education had prepared the populations to pass through modern educational programs. In other countries of the region, such as Malaysia, Indonesia, and Thailand, people of Chinese origins control a high percentage of the private economy (cf. Camilleri 2000: 109; Chua-Franz 2002: 101; Haggard 1998; Yoshihara 2000). This means that the thesis of the influence of Confucius's ethics is also validated for these countries, even if the majority of their populations is influenced by Islam or Buddhism.

If we compare China to India, the other giant in Asia, one may ask why the subcontinent has undertaken a socioeconomic development that is so much different from other countries in the region. (Gauchon 2006) If we continue to argue with cultural arguments, modern capitalism according to its Western characteristics encounters here cultural and social prerequisites that favor the denial of problems (cf. Schmitt 2004). Economic growth knew steady rates in both China and India since 1949, but China's growth rates increased at the end of the 1970s. India's growth rate in the 1990s was 5 to 7 percent lower than that of China. Foreign investments in 2002 represented US $3.2 billion in India, whereas China received US $52.7 billion (Schmitt 2004: 191). Infant mortality and life expectancy are different in the two countries; the absolute values are much more favorable in China than in India. In many development dimensions, India is still at the level of the poorest countries of the world: for example, in primary education or access to medical care. (Goldstein et al. 2006) Furthermore, the high importance of the caste system and sociocultural traditions that legitimate the huge inequalities among different social groups, which mean resignation and apathy for members of the lower castes, continue to be elements that hinder the socioeconomic development of the country. In a recent article, Van Dijk (2006) compares India and China and explains China's higher economic performance by "pointing at structural factors: land reform, relatively good education, health and social security systems and performance, superior (local) governance, and a high speed of reform" (Visser and Van Dijk 2006: 468). Moreover, Van Dijk finds that "the rate of productivity growth along with key aspects of the labour legislation (especially the part determining labour market flexibility)" (p. 468) explains the difference between China and India so that China benefited more from economic globalization than India.

The chapter by F. Wherry informs us of another socioeconomic strategy of local people in Asia: the export of cultural commodities that permit the nation-state to promote a particular image of itself. "The images become branded by the national tourism agency," as F. Wherry informs us, and "are influenced by non-local expectations." (121) Cultural handicrafts permit states to compete in global markets and to covert a symbolic capital into economic capital for former agricultural workers and tourist services. Furthermore, the state can protect its cultural traditions and define new opportunities, which create a comparative advantage for the country in the handicraft sector. This sector finds thus its place in a modern society by highlighting some of its traditional roots. F. Wherry evokes in his chapter the history of the Thai's participation in World Fairs that "set the stage for the commodification of the exotic in the global marketplace." (130) Currently, the main argument of the Thai government is that "culture pays in quality where labor loses to neighboring competitors." (130) Local Thai entrepreneurs have so become competitors on a global market of cultural goods sustained by their own government.

M. Gauvain links in her chapter the development of the informal economy to the advent of the neo-liberal credo in southern countries. She writes that processes of privatization and "an increasing national and international competition . . . led to an important unemployment for nonskilled and low-skilled people . . . this has encouraged the development of the informal economy." (139) She reports that governments in Venezuela have adopted spatial and not economic strategies in order to find a solution. This fact reveals the small possibilities of governments in southern countries confronted with this development. M. Gauvain suggests three theoretical viewpoints on the informal sector: According to the dualists, "the informal sector is just a way to provide an income to the poor, whereas economic circumstances around their inclusion into the formal job market do not exist."

(145) The structuralists consider the informal economy "according to the scheme 'dominate/dominated' . . . as a possibility to reduce the labor costs in a competitive market." (146) The legalist approach "considers informal work as a rational answer to the high costs of formalized establishments." (146)

M. Gauvain could find another recent influence of global markets on the informal economy of street vendors, in that "an increasing part of these products has originated in Asia, due to a huge network of importation and smuggling." (147) In Caracas, she found "two different types of informal workers, characterized by different incomes and a different *habitus*" (148): There are upper tier and lower tier informal sectors, differentiated by the amount of earnings. Some of these street vendors are beginning to organize themselves in cooperatives, which means "deep changes in the organization of production and selling." (148) Yet these processes can also be found in other southern countries, where, for example, organizations such as the Grameen Bank since the 1970s[1] or later on the International Labor Organization, since the turn of the millennium, promote the restructuring efforts of these groups.[2] (Africultures 2006)

The chapter by D. Kohnert tackles cultures of innovation that accrue from the informal sector, not the formal one. He asks how culture matters. According to a common definition that D. Kohnert suggests, cultures of innovation "are relatively stable modes of cognition, behavior and social organization, directed towards 'modernization' and 'development.'" (151) He argues that it is "misleading to put the blame for lacking development in Africa . . . on the cultural heritage" and that "African cultures are highly differentiated." (152) It is thus important to redirect research toward the informal sector, where the poor look for innovative solutions in their own cultures. D. Kohnert differentiates the informal sector into three groups: first, the poor, who try to assure their survival as human beings in the form of indigenous innovations; second, the middle classes, who are divided in a lower and an upper segment. The first group tries to preserve its socioeconomic status, whereas the latter tries to consolidate and improve its position. Third is the upper class, whose male members try to consolidate their power. D. Kohnert analyzes empirical examples from Benin, where competing cultures of opposition movements imposed the democratic renewal and became pioneers of transition. In another case study from Haiti, D. Kohnert could show that "the Haitian *vodun* acted as a modern driving force for democratic transition . . . against the firm resistance of the religious and political establishment." (164) In sum, D. Kohnert is able to show that cultural innovations that are based on indigenous cultures are powerful stimuli for agents of change. In this sense, they add important elements to the culture of socioeconomic change that the globalized Western development practice sustained by the development institutions tries to promote.

The chapter by N. Sylvanus demonstrates the changing socioeconomic practices of Togolese women entrepreneurs in the global textile trade. She argues that the structure of the textile market in Togo is linked to the shifts in production toward China, thus being closely linked to the reorganization of the global economy. The *Nanettes* N. Sylvanus studies "reinforce the competitiveness of the market ensuing free-trade mechanisms and the multiplication of economic players and networks." (175) She writes: "Although the opening of the market to increasing competition, de facto liberalization, has occurred, it however does not refer to an entirely new—neo-liberal—market scheme as such because, in my view, it is not more capitalistic than the previous system." (176) In this sense, the trade strategies N. Sylvanus displays "refer to an adaptation to increasing global competition in the local market." (176) The author demonstrates that the currency devaluations of the 1990s and the availability of cheap products from East and Southeast Asia affected the "informal" trade structures. One particular aspect of this activity is that "the *Nanettes* consider themselves as having brought consumption democratization to Togo" (185) insofar as the new goods have become much cheaper. N. Sylvanus shows how copies of Dutch prints have been produced since the beginning of the 21st century in China and have contributed to a multiplication of actors. The external economic relations of these women function in a highly competitive context. In 2005, the author could find ten competing Chinese firms that tried to reorganize the Togolese market and to put in question the earnings of the women entrepreneurs. The result has been a decrease of profits and a diversification of the market. The stories of these women inform us that they have been looking for a temporal success and not for "profit maximization per se." (188) In this sense, these traders have adapted to an increasing global competition in the local market: They have been obliged to be flexible and individualistic. N. Sylvanus argues finally that these practices "are not part of a new strategy or a new neo-liberal market scheme." (189) Further research that goes in this direction has been done by Evers Rosander (2005) on Senegalese women who circulate between their country and Spain in order to pursuit their economic activities as entrepreneurs. Insofar as socioeconomic practices are locally shaped, these traders react to global patterns that are linked to the functioning of the global economic system. N. Sylvanus's observations suggest that more research has to be done on the influence of global economic patterns on local socioeconomic practices in order to retrace long-term development strategies. It seems obvious that the local and the global intertwine in order to produce a result that constitutes a new element linked to a local cultural setting and influenced by global economic parameters, but we still possess too little knowledge on long-term tendencies in the socioeconomic sector.

ALTER-GLOBALIZATION MOVEMENTS AND THE ECONOMIC SYSTEM

The collected evidence of this book shows that there are multiple varieties of neo-liberal global capitalism. In this understanding, local cultures continue to force the global economic system to adapt to its seemingly "neutral" rules.

(Nichols and Sugur 2004; Pietrobelli and Sverrisson 2004; Schmitz 2004; Smart and Smart 2005) This means that current global markets depend on historical and concrete situations, despite global elites who defend neo-liberal economic schemes as the only possible solution in our contemporary world. It is obvious that the power of these groups is so important that only movements such as the alter-globalization movements have the potential to form a counterforce. Yet these movements tend to be rather disparate[3] today, as Fougier (2004) has shown in an interesting study. This leads to dispersion and an absence of efficient counterprojects. Nevertheless, these different movements that are reunited at meetings such as the World Social Summits gather so many people that as such they have already begun to influence politicians and will continue to do so if the negative effects of the current neo-liberal globalization become more obvious. The first political reactions can be seen in electoral results that no longer favor one of the old established parties but split politicians on a fifty/fifty basis (e.g., Germany, the United States, France). People are no longer convinced that political elites sustain different programs, a fact that leads to high rates of electoral absenteeism in national elections.

In this political situation, the alter-globalization movements constitute a possible force that could oblige political elites to overtake some of the topics discussed. The result will probably be that the neo-liberal economic system will improve some of its outcomes that still mean injustice, inequality, poverty, and so on. After the downfall of the Soviet system, these movements have included groups that can be considered as progressive in a historical sense, meaning that they have suggested development possibilities that may render our current world more equal and more responsible regarding social topics. The difficulty of these movements is, as Fougier has rightly underlined, that they are much too numerous so that a common strategy is missing. Moreover, the most often emphasized idea of accepting diversity and localism renders difficult the formation of a group that could become predominant on a global scale.

Meanwhile, the credo of these groups is to construct alternative local spaces that may mushroom so that in the long run values would be changed and people would ask their elites to change long-accepted values. Governments, political movements, and enterprises would then be obliged to respect aspects or demands that have been formulated by these groups. In this understanding, alter-globalization would permit transformation of economic globalization as it is currently understood. Social, political, and cultural aspects may then be integrated in a more humane form of neo-liberal capitalism than what our societies live today. In this sense, the alter-globalization movement would not put in question the neo-liberal credo as such but it would contribute to correcting some of its negative outcomes (cf. Fougier 2004). The "third way" of the cold war period that no longer exists may thus find a successor in the current alter-globalization movement and its requests for changes.

The main question at the origin of this volume has been whether another economy is possible, even if this query seems to be more or less academic and does not represent a real challenge in numerous countries where the "normal" economy has not been really settled. (Margairaz and Minard 2006) In many countries, it is still urgent to look for measures for surviving what Karl Polanyi declared to be the "livelihood of man." In countries where only a quarter or half of the population capable of work possesses more or less regular commercial, public, or private jobs, where neither the state nor the open market is sufficient to satisfy the needs of their populations, some further economic solutions are needed. It is known that alternative ways include illegal or even criminal activities, severe working conditions, traffic in drugs or arms, and so on. Obviously, these are solutions, but they are neither universal nor recommended. M. Gauvain has discussed in this volume one of the possible alternatives that has been the informal economy, but she has also stressed the limits of this approach. Yet the question remains of whether there is any alternative to the market where human beings function according to a common factor: their personal interests and their looking for monetary gains. There are scholars who think that livelihood and market are not fundamentally different in their ideal functioning.[4] Even if alternatives to the market exist (e.g., NGOs, public wealth), Caillé (2003) underlines that there are no economic alternatives insofar as public servants or subventions to nongovernmental organizations (NGOs) are paid by taxes, obtained from what the market has permitted to collect. Based on this assumption, Caillé thinks that there is only one economy and that there are not several economies. According to him, an economy based on solidarities does not form a systematic and autoregulated alternative to capitalism. The political project of this solidarity may be coherent, but it does not figure out another economic project. Even if there are economic results that may be beneficial to certain groups, no further economic system different from the market economy exists today. The socialist project of Eastern Europe is no longer discussed as another economic possibility even in countries such as China that have been opened up to the market principle for over twenty years now, with the results that Th. Pairrault has discussed in this book. Alternative economic groups support other groups than the groups that are sustained by the market principle. In this sense, there are different ways to create solidarity in social or political communities. As everybody knows, the family allows creation of economic links that are based on rules other than the market mechanism. Village members, cultural groups, migrants, or even workers of the social sector may be linked by rules that are particular for them, that create solidarity, reciprocity, and another yearning for democracy, a conclusion underlined by Jean-Louis Laville (2003).

There is enough agreement among scholars that it is an illusion to ask for the creation of an alternative economic science. Instead, it seems to be urgent to have another look at the economy, a look that is inspired by other social sciences and by an ethical and political concern that asks for improving a vision that exclusively emphasizes economic factors. (Jansen and Lee 2007)

More and more economists share this endeavor, people who know best the limits of their scientific endeavors. They have gathered around the PEKEA movement (Political and Ethical Knowledge on Economic Activities),[5] where famous scholars such as Alain Touraine, Jacques Sapir, Yves Berthelot, and Noam Chomsky are members of the scientific board. This group defends the necessity to invent new market regulations and rules that permit another way to refer to economics and to include social measures in the market economy.

J. Sapir wrote in his recent book (2006a) and in an article in *Le Monde diplomatique* (2006b) that competition and concurrence, two principles that the Organization for Economic Cooperation and Development (OECD) emphasizes, are based on faith and not on scientific principles. In fact, the OECD stated in a recent report with the title "Promoting Pro-Poor Growth: Private Sector Development" (2006):

> Competitive markets are not only more efficient in producing and dis-tributing goods and services and in allocating resources, they are es-sential for markets to work better for the poor. Competitive markets are more likely to provide the poor with opportunities to be employed or to start their own business. . . . A competition policy and law may seem to be a luxury for developing countries short of finance and skilled people but the potential gains can be enormous. (2006: 19)

However, the report agrees that "more empirical research on the effects of increasing the intensity of competition would be of value and could help deci-sion making on how to sequence reforms that promote greater competition" (19). According to J. Sapir, these arguments have been introduced in the eco-nomical and political debate because of their "objective" scientific character. In fact, they are not based on scientific evidence but are supported by economical experts influenced by the neo-liberal credo. These experts gather in institu-tions such as the World Bank and the OECD, and pretend that competition and concurrence are economical dogmas applicable to every society in the global world. This means that even poor societies in the South would func-tion according to these principles despite global inequality and the existence of powerful (and powerless) countries or institutions. As an alternative to this credo, J. Sapir has shown that the hypothesis at the basis of these theories, that of an individual actor (or a political group) whose reactions are previsible and do not depend on concrete situations, has been invalidated during the last 30 years in social sciences.[6] However, the majority of today's economists deny these results, which would put in question their models. Instead, they prefer to support what J. Sapir has called a "religious belief."[7] The studies in this book support J. Sapir's argument: The authors have described particular socioeco-nomic practices in current societies where social actors try to adapt their living to economic situations. Principles such as competition and concurrence have been discussed, but they have not been declared as scientific dogmas.

CONCLUSION

Contrary to Wallerstein's global capitalist system (1979), we have presented in this book studies that emphasize the theoretical reasons to differentiate among economic systems. The various institutional forms that the authors of this book present are the results of social and political conflicts embedded in particular geographic societies, and specific for given historical periods. Institutions that govern these economies are characterized by conventional economic mechanisms such as the state and the market. Further actors are associations, communities, and social networks that constitute historical legacies insofar as they contribute to the current shaping of socioeconomic practices influenced by global conditions. One can speak here about "path dependency," as the economical literature does (Boyer 2005: 38). Boyer even suggests "that technologies, institutions, and organizations co-evolve" (38) so that "there is no clear force that would bring about the convergence of various capitalisms" (38). Insofar as economic globalization has already stood for a restructuring of the economies of Eastern Europe and China (cf. the chapters of N. Bandelj, A. Mennicken, and Th. Pairault), and a spread of some aspects of the capitalist system in Asian (cf. the chapter by F. Wherry), Latin American (cf. the chapter by M. Gauvain), and African (cf. the chapter by N. Sylvanus) societies, we are only at the beginning of our research endeavors on the diversity of capitalism in the global world. Some of the authors in this book have pointed to reasons for this diversity, such as social and/or political disinterest, dependency, or historical legacies. Yet the results of the collected studies let us presume that each economic configuration develops its own variations and improvements (cf. Hall and Soskice 2001; Jackson and Deeg 2006). This would mean that it is not appropriate to oppose dynamic forms to inert types. Instead, further research should try to determine the given conditions of development and innovation in particular societies, and to discover the patterns that delay or hinder advances. This will go further than to find only one kind of productive socioeconomic model and will respect the varieties that are constitutive for the sociocultural diversity we can find in our global world. (Schuerkens 2004)

NOTES

1. Cf. http://www.grameenfoundation.org/pubdownload/dl.php?pubID=2, accessed January 28, 2007.
2. Cf. http://www.global-labour.org/trade_unions_and_the_informal_sector_wiego.htm, accessed January 28, 2007.
3. Cf. Fougier (2004).
4. For example, Caillé (2003: 13).
5. Cf. www.pekea-fr.org, accessed November 25, 2006.
6. Cf. http://www.prospectives.info/La-concurrence,-un-mythe_a90.html, accessed January 1, 2007.
7. Ibid.

REFERENCES

Bon, Ho Koo. 1992. *Socio-Cultural Factors in the Industrialization of Korea*. San Francisco: ICS Press.

Boyer, Robert. 1999. "The Variety and Dynamics of Capitalism." Pp. 122–140 in *Institutions and the Evolution of Capitalism: Implications of Evolutionary Economics*, ed. John Groenewegen and Jack Vromen. Northampton, MA: Edward Elgar.

Boyer, Robert. 2005. "How and Why Capitalisms Differ." MPIfG Discussion Paper 05/4. Cologne: Max Planck Institute for the Study of Societies.

Caillé, Alain. 2003. "Présentation," L'Alteréconomie. Quelle "autre mondialisation"? *Revue de Mauss* 21: 5–20.

Camilleri, Joseph A. 2000. *States, Markets and Civil Society in Asia Pacific. The Political Economy of the Asia-Pacific Region*, Vol. 1. Cheltenham: Edward Elgar.

Causa, Orsetta, and Daniel Cohen. 2006. *The Ladder of Competitiveness: How to Climb It*. Paris: OECD.

Chua-Franz, Christian. 2002. *Indonesiens Chinesen. Konstruktion und Instrumentalisierung einer ethnischen Minderheit*. Hamburg: Mitteilungen des Instituts für Asienkunde, no. 361.

Cook, Scott. 2006. "Commodity Cultures, Mesoamerica and Mexico's Changing Indigenous Economy." *Critique of Anthropology* 26 (2): 181–208.

Dunning, John H., and Jean-Louis Muccielli, eds. 2002. *Multinational Firms: The Global–Local Dilemma*. New York: Routledge.

Edelman, Marc, and Angelique Haugerud, eds. 2006. *The Anthropology of Development and Globalization. From Classical Political Economy to Contemporary Neoliberalism*. Malden, Oxford: Blackwell.

Evers Rosander, Eva. 2005. "Cosmopolites et locales: Femmes sénégalaises en voyage." *Afrique et Histoire: Revue internationale* 4: 103–122.

Fougier, Eddy. 2004. *Altermondialisme. Le nouveau mouvement d'émancipation?* Paris: Lignes de repères.

Gauchon, Pascal, ed. 2006. *Inde, Chine à l'assaut du monde: rapport Antheios*. Paris: Presses universitaires de France.

Geschiere, Peter. 1997. *The Modernity of Witchcraft: Politics and the Occult in Postcolonial Africa*. Charlottesville: University Press of Virginia.

Goldberg, Nathanael. 2005. *Measuring the Impact of Microfinance: Taking Stock of What We Know*. Grameen Foundation USA. Publication Series. PDF document http://www.grameenfoundation.org/pubdownload/dl.php?pubID=29, accessed January 28, 2007.

Goldstein, Andrea, Nicolas Pinaud, Helmut Reisen, and Xiaobao Chen. 2006. *The Rise of China and India: What's in it for Africa*. Paris: OECD.

Haggard, Stephan M. 1998. "Business, Politics and Policy in East and Southeast Asia." Pp. 78–104 in *Behind East Asian Growth. The Political and Social Foundations of Prosperity*, ed. Henry S. Rowen. New York: Routledge.

Hall, Peter, and David Soskice, eds. 2001. *Varieties of Capitalism: The Institutional Foundations of Comparative Advantage*. Oxford: Oxford University Press.

Imbusch, Peter, and Dieter Rucht. 2007a. "Wirtschaftseliten und ihre gesellschaftliche Verantwortung." *Aus Politik und Zeitgeschichte* 4–5: 3–10.

Imbusch, Peter, and Dieter Rucht, eds. 2007b. *"Ohne Druck bewegt sich nichts"— Fallstudien zur gesellschaftlichen Verantwortung von Eliten*. Wiesbaden: VS-Verlag.

Jackson, Gregory, and Richard Deeg. 2006. "How Many Varieties of Capitalism? Comparing the Comparative Institutional Analyses of Capitalist Diversity."

MPIfG Discussion Paper 06/2. Cologne: Max Planck Institute for the Study of Societies.

Jansen, Marion, and Eddy Lee. 2007. *Trade and Employment: Challenges for Policy Research*. Geneva: International Labor Organization and World Trade Organization.

"Les cultures africaines sont-elles à vendre?" 2006. *Africultures* 69.

Margairaz, Dominique, and Philippe Minard. 2006. "Présentation du numéro spécial: Le marché dans son histoire," *Revue de Synthèse*, 5e série, 2: 241–252.

Mattelart, Armand, Xavier Delcourt, and Michèle Mattelart. 1984. *International Image Markets: In Search of an Alternative Perspective*. New York: Comedia.

Miller, Daniel. 2006. "A Theory of Virtualism: Consumption as Negation." Pp. 224–231 in *The Anthropology of Development and Globalization. From Classical Political Economy to Contemporary Neoliberalism*, ed. Marc Edelman and Angelique Haugerud. Malden, Oxford: Blackwell.

Mohapatra, Sandeep, Rozelle Scott, and Jikun Huang. 2006. "Climbing the Development Ladder: Economic Development and the Evolution of Occupations in Rural China." *Journal of Development Studies* 42 (6): 1023–1055.

Nichols, Theo, and Nadir Sugur. 2004. *Global Management, Local Labour: Turkish Workers and Modern Industry*. Houndmills, NY: Palgrave Macmillan.

Organization for Economic Cooperation and Development. 2006. *Promoting Pro-Poor Growth. Private Sector Development*. Paris: OECD.

Perrons, Diane. 2004. *Globalization and Social Change. People and Places in a Divided World*. New York: Routledge.

Pietrobelli, Carlo, and Arni Sverrisson, eds. 2004. *Linking Local and Global Economies: The Ties That Bind*. New York: Routledge.

PEKEA. 2003. "*Prolegomena to the Building of a Political and Ethical Knowledge Regarding Economic Activities (PEKEA.)*, *Économies et Societés* Hors Série XXXVII (6). Paris: Les Presses de l'ISMEA.

Sapir, Jacques. 2006a. *La fin de l'eurolibéralisme*. Paris: Seuil.

Sapir, Jacques. 2006b. "La concurrence, un mythe," *Le monde diplomatique*, June. http://www.prospectives.info/La-concurrence,-un-mythe_a90.html, accessed January 1, 2007.

Schein, Louisa. 2006. "Market Mentalities, Iron Satellite Dishes, and Contested Cultural Developmentalism." Pp. 216–223 in *The Anthropology of Development and Globalization. From Classical Political Economy to Contemporary Neoliberalism*, eds. Marc Edelman and Angelique Haugerud. Malden, Oxford: Blackwell.

Schmitt, Volker. 2004. "Erfolgsbedingungen des konfuzianischen Wohlfahrtskapitalismus. Kultursoziologische und modernisierungstheoretische Überlegungen." Pp. 175–196 in *Gesellschaft mit beschränkter Hoffnung. Reformfähigkeit und die Möglichkeit rationaler Politik*, eds. Petra Stykow and Jürgen Beyer. Wiesbaden: Verlag für Sozialwissenschaften.

Schmitz, Hubert, ed. 2004. *Local Enterprises in the Global Economy: Issues of Governance and Upgrading*. Northampton, MA: Edward Elgar.

Schuerkens, Ulrike, ed. 2004. *Global Forces and Local Life-Worlds: Social Transformations*. Thousand Oaks, CA, New Delhi, London: Sage.

Smart, Alan, and Josephine Smart, eds. 2005. *Petty Capitalists and Globalization: Flexibility, Entrepreneurship, and Economic Development*. Albany: SUNY Press.

The Opportunity Continent: Africa. Web site: http://www.theopportunitycontinent.com/overview.php, accessed July 15, 2007.

Van Binsbergen, Wim, and Peter Geschiere, eds. 2005. *Commodification: Things, Agency, and Identities (The Social Life of Things* Revisited). Münster: Lit.

Van Dijk, Meine Pieter. 2006. "Different Effects of Globalisation for Workers and the Poor in China and India, Comparing Countries, Cities and ICT Clusters." *Tijdschrift voor Economische en Sociale Geografie* 97 (5): 503–514.

Visser, Evert-Jan, and Meine Pieter Van Dijk. 2006. "Economic Globalisation and Workers: Introduction." *Tijdschrift voor Economische en Sociale Geografie* 97 (5): 463–469.

Wallerstein, Immanuel. 1979. *The Capitalist World-Economy*. Cambridge: Cambridge University Press.

Weber, Max. 1984. *Die protestantische Ethik I. Eine Aufsatzsammlung*. Gütersloh: Mohn.

Weber, Max. 1991. *Die Wirtschaftsethik der Weltreligionen. Konfuzianismus und Taoismus (Schriften 1915–1920)*. Tübingen: Mohn (MWG 1/19).

Yoshihara, Kunio. 2000. *Asia Per Capita. Why National Incomes Differ in East Asia*. London: Curzon Press.

Notes on Contributors

Nina Bandelj is assistant professor of sociology, and faculty associate at the Center for the Study of Democracy, University of California, Irvine. She completed her PhD dissertation at Princeton University, for which she received the Martin Seymour Lipset Award from the Society of Comparative Research. She was a Fellow at the Max Planck Institute for the Study of Societies in Cologne and a Jean Monnet Fellow at the European University Institute, Florence. Her research interests are in economic and comparative sociology, culture, political economy, organizations, and social change. She has published in *Social Forces, Current Sociology, East European Politics and Societies,* and *Sociological Forum.* Her book *From Communists to Foreign Capitalists* is forthcoming with Princeton University Press (2007). E-mail: nbandelj@uci.edu.

Mathilde Gauvain studied literature and social sciences in a preparatory class before entering the *Ecole Normale Supérieure* of Literature and Human Sciences (ENS-LSH) in Lyon. She obtained a BA in sociology and anthropology at the University of Lyon 2. She graduated from *Sciences-Po Paris* in 2003. She obtained a diploma in economics and social sciences in 2004. In 2005, she obtained a diploma in Comparative Development Research at the EHESS, with a thesis on "Street vending and urban public spaces: the case of the *buhoneros* of Caracas." She is preparing a PhD thesis on "The dark side of Caracas: From the informal city to the secondary urban system." E-mail: mathildegauvain@hotmail.com.

Peter Imbusch is professor of conflict research at the University of Marburg. He has been coordinator of the research association on "disintegration processes" at the University of Bielefeld (Germany). He studied sociology and political science, and received his PhD in 1990 with a comparative analysis of the transformation of social structures in different Latin American countries. He studied in his "habilitation" the topic "Modernity and Violence" (2001). His research interests are political sociology, social structure, conflict and violence, and sociological theory. E-mail: imbusch@staff.uni-marburg.de.

Dirk Kohnert, economist, is deputy director of the Institute of African Affairs (IAA) at GIGA (German Institute of Global and Area Studies), Hamburg, Germany, and managing editor of the academic journal *Afrika Spectrum* since 1991. Before that, he was lecturer in development planning and senior development expert in several African countries. He has published numerous books and articles in scholarly journals on economic, social, and cultural development, planning, and evaluation. E-mail: Kohnert@iak.duei.de.

Andrea Mennicken is a lecturer in accounting at the London School of Economics (LSE). She received her doctorate from the London School of Economics in 2005 on a thesis entitled *Moving West: The Emergence, Reform, and Standardization of Audit Practices in Post-Soviet Russia*. She holds a master's degree (LSE) and a diploma degree (University of Bielefeld, Germany) in sociology. Her research interests include transnational governance regimes, processes of professionalization and standardization, and sociological studies of calculative practices. E-mail: a.m.mennicken@lse.ac.uk.

Thierry Pairault, economist and sinologist, is *Directeur de recherche* at the French *Centre national de la recherche scientifique* and member of the *Centre d'études sur la Chine moderne et contemporaine* at the *École des Hautes Études en Sciences Sociales*, where he teaches a seminar on Chinese economy. He is the scientific coordinator of the Daedalos Institute of Geopolitics. He has published numerous books and articles in learned journals on socioeconomic issues related to China. E-mail: pairault@ehess.fr.

Ulrike Schuerkens has doctorates both in sociology, and in social anthropology and ethnology, from the *École des Hautes Études en Sciences Sociales* in Paris. She received the diploma *Habilitation à diriger des recherches* from the University Paris V–René Descartes. Currently, she is senior lecturer at the *École des Hautes Études en Sciences Sociales*, Paris, France. She has published extensively on development, social change, migration, multiculturalism, and colonialism. Her latest monographs are *Transnational Migrations and Social Transformations* (ed., *Current Sociology*, 53, 4, 2, 2005); *Global Forces and Local Life-Worlds: Social Transformations* (ed., Sage, 2004); *Changement social sous régime colonial: Du Togo allemand aux Togo et Ghana indépendants* (L'Harmattan, 2001); and *Transformationsprozesse in der Elfenbeinkueste und in Ghana* (Lit, 2001). E-mail: Ulrike.Schuerkens@ehess.fr.

Nina Sylvanus obtained a PhD at the *Centre d'Etudes Africaines* at the *Ecole des Hautes Etudes en Sciences Sociales* in Paris in 2006. In her dissertation "*Des fils enchevêtrés. Des commerçantes togolaises dans les circuits mondiaux du textile*," she studied the shaping of a West African trading network and its links to broader networks of global trade exchange. She has been appointed visiting assistant professor to the University of Californa (UCLA) International Institute's Global Fellows Program, where she is working on a book project entitled the *The Fabric of Globality: West African Women in the World Commodity Trade*. E-mail: nsylvanus@international.ucla.edu.

Frederick F. Wherry, University of Michigan, is an assistant professor of sociology and a faculty affiliate at the Center for Southeast Asian Studies. He investigates culture and commerce in comparative perspective and has completed a book manuscript about how international tourism and the global market for handicrafts have affected the economic development of communities where most of the residents earn their living directly or indirectly from handicraft sales in Thailand and Costa Rica. He is currently at work on an ethnographic monograph about entrepreneurial endeavors (artistic and nonartistic) in Philadelphia's ethnic and cosmopolitan neighborhoods. The research for his article is based on materials from the book *Global Markets and Local Crafts: Thailand and Costa Rica Compared* (2008, Johns Hopkins University Press). Further publications have appeared in *Ethnic & Racial Studies*, the *Journal of Consumer Culture*, the *International Review of Sociology*, and the *Consumers, Commodities, and Consumption Newsletter*. He holds a PhD in sociology from Princeton University and a master's degree in public affairs from the Woodrow Wilson School of Public and International Affairs. E-mail: ffwherry@umich.edu.

Index

For Product Safety Concerns and Information please contact our EU representative GPSR@taylorandfrancis.com Taylor & Francis Verlag GmbH, Kaufingerstraße 24, 80331 München, Germany

T - #0126 - 270225 - C0 - 229/152/12 - PB - 9780415541350 - Gloss Lamination